50 Hikes

The ruins of the medieval fortress of Volterraio on the Island of Elba

50 *Hikes*

In & Around Tuscany

Hiking the Mountains, Forests, Coast & Historic Sites of Wild Tuscany & Beyond

First Edition

JEFF TAYLOR

The Countryman Press
Woodstock, Vermont

We welcome your comments and suggestions. Please contact 50 Hikes Editor, The Countryman Press, P.O. Box 748, Woodstock, VT 05091, or e-mail countrymanpress@wwnorton.com.

© 2007 by Jeff Taylor

First Edition

ISBN 978-0-88150-734-8

Cover design by Hespenheide Design
Text design by Glenn Suokko
Composition by Desktop Services & Publishing, San Antonio, TX
Maps by Mapping Specialists Ltd., Madison, WI
Cover photo of Castellucio (Hike 49) and interior photos by the author

Published by The Countryman Press, P.O. Box 748, Woodstock, Vermont 05091

Distributed by W.W. Norton & Company, Inc., 500 Fifth Avenue, New York, NY 10110

Printed in the United States of America

10 9 8 7 6 5 4 3 2 1

Acknowledgments

I want to start by dedicating this book to my wonderful wife, Linda Lenz. Linda introduced me to hiking some 12 years ago in the Cascades, and we've been going strong ever since. Linda spent countless hours editing the text of this guide, and accompanied me on every hike, offering ideas and companionship. When I use the word "we" in this book, that is because Linda was a critical part of this project's success. I also want to thank my 10-year-old Australian shepherd, Maile, who was a real trooper on nearly every hike, and whose excitement and energy was the inspiration to go out on those weekend days when we did not feel like getting out of bed.

I would also like to thank Kathleen Theisen and her dog, Sabo, who accompanied us often to field test and offer assistance along the way. Their excitement and support of this project inspired me to continue. Other hiking companions who offered support and advice included Gloria and Werner Lenz and Sandra Hohmann.

I received assistance from my good friends John and Emily Asante, especially on the production and marketing of the initial proposal. I also want to thank my colleagues at Livorno American High School for their support, especially Cathy Magni, for all that she has done to make living and traveling in Tuscany possible in the first place. Finally, thank you to my parents and friends for this support and encouragement.

Disclaimer

Be aware that the trails, signs, and directions described in this book are subject to change. Signs can degrade or be removed, and trails rerouted due to erosion or construction. The author has taken great care to note hazards and confusing sections that may be encountered on the trails. Nonetheless, circumstances change, and hazardous conditions may occur during any time of year.

Updating

I would greatly appreciate any comments, suggestions, or updates of trail conditions. Please feel free to email me at: jeff@ 50hikesintuscany.com. For additional pictures and information visit www.50hikesin tuscany.com.

50 Hikes In & Around Tuscany at a Glance

HIKE	LOCATION: Tuscany (unless noted)
1. Monte Argentario Loop	near Orbetello
2. Tombolo di Feniglia at Laguna di Orbetello	near Orbetello
3. Maremma South	S of Grosseto
4. Maremma Coastline	S of Grosseto
5. Maremma Cork Oak Savannah	S of Grosseto
6. Elba–Pomonte Valley Loop	Island of Elba
7. Elba–Monte Capanne Summit Loop	Island of Elba
Bonus Hike: Elba–Ruins of Volterraio	Island of Elba
8. Sterpaia Coastal Park	near Piombino
9. Piombino Coast and Punta Falcone	near Piombino
10. Island of Capraia	Island of Capraia
11. Marina di Pisa Loop	near Pisa
12. Dunes of Torre del Lago	near Viareggio
13. Livorno Hills Park and Waterworks of Colognole Loop	near Livorno
14. Lago di Santa Luce Loop–North	S of Collesalvetti
15. Lago di Santa Luce Loop–South	S of Collesalvetti
16. Archeomineralogical Park of San Silvestro	near San Vicenzo
17. Forests and Canyon of Tatti-Berignone	SE of Volterra
18. Ruins of Castelvecchio	near San Gimignano
19. Monti della Calvana	near Prato
20. Leonardo da Vinci's Home and Montalbano	Vinci
21. Monte Pisano Loop	near Pisa
22. Procinto–Monte Nona Loop	NE of Forte dei Marmi
23. Monte Croce Loop	N of Lucca
24. Arch of Monte Forato Loop	N of Lucca
Bonus Hike: Grand Loop of the Southern Alpi Apuane	N of Lucca
25. Monte Fiocca Geological Tour	NE of Forte dei Marmi

DISTANCE (in km)	ELEV CHANGE (high to low in meters)	DIFFICULTY*	WILDFLOWERS	BEST MONTHS	NOTES
17	0–578	S		Mar–Jun & Sep–Oct	Views of the lagoon of Orbetello
5–12	3	E	★	Year Rnd	Birdwatching on the lagoon
4–12.5	40–220	ME	★	Mar–Jun & Sep–Oct	Panoramic views of southern Tuscany
14.1	100	M	★	Oct–Jun	Coastal wilderness experience
6	25–200	E	★	Oct–Jun	Rare cork oak ecosystem
12.1	634	S	★	Year Rnd	Spectacular valley below granite summit
12.6	326–1,019	S		Mar–Jun	Spectacular panorama 1000 m above the sea
2.5	247–394	ME	★	Year Rnd	Incredible view of the harbor
5.3	3	E	★	Year Rnd	Beautiful wildflowers in spring
10	40	E	★	Year Rnd	Wild coastline and macchia
14	400	M	★	Year Rnd	Remote, nearly uninhabited island
7.3	3	E		Year Rnd	Coastal forest in the urban landscape
8	3	E	★	Mar–Jun	Rare dunes in the urban landscape
7.5	185–415	E		Year Rnd	Forested hills and 18th century aqueduct
10.4	40–100	E	★	Year Rnd	Beautiful farmland, rolling hills, and a lake
6.3	40–100	E	★	Year Rnd	Bird watching along marshy lake by farmland
9	280–395	ME	★	Year Rnd	Ancient mines/mineral deposits, medieval village ruins
15	134–518	MS		Year Rnd	Tuscan forest wilderness
5	337–383	E		Year Rnd	Abandoned village of the plague
13.7–17.4	125–818	M	★	Mar–Nov	Bald summit above Florence
11.4	215–629	M		Year Rnd	Boyhood home/mountain of Leonardo da Vinci
8.2	620–830	ME		Mar–Nov	Spectacular panorama above Pisa
13.1	527–1,317	MS		Apr–Oct	Rugged limestone mountains
9	757–1,314	MS		Apr–Oct	Spectacular panorama of the Alpi Apuane
9–10.5	757–1,314	MS		Apr–Oct	Limestone arch and rugged mountains
29.5	440–1,317	S		Apr–Oct	Multi-day adventure in the Alpi Apuane
12.4	920–1,711	MS		Apr–Oct	Geological tour of the metamorphic range

50 Hikes In & Around Tuscany at a Glance

HIKE	LOCATION: Tuscany (unless noted)
26. Monte Altissimo Loop	NE of Forte dei Marmi
Bonus Hike: Marble "Glacier" of Monte Corchia	NE of Forte dei Marmi
27. Monte Sagro and Quarries of Carrara Loop	above Carrara
28. Montemarcello to Monte Murlo Loop	W of Carrara
29. Cinque Terre–Portovenere to Riomaggiore	near La Spezia, Liguria
30. Cinque Terre–Riomaggiore to Vernazza	N of La Spezia, Liguria
31. Cinque Terre–Vernazza to Levanto	N of La Spezia, Liguria
32. Amphitheater of Monte Moneglia	S of Sestri Levante, Liguria
33. Promontory of Portofino	near Rapallo, Liguria
34. High Crest–Monte Sillara Loop	NE of Aulla
35. Springs of the Secchia River	NE of Aulla
36. Monte Sillano Loop	N of Castelnuovo-Garfagnana
37. Monte Cusna Loop	NE of Castelnuovo-Garfagnana
38. Monte Cimone Loop	E of Abetone
39. Glacial Cirque of Monte Giovo	W of Abetone
40. Corno alle Scale Loop	N of Pistoia
41. Monte Falco and Foreste Casintenesi	E of Pontassieve
42. Republic of San Marino	W of Rimini, Emilia-Romagna
43. Sea Stacks of Monte Conero	S of Ancona, Le Marché
44. Monte Subasio of St. Francis of Assisi	near Assisi, Umbria
45. Badlands of Civita di Bagnoregio	S of Orvieto, Umbria
46. Pian Grande Ridge Route–West	near Norcia, Umbria
47. Pian Grande Ridge Route–South	near Norcia, Umbria
48. Monte Vettore Summit Route	near Norcia, Umbria
49. Monti Sibillini Grand Loop	near Norcia, Umbria
Bonus Hike: Lakes of Pantani-Accumoli	near Norcia, Umbria
50. Great Cirque of Corno Grande	near L'Aquila, Abruzzi

DISTANCE (in km)	ELEV CHANGE (high to low in meters)	DIFFICULTY*	WILDFLOWERS	BEST MONTHS	NOTES
9.5	990–1,589	MS		Apr–Oct	Spectacular panorama above Versilia coast
7	1,160–1,675	ME		Apr–Oct	Walk through an active marble quarry
8.5	1,279–1,749	M		Apr–Oct	High above famous marble quarries of Carrara
9–10.5	280–361	ME	★	Year Rnd	Coastal hills getaway
13.5	515	M	★	Year Rnd	Famous Cinque Terre coastal cliffs
9.8	300	M	★	Mar–Jun	Visit famous villages of Cinque Terre
12.1	150	M	★	Mar–Jun	Hiking north out of Cinque Terre
7.6	520	M	★	Sep–Jun	Ecological regeneration from catastrophic fire
8	250	ME		Year Rnd	Spectacular coastal views
10	1,320–1,859	MS	★	Apr–Oct	Alpine crest of N Apennines; many tarn lakes
8	1,261–1,779	M		Apr–Oct	Springs emerging from a glacial cirque
15	1,575–1,810	M	★	May–Oct	Loop through splendid alpine meadows
14.5	1,150–2,120	S	★	Jun–Oct	Rugged climb to summit of 2nd highest N Apennine peak
12.2	1,305–2,165	MS	★	May–Oct	Climb to summit of the highest peak in the N Apennines
8.5–11.4	1,365–1,964	MS	★	Jun–Oct	Spectacular glacial features
9.2	1,413–1,945	M		May–Oct	Pleasant stroll along the crest of Apennines
15	1,296–1,654	M		Apr–Nov	Ancient forests; Arno River source; endangered plants
7.1	456–740	E		Year Rnd	World's oldest Republic and touristic oddity
6.4	240	M		Year Rnd	Dramatic sea cliffs; tilted limestone layers
7.5	750–1,290	M		Mar–Nov	Mountain of St. Francis of Assisi
6	481–240	MS		Sep–Jun	Volcanic badlands
19	1,296–1,833	MS	★	Apr–Oct	Pleasant hike along crest above Pian Grande
11.8	1,296–1,751	ME	★	Apr–Oct	Pleasant hike along crest above Pian Grande
10–12	1,530–2,476	S	★	May–Oct	Rugged climb to the summit
30	1,296–1,883	MS	★	Apr–Oct	Multi-day adventure around spectacular Pian Grande
7–13	1,547–1,790	ME	★	May–Oct	Pleasant stroll in alpine meadows to ephemeral lakes
14.3	1,640–2,450	S	★	May–Oct	Glacial cirque hike of highest peak on Italian Peninsula

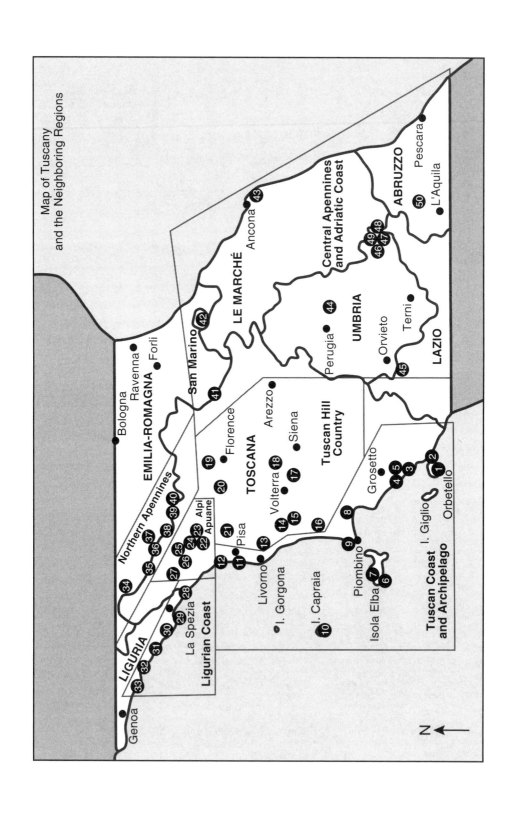

Map of Tuscany
and the Neighboring Regions

N

CONTENTS

Introduction

When people think of Tuscany, they often imagine wheat fields, sunflowers, vineyards, and olive groves carpeting the rolling hills scattered with lovely medieval villages dotting the landscape. Movies such as *Under the Tuscan Sun* invoke longings for a carefree and relaxed life, in a warm and sunny location, where wonderful food and wine are commonplace. In addition, those visiting Tuscany make it a goal to visit the wonderful Renaissance cities of Florence and Pisa, with their splendid art and architecture. However, what most people do not realize is that Tuscany is home to rugged mountains topped by alpine meadows, ancient chestnut forests, miles of sandy beaches unspoiled by resorts, chaparral scrublands strong with the scent of rosemary and thyme, remote and uninhabited islands, steep sea cliffs, and rocky shores teeming with marine life. Few visitors know of the "wild Tuscany," where wolves still roam the mountain summits, and wild boar root for truffles on the forest floor.

There are several travel guides that provide fascinating information about the sights and walks in the Chianti and Siena areas of Tuscany, where beautiful fields of sunflowers and wheat glow golden in the summer sun, and vineyards produce some of the best wine in the world. The hills of Tuscany deserve all the praise that they receive, because this is both an aesthetically pleasing place, and a restful place where one can enjoy incredible culinary experiences and a warm and friendly atmosphere. However, the aim of this guide is to introduce you to a Tuscany that does not get mentioned in the books, travel brochures, or in the movies: wild Tuscany.

Whether you are an avid hiker, naturalist, or even a weekend wanderer looking for a short jaunt in nature, *50 Hikes In & Around Tuscany* offers hikes with varying degrees of challenge, and all guaranteed to expand the mind. Actually there are 60 hiking options altogether, if you include the bonus hikes and alternate routes. This guide provides a multi-faceted picture of the fascinating ecology, geology, and human history of this region, and a glimpse into what life has been like here for thousands of years. Tuscany sits in the heart of the Mediterranean Basin, a biodiversity hotspot, containing thousands of plant and animal species. This guide offers the reader hikes ranging from high Apennine summits to the undeveloped dunes of the coast; from the volcanic columns on the island of Capraia to the metamorphic white marble cliffs of the Alpi Apuane; from the ancient chestnut forests of the Foreste Casintensi to the ruins of medieval villages in the Mediterranean chaparral.

Another aspect of Tuscany that is often ignored by guidebooks, and therefore remains unknown to many tourists, are Tuscany's incredible neighboring regions. The crest of the Northern Apennines represents the border between Emilia-Romagna and Tuscany, and is as wild and spectacular as any place you can find on the Italian peninsula. The Central Apennines, just south of Tuscany near the junction of the regions of Umbria, Le Marché, and Abruzzo, has the highest and most rugged mountains south of the Alps. The Cinque Terre in Liguria is a world-famous United Nations Educational, Scientific and Cultural Organization (UNESCO) World Heritage Site and, despite its presence in numerous other guides, is included here because the history and beauty of the area simply cannot be ignored. But there are many other places along the Ligurian coast that remain largely unknown, yet offer equally stunning scenery. The islands of the Tuscan Archipelago are rarely visited, yet they offer crystal-clear waters and protect species of plants and animals found nowhere else on Earth. Finally, the southern coast of Tuscany is among the least populated and least developed locations in all of Italy, and contains some beautiful wilderness areas.

Although there are hikes in this guide that do take in the beautiful agricultural areas of the Tuscan Hill Country, these are lesser known sites that will not be found in other guidebooks, and thus will be free from the crowds and tourism of the Chianti area.

I have separated this guide into six sections, based on the unique aspects that each area has to offer, beginning with the Tuscan Coast and Archipelago. This area is largely undeveloped, lightly populated, offers a multitude of protected natural parks, and preserves thousands of years of history dating back to the Etruscans, Romans, and medieval times. This area is home to the increasingly rare and fragmented *macchia* scrub, undeveloped beaches and coastal dune areas, riparian ash woodlands, and a rugged coastline.

I then continue with hikes in the western Tuscan hill country, where people can hike through farmers' fields, visit ghostly towns abandoned centuries ago during the bubonic plague, view migrating birds along lakeside wetlands, and gaze across at views of the snowcapped mountains to the north.

The third section focuses on the incredibly steep metamorphic mountains of the Alpi Apuane. Large quarries of high-quality marble dot the mountain summits, while beautiful stands of chestnut and beech open up into grassy alpine meadows and heath moorlands on the craggy summits. As a metamorphic core complex, this range is an amateur geologist's dream, containing an incredible array of colors, foliations, and states of deformation.

The fourth section focuses on the rugged and isolated Ligurian coast, just north of Tuscany. This section includes the famous and busy Cinque Terre, incredible scenery on the high cliffs near Portofino, the remarkable regeneration of a *macchia* pine woodland following a catastrophic fire near Moneglia, and an opportunity to get away from the crowds near Montemarcello.

For mountain enthusiasts, the Northern Apennines offer distinctive dramatically tilted sedimentary structures, Ice Age glacial features, high alpine meadows, and protected stands of chestnut, beech, and white fir. In addition to a chance to view these spectacular panoramas, colonies of Alpine marmots and the rare Apennine wolf still roam these open alpine summits. While they may be only half the elevation of the Alps, these mountains do still rise dramatically, some 2,000 meters above the sea.

Finally, this book ends with some of Tuscany's southern and eastern neighbors, in the Central Apennines and the Adriatic coast. Hikers have a chance to take in some of the highest mountains on the entire Italian peninsula, enjoy the interior cuisine, and visit some of the most important historical sights in Italy, including St. Francis's hometown of Assisi, the oldest republic in the world at San Marino, and a hike on steep limestone cliffs high above the Adriatic Sea.

50 Hikes In & Around Tuscany has more to offer than just vineyards, rolling hills, and Renaissance art, however. It also offers incredible panoramas, rugged mountain summits, and rare intact ecosystems. Whether you are just coming down to bathe on the sandy beaches, enjoy the wine, or experience the history, a trip out to one of these wild Tuscan areas will change your impression of what Tuscany, and in fact all of Italy, is about!

Logistics of Hiking in Italy

As much as I would like to recommend using public transportation to access these hikes, in all honessty—if you are on vacation and have only a limited amount of time, logistically speaking—it is much more efficient to drive down, if coming from northern Europe, or to rent a car. Most of these hikes are in rather remote locations, along long, winding roads, and public transportation is either nonexistent, unreliable, or would take an inordinate amount of time. The notable exceptions to this are the Cinque Terre hikes, where reliable train service will drop you off right at the trailhead, and at Portofino, Moneglia, Marina di Pisa, the Piombino coast, and a few others where bus service is readily available. Other hikes are possible to access by bus as well, and when this is the case, contact information is provided.

The Italian train service is offered by Trenitalia, and they are pretty reliable and quite convenient. Information on train routes and locations is available in both English and Italian, by visiting www.trenitalia.com. If you choose to visit Tuscany by train, some of the hikes in this guide are available directly by train or by connecting bus routes. However, it might be worth it to rent a car for a day or two, to visit some of the more remote locations. If you choose to rent, cars are available at the airport in Pisa and Florence, and near most significant train stations.

It is important to get a good road atlas for Tuscany when driving to the trailheads. The roads are small and winding, and many will not be shown on more generic road maps. Autogrills, located at rest stops on the Italian highway system (known as the Autostrada) sell some very good road atlases for Italy. A recommended one is *Atlante Stradale d'Italia* by L'Istituto Geografico De Agostini, also available through online booksellers.

Italians have a notable reputation for being crazy drivers, but it has been my experience that they are pretty reasonable, as long as you are prepared for anything. Be very flexible and expect anything so that you are not caught off guard. Cars pass each other readily in very tight spots, and slow vehicles will pull out onto main roads with little warning. Be prepared for a wide variety of vehicular speeds, from very slow to ridiculously fast. In summer, thousands of mopeds hit the roads, weaving freely in and out of traffic, while weekends often see teams of bicycle riders touring the main roads.

That being said, drivers here are not unreasonably dangerous and the roads are generally in good condition, although often narrow in the countryside. The most efficient way to drive in Italy is on the Autostrade (toll highways). There is an unofficial rule to getting around Italy "if you can get there by Autostrada, do it!" They have a maximum speed of 130 kph (about 80 mph), although many vehicles go well in excess of that, on straight stretches. These highways are well worth the cost, as they are in very good condition and offer efficient routes across the entire country. Once off the Autostrada, the roads are significantly slower, routes often become inefficient, and you will encounter traffic circles over and over again. The roads heading up into the mountains are extremely curvy, and they can get quite narrow in the small villages. Another general rule is to never drive into the center of any major Italian city. That is where driving is the most crazy, and the roads most confusing. Instead, park your car at a train station in the suburbs, and take the train into the city center.

Tuscany Weather Patterns and How They Affect Hikes

Tuscany has a generally warm and dry Mediterranean climate. Rainfall only totals approximately 90 centimeters (35 inches) per year. However, this region is very seasonal, and these seasonal changes can make a big difference in determining when and where you want to hike. In winter, the climate is generally cool, sunny, and dry, with little rain, only about 7 cm/month. January and February can be glorious months to hike near sea level, despite the short daylight hours. Near the sea, the temperatures rarely drop below freezing, snow is virtually unheard of, and some days can get as warm as 15 degrees C (60 degrees F) although 8–12 degrees C is more the norm. In the mountains, it is obviously significantly colder, and a blanket of snow usually covers the Apennine summits from December through early May. The Alpi Apuane may be snow-free during parts of the winter, but be aware that ice often covers the trails due to snowmelt or rain that freezes during cold nights.

Early spring brings more rain, and unpredictable weather. Temperatures here can rise above 20 degrees C (68 degrees F) or remain chilly. Many sunny days are also windy, and passing showers are common. However, rarely will the sunshine not appear at some point in the day. Generally the high mountains meadows have too much snow on them for hiking, but options in the middle elevations do open up. Wildflowers are beautiful at the lower elevations in April, especially near Maremma.

Late April through mid-June is my favorite time of year in Tuscany. It dries up significantly, sunshine is abundant, temperatures rise consistently above 20 degrees C, and the mosquitoes have not yet emerged. The landscape is green due to the early spring rains, wildflowers abound, and the mountain summits open up as the snowpack melts. June is an incredible time to hit the Alpi Apuane and the Apennines. In fact, June is the month where every hike in this book can be enjoyed to the fullest. In addition, since most of the mass tourism is still over a month away, you will have an abundance of solitude on the trail, especially midweek.

Summer in Tuscany is famous for being very hot and having virtually no precipitation (< 1 cm per month), but still somewhat hazy and humid. In the lowlands and near the sea, temperatures routinely rise well above 30 degrees C (86 degrees F) in July and August, and humidity, while not stifling, can certainly have its effects. The sun is intense and many plants turn brown due to the lack of rain. This is a time when it is not recommended to do low-elevation hikes at midday. Some of the coastal hikes would be nice to do in the early morning, before taking a swim after it heats up. Do be prepared for mosquitoes at the lower elevations, especially near water sources.

August is the month when nearly all of Italy takes their vacations. Millions of tourists and locals hit Tuscany to bathe at the beaches or to visit Florence. Traffic will be heavy, particularly near beach resorts, and crowds will cram the major historic sights and tourist destinations. However, the Apennine summits are much cooler, and are an excellent place to beat the heat and also escape the massive crowds down below.

After the peak heat and tourist seasons both die down, in September and early October, Tuscany returns to its best. In addition to May and June, these are my two other favorite months in this region. The weather cools down, but remains mostly sunny, although occasional evening thunderstorms do roll in, starting in late September. The crowds have dispersed and autumn color begins to creep into the high mountain forests and alpine meadows. The water of the Mediterranean remains warm, and swimming is an excellent choice on the now nearly deserted beaches. Every hike in the book is again available to be enjoyed to the fullest. October is an especially wonderful time to hike in the cool, sometimes misty Apennines, when they are adorned in blankets of red, orange, and golden foliage. This is also a great season to collect chestnuts falling from the trees, and mushrooms bursting from the forest floor. If you do not trust your ability to identify mushrooms, there are many roadside vendors in the countryside selling porcini and other excellent mushroom varieties.

However, in late October and November things begin to take a turn for the worse. November is, in my opinion, the worst month of the year in Tuscany, weather-wise. The weather can remain quite warm for most of the month and then will suddenly chill with a large storm front from the north. This is the monsoon season, as the warm water of the Mediterranean begins interacting with the cooler autumn air to create dangerous thunderstorms. Moisture evaporating from the warm sea rises, then cools higher up, condensing into immense clouds. These clouds grow throughout the day until sometime in the late afternoon or evening, enormous black thunderclouds form overhead.

On many nights during this season, you might be mesmerized and frightened by some of the most incredible lightshows in the world. In some storms, not one second passes between lightning bolts, and taking photos of lightning is easy, because the camera is bound to capture one while snapping shots randomly at the sky. These storms often linger until early the next morning, then break up quickly, resulting in clear skies when you awaken. That is, if you were ever able to sleep, through all the noise!

The rain during these storms is often heavy, and flash floods are common in steep mountainous areas, or along river valleys. There are sometimes large hailstones, which can damage cars. While I have luckily never been in the mountains of Tuscany during one of these storms, it is probably something you would not want to experience. If you are in Tuscany in November, and the weather is not threatening, there may be an opportunity to do one of the coastal hikes, but do not try anything too strenuous and risk being caught out there, exposed to the elements.

Some of these monsoon storms can linger into December, but generally they start becoming less frequent as the sea cools, especially after a couple of arctic fronts have come down from the north. If snow is going to happen in Tuscany, December is often the month, as cold air from the north interacts with warm moist air from the sea. However, hiking in the lowlands becomes more of an opportunity, and once January returns, the typically beautiful sunny days are back!

Autumn also has one other drawback: the beginning of hunting season. Men wearing camouflage, packs of hunting dogs, and the sound of gunfire can be seen and heard in many of the places I have hiked in the autumn. The good news is that the hunters are morning people, so you can enjoy freedom from all the gunfire and barking in the afternoon! You can also expect to encounter, or be startled by, nearly silent mushroom and chestnut hunters emerging from the woods, carrying their brimming baskets.

Hiking with Dogs

First and foremost, Italians love dogs (*cane,* in Italian). Virtually everyone has one, they walk them religiously, and they love seeing others out walking theirs. In our own town, people we have never met before stop us all the time, using our dog as a reason to start a conversation. In addition, from what we have seen in our town, in our own travels, and on the trails, Italian dogs are well treated and generally well behaved. Most Italians wisely keep their dogs inside their fenced yards, and take them for walks in the mornings and evenings. This will make your walks through villages much more relaxing, because you do not have to worry that an angry pit bull will suddenly come running out to rip your leg off. The exceptions to the note above are the hunting dogs that we often seem crammed into tiny kennels in the back of their owners' vehicles.

The dogs we have met on the trail are almost always friendly. We take our 10-year-old Australian shepherd, Maile (pronounced *my-lee*) with us on virtually every hike, and have rarely had any confrontation that was in the least scary. When we hike on trails, Italians will often say *carino* (pretty) or *bello* (beautiful), to indicate their approval of seeing our dog on the trail.

One of the most common questions we hear on the trail is *"Femmina?"* (or, "Female dog?"). Italians have a belief that two female dogs should not meet because they will fight. So, if you have a *femmina,* and they do too, they will immediately grab their dog and hold it until you walk by, usually muttering some quiet comment of frustration. If you say instead that it is *"maschio,"* they will immediately relax and say, *"Va bene."*

You may also encounter herding dogs accompanying flocks of sheep and goats in the Apennines. There are two varieties of dogs that shepherds use with their flocks. The smaller herding dogs are similar in appearance to border collies, and are used to corral the flock. Most of these that we have encountered have been friendly and are very obedient to their owners, who will almost always call them back. But we have, on several occasions, encountered the other breed: the large, all-white Maremma sheepdog. These do not always seem so friendly. The Maremma sheepdog is an ancient breed that has been bred to protect the flocks from wolves that still roam the mountains, thus they are very protective of their flock. It is recommended that you make wide tracks around any sheep you encounter, so that the sheepdogs do not feel you are threatening their flock, especially if you also have another dog with you.

With the notable exception of the Maremma Natural Park, I have never seen a sign banning dogs on trails anywhere in Italy. Also, at many of the *rifugio* or *trattoria* (eating establishments) where we have eaten, our dog has been free to sit under the table with us, while we eat. While it is preferable that you eat outside if you have a dog accompanying you, if outside seating is not an option, simply ask the waiter if the dog can come in *("Permesso per il cane entrare?"),* and often they will approve.

Dogs are frequently encountered on the trails, accompanying their hiking owners. Dogs are also allowed on the trains for the child-priced ticket, which is handy for visiting the Cinque Terre (as long as it is not the Eurostar fast train). One place where they are not generally accepted is at hotels, so plan on keeping them in your car overnight.

So, if you have a dog with you, feel free to bring them with you to hike in Italy, as they will be welcomed, and they will probably have an even more wonderful time than you!

Camping and Lodging

Lodging is not hard to find in Italy. Most significant towns have a hotel, bed-and-breakfast, or *pensione*. They range from 1-star to 5-stars. Contrary to popular opinion, and many guide books, it is not usually necessary to make reservations unless you are in a large city, or at the peak of tourist season in July and August. If you plan to come to Tuscany in midsummer, then booking ahead is probably a good idea because several million other Italians, plus Germans, Dutch, and Scandinavian tourists, will already be there. Outside of the tourist hotspots of Florence, Chianti, and the beach resorts, however, many hotels remain available. If, by chance, you arrive late and the hotel is full, they often know some other hotel nearby that still has vacancies. Not making reservations can provide for the maximum flexibility of movement and save you an incredible about of planning time, even if it can be a little nerve-racking to not know in advance where you will be sleeping.

If you are hiking in the Apennines, there is a *rifugio* (mountain hut) at the top of virtually every major mountain pass. Most *rifugi* offer overnight lodging, a bar, and a restaurant. Although some of the smaller ones not connected by road only offer food. Before starting a hike, stop by one of these in advance to check into availability, then you can enjoy your hike with a sense of relaxation knowing that you will walk right back to your lodgings in the afternoon. There are also *rifugio* in the villages at the end of almost every road heading into the Alpi Apuane. Near Maremma, and throughout much of rural Tuscany, the *agriturismo* has become common.

These are farmhouses that also serve as bed-and-breakfasts, or even campgrounds. You will see their signs on the sides of the small farm roads, and they are a wonderful way to meet real, rural Italian families maintaining a traditional lifestyle, while still embracing tourism.

Camping is certainly not like it is in America. Camping is popular in Italy, but is more like going to set up your tent at a resort than any form of wilderness experience. Italian campgrounds are densely packed and often full of amenities such as showers, bars, restaurants, mini-marts, and even occasionally, waterslides. They often have small bungalows or cabins for rent, although most of the people present will be in small RVs. Many Europeans rent RVs in the summer to tour, offering them the flexibility of using campgrounds, or parking anywhere they choose overnight.

Dispersed camping, where you set up on remote logging roads, such as in the national forests of the United States, is not done in Italy. There are not many places where you can get off the road to park, without it being on someone's property. Sometimes, the risk of encountering flocks of sheep and their accompanying sheepdogs in open fields outweighs the potential benefits. Many places are just too exposed for comfort. It can be done in some places in the Apennines, but be prepared to look around for a while, and be aware that the spot you choose might be illegal. It is probably better to find a nice bed-and-breakfast somewhere instead.

Eating in Italy

First and foremost, it goes without saying that Italian food is incredible. Every little *ristorante* or *trattoria* seems to have excellent food. In addition, the wine is cheap and of good quality. No need to get all snooty here.

Just order *un litro* (one liter) or *mezzo litro* (a half liter) of the *vino casa biano* or *casa rosso,* and you will not be disappointed. Timing of meals on the other hand can be frustrating to someone on the hiker's schedule. Breakfast *(colazione)* is virtually nonexistent in Italy, which is very disappointing for those familiar with the bread, cheese, and muesli of the Alps and the Germanic countries. When you awake at a bed-and-breakfast, you will likely be offered a single croissant (*brioche* or *cornetta*) and a cappuccino. While the cappuccino will be excellent, the lack of substantial food leaves a hiker with a long day ahead of them, and a little undernourished. The best opportunity for something more substantial is to stop at the bar on the way to the trailhead. Bars in Italy are not like liquor establishments in America. They are small cafés that serve coffee *(café),* soft drinks *(bibite),* pastries *(pasta),* and small sandwiches *(panino)* for breakfast, or in-between meal snacks. Bars are everywhere; every village will have at least two, so finding one will be no problem. Many cafés will charge more if you get a table, so just eat and drink right there at the bar.

If you stop at a bar any time of day for coffee, your primary choices are *café* (straight shot of espresso), *café macchiato* (espresso with a small dollop of foamed milk), cappuccino (espresso with foamed milk on top) and *café latte* (espresso in a glass of warm milk).

Another interesting drink that you will see Italians indulge in right after lunch is *café corretto,* which is a shot of espresso and a shot of alcohol. They will have dozens of bottles on the back shelf, and you choose the variety that you want added. I am not a fan of *corretto,* so I have no specific recommendations, but it seems *grappa,* Sambuca, brandy, and cognac are the most commonly chosen liqueurs that are added. The idea is that the alcohol will "correct" for the effects

of the caffeine. Or maybe it is just an excuse to drink during work time.

Italians do not eat lunch *(pranzo)* before 1 PM, and it is usually over by 2:30 PM. This can be a difficult window to fit into when you are out hiking. Lunch is a large meal and often consists of a *primi piatti* (first course, of pasta) and a *secondi piatti* (second course, of meat or fish). You can also order a *contorni* (side dish) instead of the *secondi.* Often, places will also serve pizzas during lunch, which can be your entire meal.

Midafternoon is the worst time to try to find food. The restaurants will not reopen for dinner until around 7:30 PM. We have been on hikes where we expected to arrive at a place for lunch, but did not make it on time and had to wait five or six hours, starving, until dinner. Even if you expect to arrive at a *rifugio* or *ristorante* in time for lunch, it is recommended that you bring some snacks along on the hike, just in case. The only other option is to find a bar, which will no longer have any fresh food, but will have some prepackaged snacks available.

Italians eat dinner *(cena)* late in the evening. Most restaurants will not open their doors until 7:30 PM, and will not start serving dinner until after 8 PM. If you arrive early, the restaurant will likely be almost completely empty. However, around 8:30–9 PM, the locals begin arriving in droves. They love to eat out, are very gregarious, and the place will be very loud with laughter, well into the night. On weekends, don't be shocked to see Italians just arriving for dinner even after 11 PM! One other interesting thing about Italian restaurants is that they do not try to push you out, like in many American establishments. The table you get is yours for the night, and if a place is full there is no waiting list, so you must move on to try another place.

Once in, it is sometimes hard to escape. Italians know that restaurants are places where people gather to talk and entertain, so unless you go seeking the check from the waiter, you will never get it. In my many dozens of times eating out, I have never been given the bill before I asked for it, and many times I have had to go into the back area to find the waiter or waitress and ask for the bill. Be prepared to sit at the restaurant for two to four hours—especially if you get the full, six-course meal and are eating with Italian friends!

At a restaurant you can ask for a table by saying *tavola per due* (table for two). The waiter will come by and ask about *bere* (drink). If you want water, you must specify between regular bottled water *(acqua naturale)* and sparkling water *(acqua frizzante)*. Many Italians have an *aperitivo* before dinner. *Amaro* is a common aperitivo, a bittersweet liqueur made of herbs, while *grappa* is also popular, distilled from the grape juice and skins. After dinner, most Italians finish off the meal with a *digestivo,* which is said to aid in digestion. One of the most common *digestivos* is *limoncello* (a strong, sweet, lemon liqueur).

Speaking and Interacting

Unlike Germany and many other European countries, most people in Italy do not speak fluent English. In the cities, there are usually people who speak English, but in the countryside, most people only know a few words and will speak almost completely in Italian to you—whether you know any Italian or not; but do not let this discourage you. Italians are extremely friendly and patient, and I have never encountered a situation where I needed help or directions and could not eventually figure out what was being said to me. When Italians realize that you do not speak Italian well, they will use hand gestures, speak slowly, ask other passing people for help, and will literally stop what they

are doing for as long as it takes to make sure you are okay. The most hilarious thing is that many older people will just stop you on the street or the trail, and start having a conversation with you in Italian. You can indicate that you do not speak Italian *(Non parlo Italiano),* but that will not stop them from telling you their story. Just be polite and enjoy the hospitality. On the trails, the most common greeting is *"Salvé."* In the cities, and sometimes on the trails, you will hear *buongiorno* (good day) in the mornings and *buona sera* (good afternoon, or evening) after lunch.

Insects and Other Animals

Italy's number one predator is the mosquito *(zanzara).* The lowland marshes and canals can be particularly bad in summer and early fall. Luckily, malaria was eliminated from Italy about 100 years ago. You are generally safe from those *zanzare* at high elevations, and from December through May. August and September are the worst months. Luckily, at least for me, their bites do not seem to linger for days, like some places I have been. When they bite, they only seem to itch for an hour or so and then it goes away. Most Italians do not use insect repellent; they just accept that they will be bitten, and they seem almost immune.

Ticks *(zecca)* are something to watch out for, with early spring (March through May) being the worst months. Watch for them when you climb through brush, especially in the *macchia.* If you have a dog, you most definitely want to use an anti-tick medication on them, and check their fur at the conclusion of each hike. In the higher elevations, small flies can be annoying, but are not hazardous.

Italy does have poisonous vipers, although they are rarely seen. They are identifiable from regular, nonpoisonous snakes by a dark zigzag pattern on their backs and by their flattened head and the pits near their noses. You are unlikely to come across one, but the best recommendation is not to pick up any snakes in Europe, and if your dog goes to investigate one, call it back. Italy also has scorpions, although I also have never seen one here. They are nocturnal, and not generally dangerous to humans.

Despite thousands of years of human occupation and development, Italy remarkably still has wolves, which inhabit the more remote, forested and alpine summits in the Apennines. They are rare, seldom seen, and very shy. Italians have a profound respect for wolves that dates back to the mythical founders of Rome, Romulus and Remus, who suckled from the teats of a wolf. Shepherds protect their flocks of sheep from wolves using the native Maremma sheepdogs, and it is illegal to shoot the wolves, which are a protected species.

Wild boar are very common in the forests and *macchia* in Italy. Generally speaking, they are nocturnal, very shy, and avoid humans. You are unlikely to see one, but will almost certainly come across some sign of their presence in the form of rooting on the forest floor near the trails as they search for mushrooms, insects, worms, and roots. When spotted, they are very cute, especially the piglets. But wild boar can be dangerous, especially if a mother wants to protect her young. If you come across any on the trail, stop, make some noise, and let them pass. Do not approach, if a boar stands its ground. While driving on remote roads at dusk or dawn, stop if you spot a boar crossing the road. More than likely, several young piglets will also cross shortly thereafter. We had an incident where some 10 piglets dashed across the road after the mother, one at a time, over a 30-second period. Had we continued sooner, we likely would have killed one.

ECOSYSTEMS AND HABITATS OF WILD TUSCANY

Tuscany contains a varied and rugged landscape that allows for a multitude of ecosystems containing thousands of plant and animal species. Tuscany is located in one of the world's most important biological hotspots, the Mediterranean Basin. Here, an inordinate number of species are clustered together due to a unique convergence of environmental conditions, including: warm and humid weather patterns with dramatic seasonal variation in precipitation; a variety of soil types due to a complex geological history; diverse topographic and elevational regimes; and being located near the intersection of three continents. Some 22,500 species of vascular plants can be found in this region—four times the number that can be found in the rest of Europe, combined.

While it is not practical to list every ecosystem in Tuscany, and the species that occupy them, below is a list of the major ecosystems and primary constituent species that are encountered in the hikes of this book.

Beaches and Sand Dunes

All along the Tyrrhenian Sea, on Tuscany's western coast, are strands of sandy beaches backed up by sand dunes and sandy soil deposits as far as several kilometers inland. The sand dunes that experience a significant disturbance regime, due to wind and wave action, tend to be barren, except for grasses, annual wildflower plants (such as goldenrods, curry plants, and lilies), and a few hardy drought-tolerant woody plants which are stunted in growth, such as juniper *(Juniperus oxycedrus)*, maritime *(Pinus pinaster)*, and Aleppo pines *(P. halepensis)*. Sand dune ecosystems can be found in Sterpaia, Maremma, Feniglia, Torre del Lago, and various other locations along the coast.

Pineta (coastal pine forests)

Further inland, where sand deposits have stabilized, umbrella, or stone, pine *(P. pinea)*, maritime pine, European black pine *(P. nigra)*, and Aleppo pine predominate. These *pineta*, are characterized by large, widely spaced pine trees with flat wind-shaped crowns, and an open-to-scrubby understory. The umbrella pine is quite beautiful, with its wide circular canopy and large cones, and produces the pine nuts (also called *pignoli*) commonly found in Italian cuisine. The understory consists of myrtle *(Myrtus communis)*, phyllireas *(Phyllirea sp.)*, various oak species *(Quercus sp.)*, vines of ivy *(Hedera helix)* and common smilax *(Smilax aspera)*, laurel *(Laurus noblus)*, and buckthorn *(Rhamnus sp.)*. These *pineta* can be seen in Marina di Pisa, Torre del Lago, Sterpaia, Maremma, Feniglia, and many other coastal locations.

Macchia

The *macchia,* or chaparral, habitats in Italy occupy low-elevation slopes that are well drained and exposed to the sun. These dense evergreen thickets of large shrubs and small trees are virtually impenetrable. The low canopy, generally only 2–3 meters high, is dominated by holm oak *(Quercus ilex)*, black pine, phyllireas, tree heather *(Erica arborea)*, strawberry tree *(Arbutus unedo)*, mastic tree *(Pistacia lentiscus)*, and various broom species *(Ginestra* and *Sparticum sp.)*. In the understory, rosemary *(Rosemarinus officinalis)*, lavender *(Lavandula augustafolia)*, spiny oak *(Q. coccifera)*, rock roses *(Cistus sp.)*, and a multitude of other species offer fragrant and colorful displays in spring when they burst into bloom. This is the ecosystem that has the most biological diversity in the Mediterranean Basin. These *macchia* are highly susceptible to fire, due to their high vegetative density, the flammable oils found in many of the plant leaves, and the arid, sun-exposed locations. They are now becoming increasingly fragmented in Italy, due to over-development and desertification of the Mediterranean Basin. Examples of undisturbed *macchia* ecosystems can be found on Capraia, Elba, in the Livorno Hills, Maremma, Piombino, San Silvestro, and other rocky slopes near to the sea.

Oak Woodlands

Oak woodlands occupy low- to medium-elevation sites that retain more water and offer more shade than *macchia* sites, such as north-facing slopes or streambeds. They occur up to about 500 meters elevation and are the most common ecosystem in Italy. These evergreen woodlands are very dense, with holm oak being by far the most common tree species. Other oaks include sessile oak *(Q. petraea)*, Hungarian oak *(Q. farnetto)*, and turkey oak *(Q. laevis)*. These woodlands also contain buckthorns, strawberry tree, introduced black locust *(Robinia psuedoacacia)*, and various pine species. Ash *(Fraxinus sp.)*, laurel, and elm *(Ulmus sp.)* can also be found in sheltered streambeds. The understory is often almost impenetrable due to the high density of holm oak trunks, as well as smilax vines and wild asparagus *(Asparagus acutifolis)*. Oak woodlands will be encountered in virtually every low elevation hike in this book, especially on shadier, north-facing slopes.

Riparian Ash Woodlands

In wet, poorly drained soils at low elevation, where the water table is sufficiently close to the surface, beautiful riparian ash woodlands predominate. These ash can grow very large, and in spring have a fresh green burst of growth. Ash are made obvious by their pinnate leaves, branching perpendicular to the stem. These woodlands often have a lush understory of grass and other annuals, as well as riparian trees such as poplars *(Populus sp.)*, alders *(Alnus sp.)*, willows, maples *(Acer sp.)*, and elderberry *(Sambucus nigra)*. Pure stands of ash have become quite rare, but an old-growth stand can be found at Sterpaia. Riparian woodlands can also be found at Marina di Pisa and other lowland areas near the Pisa plain.

Chestnut Forests

At medium elevation sites in the foothills of the Alpi Apuane and the Apennines, European chestnut stands *(Castanea sativa)* become the dominant forest type. These forests are, in many places, virtually monospecific. Chestnuts prefer cooler, northern aspects, while more exposed southern slopes at the same elevations may still retain oak woodlands, up to 500 meters. Forming a dense canopy, chestnut forests are dark and moist, allowing for an understory of ferns and other water-loving annuals. Chestnuts grow to a height of 30 meters or more, and in fall, produce prodigious quantities of nuts. They are fun to collect on the way down from a mountain hike, and still remain a vital part of the income for many rural Italian villages. The only other chestnut species that grows to canopy height is the now virtually extinct American chestnut. Although the chestnut blight did affect the European species, it proved more resistant to the disease and many forests of large chestnut trees remain intact. Other trees that can be found associated with chestnuts include hop-hornbeam *(Ostrya carpinifolia)*, European hornbeam *(Carpinus betulus)*, maples, and quaking aspen *(Populus tremulus)*.

Beech Forest

At higher elevations (above 1,000 meters) chestnut forests begin to give way to the European beech *(Fagus silvatica)*, especially on northern slopes. Significantly shorter and thinner than beech trees north of the Alps, these stands of beech often grow like dog-hair forests, with a dense light-green canopy, and virtually no understory. However, near springs and on northern slopes, ferns and other water-loving plants can be found in the understory. In some locations, white fir *(Abies alba)* and mountain ash *(Sorbus sp.)* can be found in scattered clumps, and birch *(Betula sp.)*, hop-hornbeam, and aspen can be found along streambeds. Valued for their timber, many forests were harvested over the centuries, and regrowth is now in progress. Beech forests can be found near treeline throughout the Alpi Apuane and Apennines, and their distribution is often controlled by the grazing activity of sheep and goats. In many locations, stands of beech will suddenly end at a fence or cling precariously on a steep slope, where they are out of reach of grazing animals. A stand of older, larger beech trees can be found at the Springs of the Secchia River.

Alpine Meadows and Heaths

The treeline in Tuscany is quite low compared to other locations in Europe or North America. At only 1200–1500 meters, beech forests will give way to grassy alpine summits along the ridgelines of the Alpi Apuane and the Apennines. Some of these alpine meadows are maintained below their natural elevations, due to the grazing of sheep and goats. In other cases, poor rocky soils, hot dry summers, and exposure to high winds and winter cold have combined to create an environment where only the hardiest plants and spring annuals can survive. Grasses, stunted blueberries *(Vaccinium sp.)*, and alpine wildflowers predominate in these open habitats, while low common juniper *(J. communis)* also creeps along rocky areas. In terms of scenery, these are the crown jewels of Italy. Glacial features from the last Ice Age, such as cirques and tarns, are also visible on the mountain slopes.

RARE ECOSYSTEMS

Cork Oak Savannah

An increasingly rare ecosystem in Tuscany is the cork oak savannah. These magnificent oaks *(Quercus suber)* with incredibly thick bark are stripped every seven to fourteen years to make cork for wine bottles. Cork oaks are obvious because they are stripped up to 4 meters above the ground. Where they are found, cork oaks typically grow widely spaced, in exposed dry areas with a grassy understory. They are more common in the western Mediterranean, such as on the Iberian peninsula. Cork oaks can be seen along the A3 trail at Maremma, and on eastern Elba.

White Fir Forests

The European white fir once dominated the mid-to-higher elevation forests of Italy. Relics of the Ice Age, they rely on moist, well-shaded slopes. They were heavily harvested for centuries, for the construction of wooden sailing vessels. Like the closely related Spanish fir *(Abies pinsapo)* and the extremely endangered Sicilian fir *(A. nebrodensis),* European white firs faced their greatest exploitation during the era of the Roman Empire, and then again during the explosion of trade and exploration of the Renaissance. Where they were once dominant, white firs have generally been replaced by chestnuts and beech. White firs can still be seen in isolated patches and individual trees in the Alpi Apuane, in the Northern Apennines, on Monte Falco, and on Montalbano.

Garigue

Usually associated with the *macchia,* these open grassy areas are created by the effects of strong sea breezes, high soil salinity, arid conditions, and high solar radiation. Only very hardy plants can survive in these areas. Curry plants *(Helichrysum italicum),* thyme *(Thymus sp.),* euphorbs *(Euphorbia sp.),* and salt grass *(Distichlis spicata),* are often the only plants that can survive in these harsh locations. Along the fringes, rock roses and tree heather can also be found, as well as the thorny dwarf broom on Elba. Usually found more commonly in southern Mediterranean locations such as Malta and Greece, garigue can be found on the saddles at the edge of the summit ridge of Capraia, along the exposed ridges of western Elba, on other Tuscan Archipelago islands, and at certain locations in the Livorno Hills.

Mediterranean Fan Palm

The Mediterranean fan palm *(Chamaerops humilis)* is an extremely rare species in Tuscany, with natural populations occurring only on the cliffs of Capraia, and on the Tombolo of Sterpaia. These small palms grow as shrubs in the understory of pine and oak woodlands, and are more commonly found in the southern and western Mediterranean basin. However, they are relatively easy to maintain as ornamental plants, and are commonly seen in urban landscaping.

LIST OF IMPORTANT ITALIAN WORDS AND TRANSLATIONS FOR THE TRAIL

Directions and Greetings

Aperto	Open
Buona sera	Hello (after lunch)
Buongiorgno	Hello (before lunch)
Chiuso	Closed
Destra	Right
Dietro	Behind
Diretto	Straight ahead
Salvé	Italian trail greeting
Sinestra	Left
Sopra	Above
Sotto	Below

Trail Markers, Features, and Common Signs

Caccia	Hunting
Capanna	Hut
Chiesa	Church
Croce	Cross
Divieto	Prohibited
Foce	Pass
Forca	Pass or fork
Galera	Prison
Galleria	Tunnel
Itinerario	Trail route
Porto	Port
Punta	Point
Ritorno	Return
Sella	Pass
Sentiero	Trail or path
Strada	Street
Diretto	Straight ahead

Geographic, Geologic, and Biological Features

Albero	Tree
Arco	Arch
Bocca	Mouth
Bosco	Woodland
Cala	Cove
Campo	Field
Canne	Reeds or canes
Cascata	Waterfall
Cima	Summit
Colle	Large hill
Corno	Horn
Cresta	Ridge
Fiume	River
Fontana	Fountain
Fonte	Spring
Foresta	Forest
Fosso	Pit or gulch

Geographic, Geologic, and Biological Features (cont.)

Ghiaccio	Ice
Gola	Gorge
Grotta	Cave
Lago	Lake
Laguna	Lagoon
Lido	Shore
Macchia	Mediterranean scrub
Monte	Mountain
Neve	Snow
Palude	Marsh
Passo	Pass
Piano	Plain or flats
Poggio	Small hill
Prato	Meadow
Rocca	Rock
Sasso	Stone
Sorgente	Spring or source
Spiaggia	Beach
Tombolo	Forest on sandy soil
Torrente	Torrent or stream
Valle	Valley

Common Tree Species

Abete	Fir
Abete Rosso	Spruce
Acero	Maple
Betulla	Birch
Castagna	Chestnut
Ciliegio	Cherry
Cipresso	Cypress
Faggio	Beech
Frassino	Ash
Larice	Larch
Olmo	Elm
Ontano	Alder
Pino	Pine
Pioppo	Poplar or cottonwood
Plantano	Plane or sycamore
Quercia	Oak
Salice	Willow
Sorbo	Mountain ash
Tiglio	Linden

Common Animal Species

Bestiami	Cattle
Capra	Goat
Cavallo	Horse
Cervi	Deer
Cinghiale	Wild boar
Falco	Hawk or falcon
Lepre	Hare

Common Animal Species (cont.)

Lupo	Wolf
Marmotta	Marmot
Pecore	Sheep
Pesce	Fish
Rana	Frog
Riccio	Hedgehog
Scoiattolo	Squirrel
Serpente	Snake
Tasso	Badger
Uccello	Bird
Volpe	Fox

Important Rules for Sounding Out Words in Italian

The C followed by an i or e is pronounced CH.
The C followed by any other letter is pronounced K.
>   EXAMPLE: *Caccia* is pronounced Ka-chia.

The G followed by an i or e is pronounced Jh.
The G followed by any other letter is pronounced Ga.
>   EXAMPLE: *Faggio* is pronounced Fajh-io, while *Lago* is pronounced La-go.

The G before an N is pronounced nya.
>   EXAMPLE: *Castagna* is pronounced Castan-ya.

The G before an L softens the L, but the G is silent.
>   EXAMPLE: *Ameglia* is pronounced Amay-lia.

The S before a Ci or Ce is pronounced Shi.
The S before a C with any other letter is pronounced Sk.
>   EXAMPLE: *Cascina* is pronounced Kas-shina.
>   EXAMPLE: *Scandicci* is pronounced Skan-deechi.

Z is pronounced S; but, ZZ is pronounced TSZ.
>   EXAMPLE: *Senza* is pronounced Sen-sa.
>   EXAMPLE: *Stazzema* is pronounced Stats-zema.

If A is followed by IO or IA it is pronounced Eye-O or Eye-A.
>   EXAMPLE: *Portoferraio* is pronounced Portoferr-eye-o.
>   EXAMPLE: *Cenaia* is pronounced Chen-eye-a.

LL together do not make a Y sound as in Spanish; it is pronounced L.

I

The Tuscan Coast and Archipelago

Introduction to the Tuscan Coast and Archipelago

With cities the size of Florence, Pisa, and Livorno, one might think of Tuscany as one of the more densely populated regions in Italy. With a population of over 3.5 million people in an area about the size of New Hampshire, it does have a relatively high population density. However, if you fly over the region on a flight from Rome to Pisa, most of Tuscany seems empty, except for scattered farms and quaint medieval villages. In fact, looking at a nighttime light pollution map of Italy, you will see that the Pisa plain to Florence is quite bright and really stands out, while one of the darkest areas on the entire peninsula is found in southern Tuscany.

The coastline and the islands of Tuscany represent some of the last bastions of non-mountainous, wild Italy. Here, there are extensive parks covered in forests and *macchia* vegetation. Wild boars run free, while falcons soar above. Pristine coastline and marine sanctuaries protect the precious marine resources that have sustained the economy and Italian heritage of fishing for centuries. This is a remote land, where towers were built on hilltops to keep watch for Saracen pirates, and Etruscan ruins still stand after 3,000 years.

From the promontory of Monte Argentario in the south, through the beautiful forested hills and spectacular cliffs of Maremma and Piombino, the sand dunes and old growth ash woodlands of Sterpaia, to the pine woodlands near the mouth of the Arno River, the Tuscan Coast has much to offer visitors seeking solace from the crowds.

For those who make the extra effort to board a ferry, the islands of the Tuscan Archipelago offer remote and exhilarating experiences, as one climbs the sea cliffs of the island of Capraia, through the arid scrubland of the Pomonte Valley, or through lush chestnut forests to the remarkable alpine summit of Monte Capanne on Elba. The Tuscan Archipelago consists of seven major islands and dozens of islets. These islands are arid landscapes, receiving only about 500 millimeters (19 inches) of rain per year. They contain unique species and ecosystems, due to their isolation and aridity. Montecristo, Giglio, and western Elba are granite landscapes formed by magmatic intrusions some 6 million years ago. Capraia was the site of an eruptive volcano that occurred at about the same time, and as such contains pumice and andesite lava columns. Capraia was also the site of a former penal colony, while the tiny island of Gorgona still remains a penal colony today. Not to be outdone, the flat limestone island of Pianosa was a maximum security prison where some of the most notorious mafia leaders were held until it closed, only recently. Of these islands, only Elba, Capraia, and Giglio can be visited without special permits. Thus, the remote, rugged nature of these islands has preserved a wonderful landscape to explore.

As for the Tuscan coast, while millions of tourists flock to the manicured sandy beaches of the Italian Riviera in Versilia, Tirrenia, and San Vincenzo, few venture out to the beautiful remote beaches of Maremma or Sterpaia. While tanned bodies lay on beach chairs baking in the summer sun, virtually no one is to be found exploring the isolated hill-top towers, or smelling the sweet scent of rosemary in the *macchia*. While thousands pack the trains and ferries of the Cinque Terre to see the rugged Ligurian coast, the cliffs of Piombino remain empty. If you want to see Tuscany, as it has existed for thousands of years, then get off the beaten trail and head to Tuscan Coast and Archipelago.

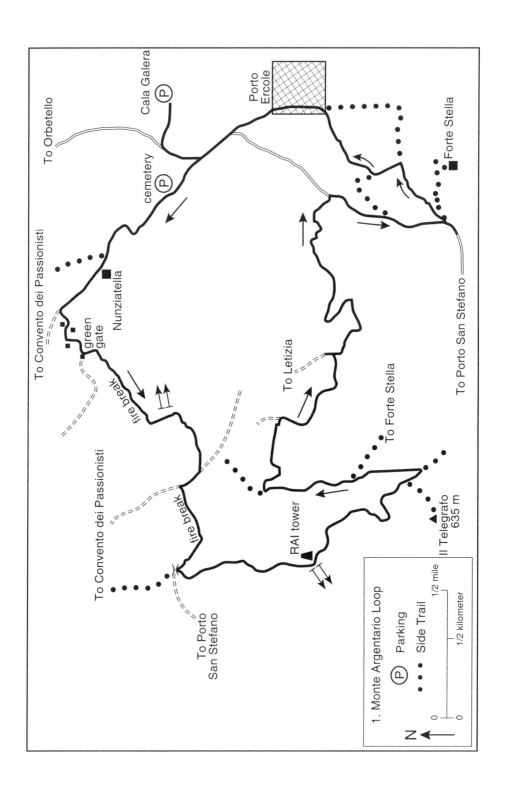

To Orbetello

Cala Galera

cemetery

Porto Ercole

Forte Stella

To Convento dei Passionisti

Nunziatella

green gate

fire break

To Convento dei Passionisti

fire break

To Porto San Stefano

To Letizia

To Forte Stella

RAI tower

Il Telegrafo
635 m

To Porto San Stefano

1. Monte Argentario Loop

Ⓟ Parking

••• Side Trail

0 ———— 1/2 mile

0 ———— 1/2 kilometer

N

1

Monte Argentario Loop

A loop hike to the summit of Monte Argentario, above the lagoon of Orbetello.

Distance: 17 kilometers (10.6 miles)

Elevation: Sea level to 578 meters (0–1,895 feet)

Hiking time: 5–6 hours

Difficulty: Strenuous

Time to visit: Year round; avoid midday during summer

Recommended time: Spring and fall

Down at the southernmost tip of Tuscany sits a large promontory, a mountain really, that rises over 600 meters above the sea, and is connected to the mainland only by two narrow strips of sand called *tombolo,* with a large lagoon in the center. The promontory of Monte Argentario is an obvious landmark for anyone riding the train or flying between Pisa and Rome. It is a fascinating geological oddity that offers spectacular views, beautiful wildflowers, layered rock strata containing fossils, historical structures, and quaint port villages. Do take into account that Monte Argentario is a heavily altered landscape, with a long history of human activity. Much of the lower slopes are covered with summer and weekend estates owned by the Roman elite or northern European expatriates. The summit is occupied by several large radio and TV towers. However, once above the estates, you enter a beautiful *macchia* woodland full of rock roses in spring, and you are unlikely to see any other people along the way. Once at the summit, the enormous towers can be excused when you look across at the spectacular views of the promontory, the islands offshore, the southern Tuscan landscape, and the lagoon of Orbetello below.

To get to Monte Argentario from Pisa or Rome, take the SS1 until the Orbetello exit. Follow signs to Porto Ercole. Just after passing the turn for the yacht harbor of Cala Galera, take the first right, which turns sharply back. Follow the road a short way until the cemetery, and park there. Alternatively, if there is not enough space, you can

View of Porto Ercole

park in the large gravel lot of Cala Galera. You can reach the area by taking the train from Rome or Pisa to the Orbetello station, and then reaching Porto Ercole by bus using RAMA. Contact RAMA at www.gri forama.it or 0564/475111.

From the cemetery, walk along the narrow paved road, working its way uphill, accompanied by the songs of nightingales in the roadside shrubs. This is a minor dead-end road with virtually no traffic. When you reach the first intersection, stay left, following signs for Nunziatella. The road will pass the fenced-in estate of Nunziatella, and you take the first left after the fences and gates. Follow this road up past several homes until you reach the end of the pavement and then continue on until you reach a T-junction with a green fire gate on the left. Walk past this green gate to the fire break, a large open strip cut through the woods that heads in a straight line up the mountain. The fire break provides a convenient, open, and

beautiful route, devoid of people, but full of flowers, as you ascend the next 400 meters up to the summit.

Shortly after beginning the ascent up the fire break, views of the lagoon, *tombolo,* and the southern Tuscan landscape start to open up before you. This stretch of the route is steep and strenuous, and potentially slick with loose rock, which is why it is better to climb it rather than descend it. The fire break rises 150 meters in elevation to the base of a hill, before turning sharply to the left. At this turn, views to the south provide a glimpse of several medieval towers, and the coastline of Lazio. The fire break will then turn right again, offering views of the summit about 200 meters above. The fire break climbs upward until it reaches a dirt road. At the road, turn right and then immediately rejoin the fire break to the left which climbs straight up along another very steep stretch. At the top of this steep stretch, the fire break turns right and then meets the

View from Il Telegrafo

paved radio tower access road. From the summit road, turn left and follow the summit road until reaching the RAI tower.

The road will pass just right of the tower, and just off to the right of a small pullout is a ledge offering spectacular views across almost the entire promontory, as well as the island of Giglio offshore to the west, and the small island of Giannutri to the southwest. This is an excellent place to sit down on the rocks, soak in the atmosphere, and eat lunch.

Once finished, continue up the summit road toward the peak of Il Telegrafo and the other radio towers. The road will go uphill to the top of the peak, but access to the actual summit is restricted. Just before reaching those towers, there will be a dirt road branching left with some red/white blazes. This is your route back down. The dirt road will wind its way down the mountain all the way to the village of Porto Ercole. Most of the way down, the route will be marked with red/white blazes. At each of the intersections you encounter, stay left and continue downslope. The route will descend through a beautiful elm and oak forest, with maples mixed in—one of the prettiest forests I have seen in Italy. The route will emerge in a brief clearing and then after another segment of forest, when you reach the first fenced estate, the route will branch. Stay right, following the sign for Porto Ercole. The route will eventually take you past more and more homes, until it ends at a major paved road that links Porto Ercole and Porto San Stefano.

At this paved road, you have a choice. The shorter route back is approximately 2 kilometers, accessed by turning left and following the busy road until you reach the cemetery road. This route does not actually enter the village of Porto Ercole. However, if you turn right, walk along the paved road until reaching the access road for the old lookout of Forte Stella, located on a rocky hill overlooking the sea. At the base of this access road, next to the gate, there is a small trail dropping into the brush to the left. Either after or instead of visiting the fort, follow this trail through the dense *macchia* woods, until it descends steeply to the bottom of a drainage, where a fire break climbs steeply up the opposite hill.

The turn at the bottom of the drainage is to the left, downslope into Porto Ercole. *Do not* go up the steep fire break. The route to the left can be difficult to spot, due to branches crossing over the trail, but just push through the shrubs and you should see it shortly. The trail will emerge onto a side street of Porto Ercole, which is a beautiful little seaside village and a great place to get a *gelato* and see the harbor up close. From Porto Ercole, follow the main road out of town and back toward Cala Galera, which is about 1 kilometer away. You will walk right past the cemetery road just before reaching the Cala Galera parking area.

2

Tombolo di Feniglia at Laguna di Orbetello

A nice easy walk through a beautiful stone pine forest alongside sand dunes, as well as bird watching in the lagoon, or strolling on the beach.

Distance: 5–12 kilometers (7.5 miles)

Elevation: Sea level

Hiking time: up to 5 hours

Difficulty: Easy

Park: Riserva Statale Duna Feniglia

Time to visit: Year round

The promontory of Monte Argentario is connected to the mainland by two narrow strips of sand known as *tombolo.* In between these *tomboli* is a brackish lagoon which is a haven for wading birds, most notably the greater flamingo. The northern *tombolo* is heavily developed with beach resorts and the main road heading onto Monte Argentario. The southern *tombolo,* however, is completely closed to traffic and is protected as a nature reserve. It contains a wide variety of wildlife, including badger, deer, foxes, and hedgehogs, as well as being an important estuary protecting sensitive dune habitats, and providing a wonderful area to walk or ride your bike. This park is popular with tourists from Rome, especially those who rent bikes at a nearby stand and ride along the dirt road that runs down the center of the park. There are numerous trails and fire breaks that span the entire length of the *tombolo* or cross over from the lagoon to the beach, allowing a comfortable and peaceful exploration of this rare dune habitat. The Tombolo di Feniglia is 6 kilometers long and only 800 meters wide, so you can chose to walk as little or as far as you wish. The map and description below details a short 5 kilometer loop that encompasses every habitat on the *tombolo,* as well as the bird-watching blinds on the lagoon, and the short botanical nature loop. However, it is certainly possible to walk or ride your bike the entire 6 kilometer length, for a route of more than 12 kilometers, roundtrip.

To get to the Tombolo di Feniglia, follow the directions for Monte Argentario dis-

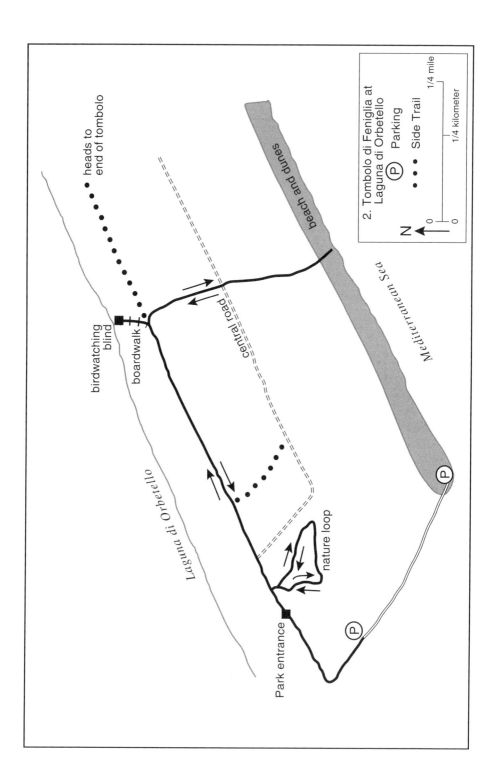

heads to
end of tombolo

birdwatching
blind

boardwalk

central road

Laguna di Orbetello

nature loop

Park entrance

beach and dunes

Mediterranean Sea

2. Tombolo di Feniglia at
Laguna di Orbetello

(P) Parking
••••• Side Trail

0 ___ 1/4 mile
0 ___ 1/4 kilometer

N

Pine forest

cussed in Hike 1. Near Porto Ercolo, follow signs for Tombolo di Feniglia. As the road curves around, look for a yellow sign and a dirt road on the left, labeled CORPO FORE-STALE DI STATO–DUNA FENIGLIA. There will also be a sign for NOLEGGIO BICI or bike rentals. Continue past this sign for a few meters, and look for the parking lot on the left. You will walk back to the yellow sign, turn right, and walk to the end of the road where there is a gate and the park entrance. There is no public bus service to the trailhead, but RAMA does offer service to Porto Ercole. Contact RAMA at www.griforama.it or call 0564/475111 for more information.

At the park entrance there are several in-terpretive signs, including a map of the park. Just past these interpretive signs is a short botanical nature loop on the right, with a wooden railing. This loop is interesting, as it has placards discussing each of the impor-tant plants and animals of the *tombolo,* their natural history, and historical uses. Some highlighted material includes the uses of stone-pine resin and wild rosemary, the iden-tification of native animal tracks, among other displays.

After the botanical loop, continue down the path and shortly there will be a branch. To the right is the main dirt road the bike rid-ers use, while a smaller and less-developed fire break continues straight ahead. Follow this fire-break route for about 1 kilometer, going through some absolutely gorgeous pine-ash savannah, and you will arrive at a boardwalk that heads left to the lagoon. At the end of the boardwalk are several bird blinds that allow viewing access of the wad-ing birds such as flamingoes, herons, and stilts, various ducks, as well as numerous plovers and other shorebirds, that feed on invertebrates in the mud. Across the lagoon you can see the city of Orbetello.

After the lagoon, walk back toward the main route. You can continue down the fire break for another 5 kilometers. To access

Orbetello Lagoon

the dune and beach area, instead of getting back on the fire break, continue straight across the *tombolo,* and 800 meters later you will arrive at the coastal sand dunes, covered in juniper and rock roses. At the top of the dunes, you can look across, over the flat stone pine canopy that covers the *tombolo.* On other side of the dunes is the beach with beautiful views of the summit of Monte Argentario and down the Lazio coast. Along the beach, you may find lightweight pumice stones that floated on the sea, and washed up onshore from the numerous volcanoes that occur throughout Lazio and southern Tuscany.

The route to get back to your car is your decision. You can walk the dirt road that has many bike riders on it, or you can walk across the *tombolo* and another route offering more solitude. There are a myriad of small paths to choose from. You may also continue farther down the *tombolo.* The choice is yours on this easy, but beautiful, hike!

3

Maremma South

Loop hikes through the macchia *to a panoramic point overlooking all of southern Tuscany.*

Distance: Approximately 7.5 kilometers (4.6 miles)

Other options:
Short route—T1 is only approximately 4 kilometers round trip (2.5 miles)
Extended route—add T3 spur; approximately 12.5 kilometers roundtrip (7.8 miles)

Elevation: 40–220 meters (130–722 feet)

Hiking time: 2–3 hours

Difficulty: Moderately easy

Park: Parco Naturale della Maremma

Time to visit: Spring and fall

Pets: Not allowed

The Parco Naturale della Maremma in southern Tuscany is located in one of the most unspoiled and uninhabited areas in Italy. This area of green hills, quaint farms, beautiful golden beaches, and azure-blue waters is a jewel yet to be discovered by the average traveler. This park is as close to a wilderness as exists in Italy. The park is completely fenced off from the outside, dogs are not allowed, and access is strictly regulated in places. The intact *macchia* and oak woodlands protect an abundance of wildlife, including fallow deer, foxes, hedgehogs, badgers, and ubiquitous signs of the park's symbol: the wild boar *(cinghale).*

Most visitors to the park explore its northern areas (Hikes 4 and 5), while the southern stretch is virtually unknown. In three visits to these southern trails, we did not encountered another hiker. The hikes of Maremma South head along the wooded limestone ridge of Monti dell'Uccellina, containing *macchia* ecosystems and dense oak woodlands, and descend into unspoiled coves, which provide incredible snorkeling opportunities.

From either Rome or Pisa, take the SS1 and head toward Grosseto. From either location the drive should take about two hours. About 30 kilometers south of Grosseto, take the Fonteblanda-Talamone exit. Follow the signs for Talamone, located 3.5 kilometers west. Just before reaching the town of Talamone, located on a rocky point above the water, you will see a dirt road on your right with a green sign for the T1 trail.

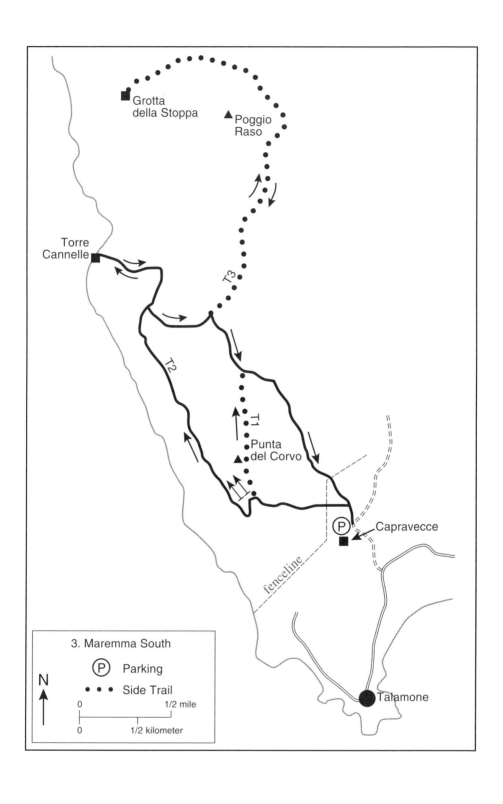

Grotta
della Stoppa

▲ Poggio
Raso

Torre
Cannelle

T3

T2

T1

Punta
▲ del Corvo

fenceline

Ⓟ

Capravecce

Talamone

3. Maremma South

Ⓟ Parking

••• Side Trail

N

0   1/2 mile

0   1/2 kilometer

Spring flowers with spider

Take that dirt road for approximately 500 meters to a parking area. You can also reach the area by taking the train from Rome or Pisa to either the Orbetello or Grosetto station and then reach Talamone by bus, using RAMA. Contact RAMA at www.griforama.it or 0564/475111.

The three routes located here offer hikers short, medium, and longer route options to explore this wonderful wilderness park. If you are in a hurry, the short T1 trail is an excellent opportunity to stop and stretch your legs. If you have a little more time, the T2 and T3 trails provide some of the best prospects anywhere in Italy for exploring the *macchia* ecosystem.

The T1, T2, and T3 trails all leave the parking area at Caprarecce, where there is an old farmhouse, and start by following along the perimeter of a centuries-old olive grove. Before long, the trail enters the *macchia* and begins slowly climbing the hill. One the first things you will probably notice are the thick shrubs of rosemary, lavender, and tree heather, in addition to the red and orange fruits of the strawberry tree. These fruits are edible and can be quite tasty, but sometimes they are very mealy. In spring, small purple and pink flowers perfume the air with a wonderful aroma.

About one half kilometer from the start of the trail, after crossing a fence used to keep the wild boar inside the reserve, the trail enters a dense holm oak stand. Look for an old wooden hut on the right, similar to those used by medieval monks making their way on the pilgrimage to Rome. The trail then emerges from the woods and back into the *macchia.* After 1 kilometer, the trail splits, with the T2 headed left and the T1 going right. Even if you are taking the T2, turn right and walk a few meters until you see the sign for the PUNTA PANORAMICA ("scenic overlook") going up to the left. After a brief climb, you reach the highest point of the hike, 220 meters above the sea at the summit of Punta del Corvo (Point of the Raven). From the top, a truly spectacular panorama provides a 360-degree view. To the north, you can see the entire length of the Monti dell'Uccelina to the northern portions of the park, and can spot the island of Elba, where Napoleon was exiled the first time. To the south, Talamone Bay and the promontory of Monte Argentario (Hikes 1 and 2) are visible. To the east and southeast stretch the fields and forested rolling hills of southern Tuscany, as well as the conical volcanic summit of Monte Amiata, the highest point in southern Tuscany. Out to sea, you can see the islands of Giglio and Montecristo, and if it is an exceptionally clear day, the mountains of Corsica some 150 kilometers away.

If you are following the T1 trail, descend back to the trail and turn left. This trail then follows the ridgeline for about 1 kilometer, in a semi-open *macchia* woodland. Look for signs of wild boar rooting along the sides of the trail. After 1 kilometer you will encounter an intersection where the T2 and T3 rejoin the route. Turn right, and the trail will emerge from the dark woodland, before descending down the drainage.

If you are following the T2 from the *punta panoramica,* return to the trail intersection and head right. This trail will begin to

Coastline view

descend down the slopes towards the sea. After 3 kilometers, the trail will meet a side trail that descends to a small beach at Torre Cannelle. Enjoy the wonderful view and the azure waters with a great place for lunch. You will have to climb back up the slope and will continue on the T2 as it climbs 200 meters in elevation. About 1.5 kilometers from the beach, the trail merges with the T3. If you are interested in extending this hike, you can turn left and follow the T3 for approximately 2 kilometers to its end at the Grotta della Stoppa (a small cavern in the limestone). Otherwise, turn right and shortly thereafter the trail also meets up again with the T1.

Once all three trails merge together again in the dense oak woodland, the trail will emerge into the open and will begin to descend down a fairly steep drainage. The rock here is loose, and footing can be difficult. The trail descends for a little more than 1 kilometer, before entering a dark oak woodland along a dry streambed. Eventually the trail reemerges at the ancient olive grove where there is a fence you must cross. After a brief walk through the olive grove, you will arrive at the parking area.

4

Maremma Coastline

Panoramic hike along the Tuscan coast through the Maremma macchia, to the isolated beach of Cala di Forno.

Round trip: 14.1 kilometers (8.75 miles)

Elevation: Sea level–100 meters (328 feet)

Hiking time: 4.5 hours

Difficulty: Moderate

Park: Parco Naturale della Maremma

Time to visit: October to June

Pets: Not allowed

Southern Tuscany's Parco Naturale della Maremma is situated in one of the most unspoiled and uninhabited areas in Italy. This area of green forested hills, open farmland, beautiful beaches, and azure-blue waters is a treasure yet to be discovered by the most visitors. The park contains a range of wooded limestone ridges known as the Monti dell'Uccellina, intact coastal dune ecosystems that come alive with wildflowers in the spring, marshlands teeming with birds and amphibians, undisturbed *macchia* woodlands, and long stretches of undeveloped sandy beaches. Wildlife abounds, including fallow and roe deer, foxes, badgers, hedgehogs, and the park's symbol, the wild boar.

This region remained sparsely populated for hundreds of years due to a high prevalence of malaria in the lowland marshes. With malaria now gone, this area stands as one of the most intact coastal ecosystems in Italy, preserving the upland *macchia* woodlands, and undeveloped coastal dunes and beaches. The only signs of past human habitation in the park are the medieval towers erected on the cliffs to look for pirate ships and invading armies off the coast, and an ancient olive grove. The ability to see almost no human development for as far as the eye can see, as well as the views of the islands of the Tuscan archipelago, makes this one of only a few true wilderness areas left in Italy.

From either Rome or Pisa, take the A12 Autostrada, which merges with the SS1, and head toward Grosseto. From either location

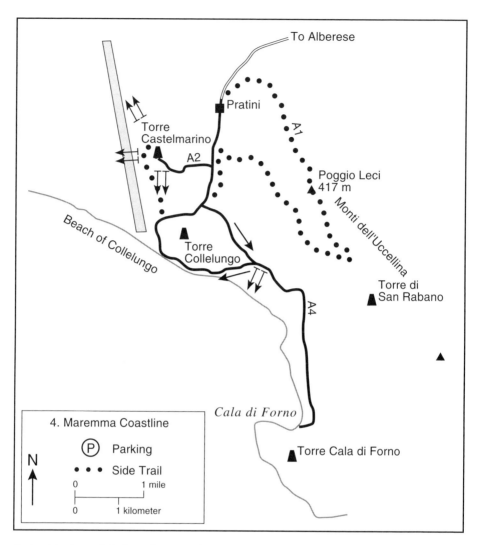

To Alberese

Pratini

Torre
Castelmarino

A2

A1

Poggio Leci
417 m

Monti dell'Uccellina

Beach of Collelungo

Torre
Collelungo

Torre di
San Rabano

A4

Cala di Forno

4. Maremma Coastline

N

Ⓟ Parking

• • • Side Trail

0   1 mile

0   1 kilometer

Torre Cala di Forno

it should take a little less than two hours. About 8 kilometers south of Grosseto, take the Rispecia-Alberese exit and follow the signs for the small village of Alberese, which you will reach in approximately 7 kilometers. There is a parking area across from the visitor center on the main road into town. Alberese can also be reached by bus from Grosetto. Contact the RAMA bus company at: www.griforama.it or call 0564/475111 for more information.

Access to the heart of the park is strictly regulated. In order to access the trails, you need to enter the visitor center at Alberese and purchase a day pass for €8, which is well worth the price! Then you will board a shuttle bus that leaves from the visitors center and takes you into the park. The bus ride is about 10 minutes long, and drops you off at Pratini, a bus turn-around spot. Spring is the best time to visit, due to the moderately warm temperatures and the prevalence of

Pirate watch tower above Valle dell'Ombrone

wildflowers. The park closes access to visitors from July 1 until September 15, due to the high heat, and fire danger.

From Pratini, the A1 trail leaves immediately to the south, and climbs steeply to the highest peak in the park. Instead, walk down the paved road—called the Strada degli Olivi, and which is closed to traffic—for 1 kilometer, until you see a sign for the A2 (Le Torri) leaving to the north. This path will lead you to the top of a hill where a medieval tower stands at the edge of a cliff, offering panoramic views across the entire northern Maremma area. You can see the island of Elba to the north, where Napoleon was exiled the first time, and the island of Giglio to the southwest. This breathtaking view is best enjoyed in the morning light before it gets hazy. You can almost imagine being stationed here 700 years ago, looking for pirates offshore. An extensive umbrella

pine woodland shades the wetlands below. You can descend straight down the cliff on the A2 to the beach, but it is recommended to retrace your steps back to the Strada degli Olivi and continue down through an ancient olive grove and until you see a sign for A4–CALA DI FORNO to the left. Along this stretch, and in the abandoned field below, look for the semi-wild Maremma cattle grazing in the tall grass.

For the first two kilometers on the A4, the trail passes through a beautiful Mediterranean scrub called the *macchia,* thick with rosemary, rock roses, and strawberry trees. In April and May, a strong perfume hangs in the air from the numerous wildflowers and it is abuzz with pollinating insects. For much of this route you will have panoramic views of the tower and beach of Cala di Forno in front of you, the promontory of Monte Argentario in the distance beyond, the beach of

View from Torre Castelmarino

Collelungo below, the Monti dell'Uccellina above, as well as the island of Giglio offshore. On an exceptionally clear day, the mountains of Corsica can be seen over 150 kilometers off shore. About 1 kilometer from the beginning of the A4, you will see a small trail headed down the cliff which says A4–RITORNO. That is for your return, so for now, continue straight ahead. Eventually the trail enters thicker brush and a dense pine-juniper woodland. Along this stretch, in the spring, be sure to have applied insect repellent for protection from ticks. At 4 kilometers from the start of the A4, the trail emerges on to the beach at Cala di Forno. This cove is very shallow and you can walk out over a hundred meters before the water gets above your waist. Continue to the far end of the beach to view undercut limestone cliffs and a variety of sea life in these tidal crevices, including sea anemones, hermit crabs, snails, oysters, and maybe even cuttlefish.

For the return, follow your way back for 3 kilometers until you see the A4–RITORNO sign. This small rocky trail descends the limestone cliff. In places it gets a little rough, and you will need to watch your hands, as the weathered limestone is razor sharp. The descent enters a pine woodland, then emerges into a wonderful untouched coastal dune habitat, full of stunted junipers and wildflowers in spring. At the beach, turn north, and follow it until just past the small promontory with the Tower of Collelungo on top. You will see a sign for the A4 headed inland on the other side of the tower, which will meet up with the paved road. Follow the paved road 3 kilometers back up the hill to Pratini, where you can catch the shuttle bus back to the visitors center.

The Tuscan Coast and Archipelago

5

Maremma Cork Oak Savannah

Twin loops through a cork oak savannah and holm oak woodland.

Round Trip: 6 kilometer (3.75 miles)

Elevation: 25–200 meters (82–656 feet)

Hiking Time: 2 hours

Difficulty: Easy

Park: Parco Naturale della Maremma

Time to Visit: October thru June

Pets: Not allowed

Located near the village of Alberese, the Parco Naturale della Maremma protects a small, but vital ecosystem and an important piece of Tuscan history, the cork oak savannah. The bark of the cork oak has been used for centuries to provide the corks for wine bottles, gaskets between metal seals, insulation, and flooring. The cork oak produces a very thick, lightweight bark that can be peeled off the tree approximately every 7–14 years, without causing much harm to the tree. The cork oak savannah contains an open understory covered by grasses and annual wildflowers, which are vital for populations of deer, small mammals, and many species of birds. Cork oak grows best in the exposed, flat lowlands of the Mediterranean region. Unfortunately, this is also the ideal area to clear for agriculture, which has resulted in a dramatic reduction of cork oak savannahs in Italy and elsewhere. Cork oaks can still be commonly seen on the Iberian peninsula, and Portugal produces 50 percent of the world's cork bark. This short and easy trail offers you an opportunity to see these beautiful trees up close, ample prospects to see wild deer, and to appreciate the history of this important ecological treasure.

To get to the park from Pisa or Rome, follow directions for Hike 4, Maremma Coastline. Walk from the visitors center to the church and turn right onto the road. A track will branch right and past a field toward a fenceline. At the fence, there will be gate where you may enter the park, designed to keep wildlife in and hunters out.

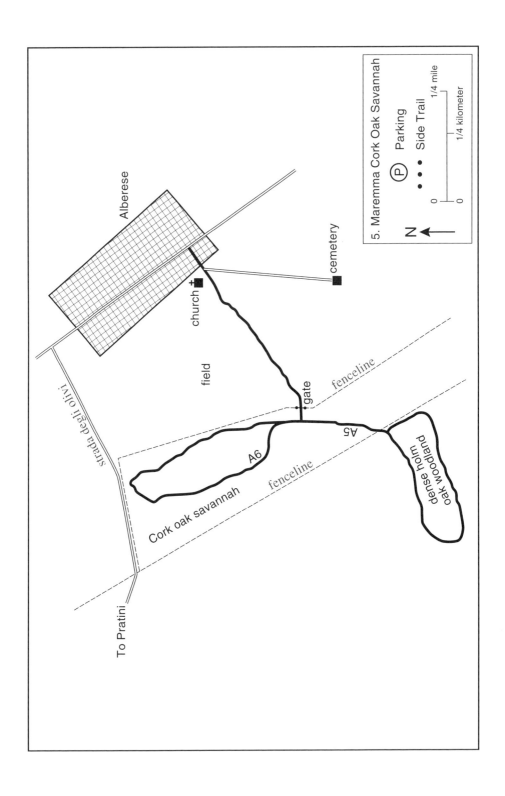

Alberese

church

field

cemetery

strada degli olivi

fenceline

gate

A6

A5

Cork oak savannah

fenceline

To Pratini

dense holm
oak woodland

N

5. Maremma Cork Oak Savannah

Ⓟ Parking

• • • Side Trail

0   1/4 mile
0   1/4 kilometer

Deer in the cork oak savannah

This hike actually consists of two short trail loops. To the left, the A5 loops through a dense holm oak woodland, up a steep slope, and down along an old rock wall. This loop begins in an open savannah, which is filled with wildflowers in spring, climbs over an old rock wall, and then enters the dark woodland. This route offers the visitor a chance to sample one of Italy's most common ecosystems. Once that loop is complete, return to the gate and then take the A6 loop. The loop will pass large cork oaks—stripped of their bark up to three meters high, and in varying stages of regrowth.

This is where the open cork oak savannah is present—protected from development, hunting, and other disturbances. This area contains a large herd of fallow deer, which likely will be visible grazing on the grasses and shrubs that make up the understory of these majestic oaks. Wild boar, badger, weasels, foxes, and hedgehogs are also common in these forests, but are more nocturnal. Once the second loop is complete, go back through the gate and back to the village of Alberese. In town, the park visitors center has additional information about other ecosystems it protects.

Hiking in the cork oak savannah

Maremma Cork Oak Savannah

6

Elba–Pomonte Valley Loop

A rugged loop high above the Pomonte Valley and then down the lush valley bottom at the base of Monte Capanne.

Round trip: 12.1 kilometers (7.5 miles)

Elevation: Sea level–634 meters (0–2,080 feet)

Hiking time: 5–6 hours

Park: Parco Nazionale della Arcipelago Toscano

Difficulty: Strenuous

Time to visit: Year round; avoid midday in summer

Recommended time: Late spring

The western half of the island of Elba is an open and arid landscape, which appears more similar to Andalucía, Spain than the rest of Italy. Open xeric scrublands of rock rose, tree heather, and lavender dominate the ridgelines. These exposed landscapes are highly susceptible to fire, and evidence of these burns is common across the island. In contrast to the dry ridges, narrow fingers of forests located in the deep valley bottoms contain chestnuts, alder, and hornbeam. Just above the drainage beds, Aleppo pine, holm oak, and strawberry tree occur where there is some summer shade from the ridge above. Aspect and elevation affect these ecosystems dramatically, in this harsh climate. The Pomonte valley is a deep southwest-facing valley that receives intense sun during the long summer drought. High above the valley, the 1,000 meter monolith of Monte Capanne dominates the landscape. A hike in the Pomonte valley is a rugged climb to the ridgeline high above the valley, into the xeric scrubland and garigue, and then a descent into an almost subtropical riparian woodland which contain enormous alder trees and chestnuts, draped by old ivy vines and interspersed with huge sword ferns.

To get to the Pomonte valley, follow directions for the Piombino Coast (Hike 9) and then follow signs for the various ferry companies to the port. Two ferry companies (Moby Lines Ferries and Toremar Ferry Company) offer regular service to Portoferraio on Elba. The trip takes about 1 hour. Upon arriving at Portoferraio, follow signs for

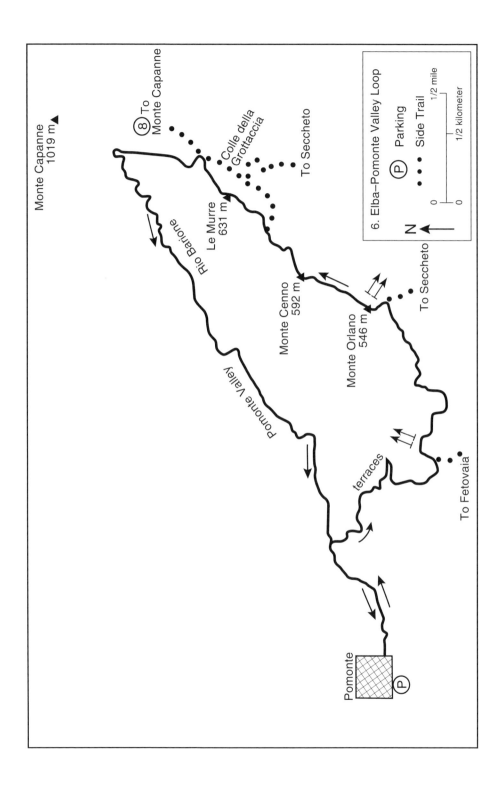

Monte Capanne
1019 m ▲

⑧ To Monte Capanne

Colle della Grottaccia

To Seccheto

Le Murre 631 m

Rio Barione

Monte Cenno 592 m

Pomonte Valley

Monte Orlano 546 m

To Seccheto

terraces

To Fetovaia

Pomonte

Ⓟ

6. Elba–Pomonte Valley Loop

Ⓟ Parking

•••• Side Trail

1/2 mile
1/2 kilometer

0
0

N ←

Pomonte Valley

Procchio (SP24) and then for Marina di Campo (SP25). At Marina di Campo, continue following the SP25 along the south coast, toward Fetovaia and Pomonte. As you enter Pomonte, pull into the parking area to the left, below the road, and start from there.

The route begins by walking into the village and turning right at the church. Follow this road until it reaches the back of the village as it heads up into the valley. To the right, a small footbridge will head toward some gardens, and signs will indicate Trails 31 and 9, headed to Monte Capanne and Colle della Grottaccia, respectively. The trail begins by heading through gardens growing grapes, berries, and figs. Elban wine is becoming quite famous in Italy because of the intense sun and excellent growing conditions, and is worth a try.

After about 1 kilometer, the trail will branch and the loop begins. Either direction is acceptable, but for several reasons, it is recommended to go right on Trail 31, heading up to the top of the ridgeline. First of all, it is generally easier on your knees to climb up steep slopes than descend them. Second, this is a very exposed valley and it is best to do all of the climbing in the morning while it

is still cool, rather than in the heat of the midafternoon. Third, it will get you to the spectacular panoramic views all the more quickly, and you will be able to see Monte Capanne for the entire length of the ridgeline.

The climb up the ridgeline is steep and rocky. It will ascend through some overgrown terraces, now containing large tree heathers that shade the route. If you are sweating in the heat, just imagine the local villagers of old who had to climb this slope every day to work this land. Across the valley on the opposite ridgeline is a burned area, where many more high terraces are now visible.

The higher you climb, the thinner the vegetation gets. By the time you reach the top of the ridge, 1.5 kilometer from the trail intersection, only scattered shrubs of rock rose and lavender remain upon the rocky ground. Once you reach the ridgetop, incredible views open up across the sea. The islands of Montecristo and Pianosa are visible to the south. Giglio and the promontory of Monte Argentario (Hike 1) are visible to the southeast. The mountains of Corsica are to the west, and Monte Capanne rises up, above the back of the valley.

A caprile and Monte Capanne

The trail continues its gradual ascent following the ridgeline, passing several stone goatherders' sheds *(caprile),* and through open xeric scrub and garigue grasslands. The area contains evidence of past fire activity, and in many locations strawberry trees and rock roses have resprouted from the scorched ground. Following this trail, you will encounter a major intersection at a *caprile,* where a route will head down toward the village of Seccheto alongside the sea, where the sandy beach covered in sunbathers is visible far below. Turn left, and continue heading upslope. Shortly thereafter, you will come to the summit of Monte Orlano and a magnificent 360-degree panorama of the entire Pomonte valley, and down the length of southern Elba.

Continuing along the ridgeline, the terrain remains rocky and exposed, but the views get more expansive. The trail will skirt just to the east of Monte Cenno and then will approach the large open saddle of Colle della Grottaccia, 1.6 kilometers after the intersection with the Seccheto trail. Just before reaching the saddle, a beautiful old dry-stone *caprile* with a rounded roof is back-dropped by the rocky wall of Monte Capanne. The trail will descend to a low saddle and then will continue uphill, while another trail to Seccheto heads right. Climb up the slope a short way and you will come to another intersection.

Trail 8 will continue up the ridgeline, eventually heading to the summit of Monte Capanne, some 350 meters higher. It is possible to reach the summit about 3 kilometers further along, by following Trail 8, until it joins with Trail 5. Then follow Trail 5 until it meets up with Trail 1, which climbs to the summit. However, there are other options for reaching the summit, including following Hike 7 in this book, or using the cableway from Marciana.

To descend into the Pomonte valley, turn left, following Trail 9. The trail will gradually descend into the valley, soon entering a strawberry tree and holm oak woodland. Once you reach the cool waters of the Rio Barione, the forest type changes over to a riparian woodland of giant alders and chestnuts, with huge ivy vines climbing to the canopy, and beautiful sword ferns emerging from the moist rocks. In the stream, tadpoles of the Sardinian tree frog may be seen. Along the way, blackberries offer a delicious treat in late summer. The trail headed back is very relaxing, as it gradually descends for the next 1 kilometer and is shaded near the stream bed for long stretches. The trail will emerge from the woods for good approximately 2.5 kilometers from the village of Pomonte, as it enters scattered garden plots and *macchia* vegetation. Once in Pomonte, several bars offer drinks and *gelato,* to celebrate the end of a wonderful hike. The waters are crystal clear, so why not cool off with a swim?

7

Elba–Monte Capanne Summit Loop

A rugged climb up the granite mountain of Monte Capanne, the highest point on Elba.

Round trip: 12.6 km (7.8 miles)

Elevation: 326–1,019 meters (1,069–3,348 feet)

Hiking time: 5–6 hours

Park: Parco Nazionale della Arcipelago Toscano

Difficulty: Strenuous

Time to visit: Year round; avoid midday in summer and watch for ice in winter

Recommended time: Late spring

Monte Capanne, at over 1,000 meters in elevation, is the highest point in the Tuscan Archipelago and of all of southern Tuscany, except for the remote volcano of Monte Amiata. It is a granite pluton formed approximately 6 million years ago by igneous intrusions, during the volcanism that also formed the islands of Capraia, Giglio, and Montecristo. From the summit of Monte Capanne, the entire island of Elba can be viewed from above, and a spectacular vista is available that spans the entire Tuscan Coast and Archipelago, from the Alpi Apuane in the north, to Monte Argentario to the south, as well as a wonderful view of Bastia and the rugged mountains on Corsica. The trail climbs up the northern slopes of the mountain, however, thus offering shade for lush chestnut forests, Aleppo pine and oak woodlands, and beautiful *macchia* scrub, blooming with rock roses in spring. The north-facing amphitheater created by the mountain also provides habitat for Sardinian tree frogs and rare yew trees.

The trail for Monte Capanne departs from the village of Marciana, perched 300 meters up the slopes above the azure-blue waters. To get there, follow directions for the Piombino Coast (Hike 9) and then follow the plentiful signs for the various ferry companies at the port. Two ferry companies (Moby Lines Ferries and Toremar Ferry Company) offer regular service to Portoferraio on Elba. The trip takes about 1 hour. Upon arriving at Portoferraio, follow signs for Procchio (SP24), drive through the village, and then follow signs for Marciana (SP25). Park in the

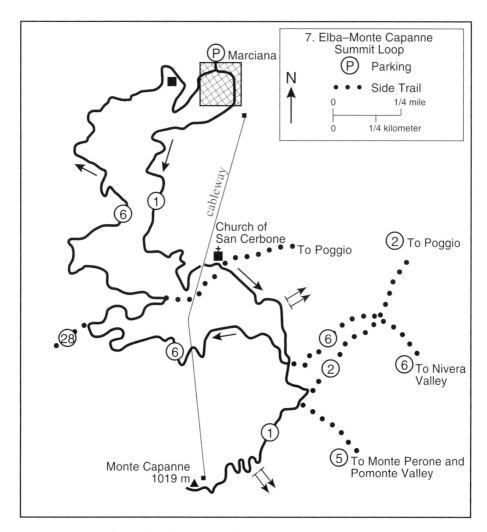

7. Elba–Monte Capanne
Summit Loop
Ⓟ   Parking
•••   Side Trail
0   1/4 mile
0   1/4 kilometer

Ⓟ Marciana

N

cableway

Church of
San Cerbone
† •••• •To Poggio

②To Poggio

②8

⑥

①

⑥

⑥

②

⑥To Nivera
Valley

①

⑤To Monte Perone and
Pomonte Valley

Monte Capanne
1019 m

free parking area located at the bottom of the village to the right.

Just before reaching the village, a cableway station offers visitors an opportunity to take a cable car to the summit for €10 one way. Thus, it is possible to make the climb up and ride the cable car down, to save the strain on your knees. Or, take the cable car up and then hike down. Either way, there is an option available if the weather is too hot or cold, time is a factor, or you simply are not prepared to hike that day.

The route to the summit begins initially by crossing the main street through Marciana, turning left into the narrow alleyway, and then walking toward the back of town. Red/white blazes on the buildings will assist you in finding the way. Trail 1 leaves from town and heads directly into a chestnut forest and through overgrown terraces. During the first 1.5 kilometers, the trail is a gentle stroll through the forest and across some nice streambeds heading down the slopes. After 1.5 kilometers, the trail will pass under

A view of the Elba coastline from the Monte Capanne trail

the cableway, heading upslope towards the summit.

From here, you get a good idea of what is ahead, as the summit of Monte Capanne stands 500 meters directly above. Right next to this cableway crossing is the 6th-century church of San Cerbone, which was reconstructed in 1421. In the courtyard area, enormous chestnut and atlas cedars are present, which most likely have been protected from the axe for centuries. Go just past the church, ignoring the dirt access road, and look to the right, as the trail begins climbing up the slopes of the mountain. The trail initially heads through second-growth chestnuts that sprout from enormous cut stumps. Soon, the trail emerges into an open *macchia* scrub with some beautiful views of the coastline and the medieval village of Poggio below. The climb is steep, but rock steps have been placed on the trail to assist hikers.

From here, the trail climbs steeply, reenters the woods, and then comes to an intersection with Trail 6. Take note: On the return, you will head to the right here (left, as you are coming down). Continue straight up the steep slope as it climbs relentlessly to the ridgeline above. You will soon encounter another intersection near a goat shed *(caprile),* this time, with Trail 1 heading towards the right for Monte Capanne and Trail 2 heading left, back down to Poggio. Continue heading up towards the summit, as the trail climbs above the last of the Aleppo pines and above the treeline. The treeline here is very low, even by Italian standards, due to the relatively sparse precipitation, the rocky substrate, poorly developed soils, and intense winds experienced during winter storms. Trail 5 will soon branch off to the left, toward the saddle in the ridgeline visible across the drainage, but continue following Trail 1 towards the summit.

The trail will now climb very steeply across a talus slope, with tall bracken ferns and some hardy green ash trees sticking out of the rocks. Near the summit, thorny

View of Pomonte Valley from the summit

dwarf broom creates a carpet of sharp needles on the ground. I have not seen this species elsewhere in Italy, although it is common in Andalucía, Spain. The summit and its radio towers still sit high above, but just under 1 kilometer from the last trail intersection, the trail switchbacks back and forth several times, and then arrives at the summit area, where there is a small bar and the cableway station. Here, you will likely encounter a fair number of people milling about, but the real summit still beckons a little higher up, where the radio towers are. At the actual summit, a viewing platform offers sweeping views across the sea, and down the coast. Other than Capraia (Hike 10), no other place offers such extensive views of Corsica. In addition, the incredible granite fortress island of Montecristo sits offshore, to the south. It is easy to see how this island inspired Alexandre Dumas to write *The Count of Monte Cristo.*

To the southwest, the long Pomonte Valley (Hike 6) extends to the sea. The ribbon of dark green forest extending down this valley follows the streambed. Above the valley, the slopes appear barren and rocky, evidence of the arid conditions on the island. The flat island just off shore from Pomonte is Pianosa, where a former high-security penal colony sits on an uplifted limestone terrace. To the northwest, the island of Capraia (Hike 10) is visible just offshore, as well as Gorgona, a little further out. To the southeast, the island of Giglio sits just right of Monte Argentario (Hike 1), which also looks like an island. While due east, the Piombino Coast (Hike 9) and the mines of San Silvestro (Hike 16) are visible, as well as the high volcanic summit of Monte Amiata well off in the distance.

For the return, retrace you steps until you return to the intersection with Trail 6. Turn left and follow this beautiful, gentle trail as it gradually descends toward Marciana. The trail will cross the cableway again, and head past some moist seeps which contain the tadpoles of the Sardinian tree frog. The trail then enters thick stands of pine, oak, and chestnut, and you may be able to see the elusive grey asp sliding into the leaf litter.

Soon you will encounter the intersection with Trail 28 heading upslope to the left. Stay right, however, and head downslope following Trail 6. The trail will come to a dirt track used by park personnel. Turn left and follow this road, as it remains Trail 6 heading for Marciana. The route will soon pass a catchment basin filled with tadpoles. The route continues through forests and open stretches, as it follows the amphitheater of the mountain, which offers different perspectives of the mountain and the surrounding landscape. After the steep initial climb to the summit, this is a pleasant way to return to Marciana, without the knee-shattering descent. Just above the village of Marciana, there will be an intersection of two dirt roads. Stay right, and follow the track downslope. The road will gradually get more pavement-like, before becoming fully paved, upon reaching the fortress ruins at the top of the village. From the fortress, take the stairs down into the heart of the village and continue downhill until it reaches the parking area.

Bonus Hike

Elba–Ruins of Volterraio

A rugged climb up the granite mountain of Monte Capanne, the highest point on Elba.

Round trip: 2.5 kilometers (1.6 miles)

Elevation: 247–394 meters (810–1,292 feet)

Hiking time: 1 hour

Park: Parco Nazionale dell'Arcipelago Toscano

Difficulty: Moderately easy

Time to visit: Year round

The ruins of the medieval fortress of Volterraio are located in the *macchia* and pine-covered hills on eastern side of Elba. This fortress was built in 1281 by the Pisan empire, high above the harbor of Portoferraio, on the ruins of an Etruscan site. Its purpose was to watch over the trade routes from the mainland into Elba, particularly Saracen pirates and other potential enemies. At the time, Portoferraio was a particularly important port, due to the large quantities of iron and other metals which were mined on Elba, and shipped across the sea. In the long history of Elba, it is the only fortress on the island that was never captured by enemy invaders. In fact, in 1534 it served as the primary refuge for the residents of Portoferraio, when the Barbary pirate Barbarossa attacked and destroyed the city. Today, the fortress still stands high above the city, offering grand views of the harbor and of much of the island, including Monte Capanne (Hike 7). The trail to the top is steep, but very short, allowing you a bird's-eye view that you may likely never forget.

To get to Volterraio, take the SP26 out of Portoferraio towards Porto Azzurro. Then, look for signs for Rionell'Elba, heading to the left. Follow the SP28 and then the SP32, following signs for Rionell'Elba. As the roads climbs up over the hills, you can see the fortress high above. Volterraio sits on the large, cone-shaped peak just south of the main hills. As the road switchbacks up the ridgeline, look for a parking area on the left at the base of the hill. There is only a small

View of Portoferraio

Volterraio ridge

sign here indicating the trailhead, so watch for the parking area carefully.

The ruins can be seen 150 meters up above the parking area. The trail is steep and rocky, but easy to follow. The first part of the climb has some loose stones, while the top is very rocky. From the top, the view is spectacular, with Monte Capanne and Portoferraio being the most obvious sights. You can also look to the north, and follow the coast of mainland Italy. To the east and south are the forested hills of the eastern and central part of Elba. Retrace your steps back to the parking area.

Sterpaia Coastal Park

Loop trail through a variety of coastal habitats including beach, dunes, bogs, pine woodlands, and an old-growth ash forest.

Round trip: 5.3 kilometers (3.3 miles)

Elevation: Sea level

Hiking time: 1–2 hours

Park: Parco Costiero della Sterpaia (Val di Cornia)

Difficulty: Easy

Time to visit: Year round

Located just outside of the industrial center of Piombino is the beautiful coastal nature reserve of Sterpaia. Protected within its 269 hectares are a variety of fragile ecosystems, including an extremely rare old-growth ash forest (Bosco della Sterpaia). In addition, this preserve protects coastal dune, bog, and grassland habitats, *macchia*-juniper thickets, and pine woodlands. Even the rare Mediterranean fan palms can be found within the park, near the northernmost edge of their range. On summer days, the beaches of Sterpaia are covered with sun-bathers. However, away from the beach, visitors can still escape the crowds by walking through the forests and fields. In winter, Sterpaia is an excellent place to take advantage of the clear, sunny days, as the beaches are empty.

To get to Parco Costiero della Sterpaia, take the SS1 south from Pisa. Just south of Piombino, leave the SS1 and take the Vignale-Riotorto exit. After exiting the SS1, look for brown signs for Parco della Sterpaia, and follow the road which will go under the highway and toward the coast. Immediately after crossing the overpass and rail line, there will be a series of brown signs pointing left for parking areas at Sterpaia, including Carbonifera, Il Pino, and Mortelliccio. Ignore this road and continue for about one kilometer more, until you see a brown sign pointing left for the Bosco della Sterpaia and Carlappiano. Follow this road to the end at the beach area. There will be a large parking area on the left. Directly next to the large parking lot, take a left onto the

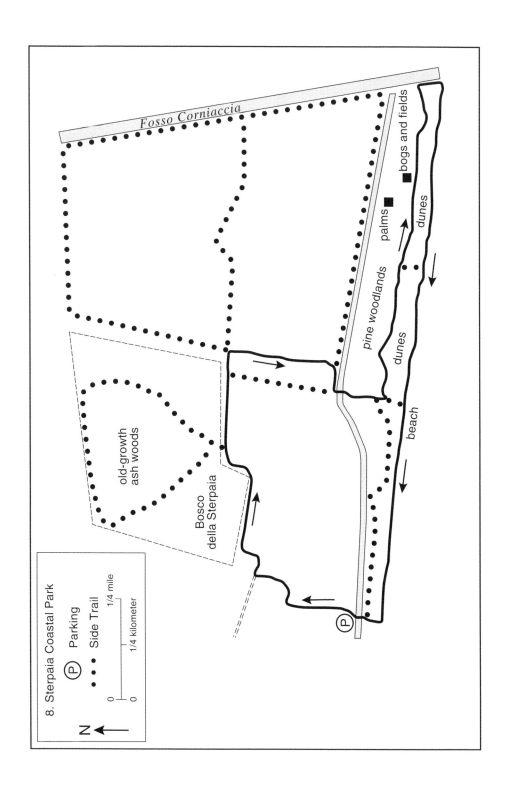

8. Sterpaia Coastal Park

Ⓟ Parking
• • • Side Trail

N ←

Fosso Corniaccia

old-growth
ash woods

Bosco
della Sterpaia

pine woodlands

palms

bogs and fields

dunes

dunes

beach

Ⓟ

0 ⌞___⌟ 1/4 mile
0 ⌞___⌟ 1/4 kilometer

Dunes at Sterpaia Coastal Park

dirt road that heads toward the woods, and park at the smaller lot at the end. It is possible to reach Sterpaia by bus from the train station at Campiglia Marittima. Contact ATM Piombino for more information at www.atm.li.it or 0565/260111.

From the far end of the parking area, the route begins on the dirt path heading inland from the canal and coast. After about 400 meters, the route meets a closed gate on the right and a road heading left. Go past the gate, and follow this route along the fenced Bosco della Sterpaia. This is an old-growth ash forest, unique in the region. These types of woodlands were far more common in the past, but draining of the wetlands and deforestation for agriculture have now left them fragmented and rare. Throughout the stand, there are some truly massive ash and deciduous oak trees. The area is protected, and access is available only through reservations being made with park officials.

This route follows the fence for about 470 meters, offering tantalizing glimpses inside, while two interpretive signs outside the fence provide information about the ecosystems of the park. The route them emerges from the woods at a field, and there will be an access gate for the ash forest, which is normally locked. If you have obtained the keys for the gate from the park office, or are with a guided tour, you can take the pleasant walk along the 1+ kilometer loop.

About 200 meters after the gate, there will be two parallel roads headed toward the sea. You can choose between the first, which is lined with tall trees to provide shade in the summer heat; or the second, which goes through the open field, providing warming sunshine in winter. Once you reach the canal, cross the bridge and enter the coastal pine forest. After about 130 meters, turn left at the sign for A13. There are 22 access points to the sea at Sterpaia, and you may choose to use any of them.

The beach at Sterpaia Coastal Park in winter

However, in order to see the maximum variety of ecosystems in the park, wait until the last access point (A22) to head to the sea.

For a little more than 1 kilometer, the A-route will go through interesting macchia thickets, umbrella and maritime pine woodlands, and eventually into open, grassy, coastal bogs. Along the edges of the bogs, some scattered clumps of the rare Mediterranean fan palm are visible on the left. Once you reach A22, turn right and head onto the beach, to enjoy the beautiful view down the Tuscan coast and across to the island of Elba.

From here it is 1.8 kilometers back along the beach to the A4 access point, which will lead you back to the parking area. From A22, it is also possible to cross the large canal and continue down the beach for an additional 5 kilometers in the other direction. All along the beach, there are some lovely dunes, covered in wildflowers in the spring. For shell collectors, clams and oysters of amazing colors and varieties are scattered across the beach.

Other Notes: In summer, a tram service drives down the A-route to drop visitors off at all these access points. To explore more of Sterpaia, there are other hiking routes north of the canal, which provide an additional 3 kilometers or so, where hikers can escape the crowds by walking along pleasant oak, ash, and pine woodlands. See the attached map for these alternate loops.

To access the old-growth ash forest of Bosco della Sterpaia, there are two options: You can take a guided tour on Saturdays, Sundays, and Wednesdays at 15:00 (3 PM) and 16:30 (4:30 PM), or take a solo tour with reservations in advance. For reservations and more information, call the park office at +39/348/888/3165.

9

Piombino Coast and Punta Falcone

Hike along the coast near Piombino, from Punta Falcone to Punta Galera via Fosso alle Canne.

Distance: 10 kilometers (6.2 miles)

Elevation: Sea level to 40 meters (0–130 feet)

Hiking Time: 3–4 hours

Park: Parco Val di Cornia and Parco di Punta Falcone

Difficulty: Easy

Time to visit: Year round

The rugged coast near the city of Piombino offers some unexpected and extraordinary scenery that rivals that of the more famous, and significantly more touristy, Cinque Terre. With the beautiful, but busy, island of Elba just offshore, many people pass right by this beautiful coastline without even noticing what this area has to offer. Piombino is an industrial town most people know best as the place to catch the ferries to the island of Elba. However, just to the north of the city is an unspoiled coastline with virtually no signs of civilization. While most tourists make a beeline through the city to the ferry docks, seldom do they stop and hike along the rugged, wild coastline that makes up the promontory between Piombino and the Estruscan ruins of Populonia. The coast along this stretch offers spectacular views of Elba, Corsica, and the Tuscan archipelago; isolated coves and beaches; azure-blue waters and spectacular snorkeling; the sweet scent of *macchia* wildflowers in spring; and most importantly, year-round solace from the rush of tourism that hits other more famous coastal areas.

To get to the Piombino coast from Pisa, take the SS1 headed south to Grosseto and Rome. After about 45 minutes on the SS1 near the town of Venturini, get on the SS398 toward Piombino. Beware that prior to Venturini, there will be an exit at San Vincenzo, which also says Piombino. Ignore this exit, as it gets onto a small and very slow road that adds extra time. As you approach Piombino, you will see refineries and iron-smelting facilities on the left. Look for the road turning

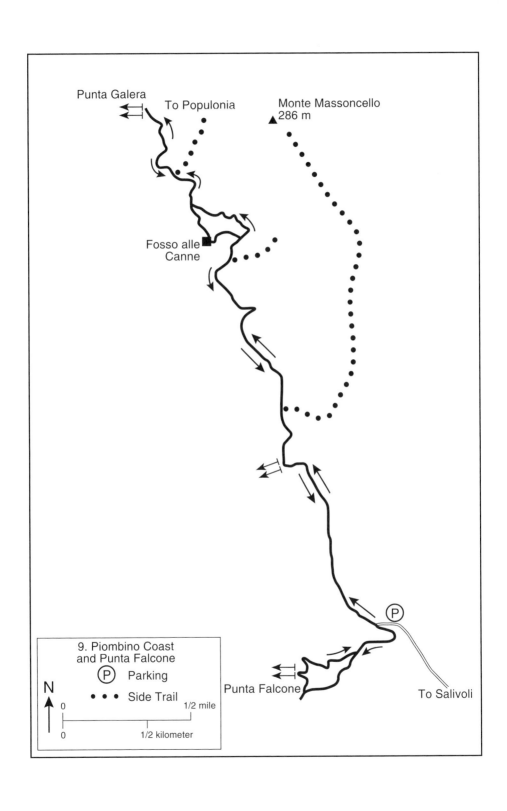

Punta Galera

To Populonia

Monte Massoncello
▲ 286 m

Fosso alle
Canne

Ⓟ

To Salivoli

Punta Falcone

9. Piombino Coast
and Punta Falcone

Ⓟ Parking

• • • Side Trail

N

0 _____ 1/2 mile

0 _____ 1/2 kilometer

Punta Falcone

to the right, toward Salivoli. Follow the road into Salivoli, then when in town, look for a left turn that goes down the hill toward the sea, with brown signs for Punta Falcone. At the bottom of the hill, turn right and the road will end very soon at a park. Parking is located just up above on the left, where the road turns 180 degrees. Buses from Piombino to Salivoli are also available. Contact ATM Piombino at www.atm.li.it or 0565/260111.

The route has two segments: a short 1.6 kilometer loop to the end of Punta Falcone; and the main stretch to the north from where the road ended. You may either do the short loop at the beginning or at the end, but either way you will walk past your car again. To do the Punta Falcone loop, walk up from the parking lot via a small trail in the grass, to the dead-end road above. Turn right on the road, and walk to the end where Parco di Punta Falcone begins. The trail entering the park leaves from a metal gate. Almost immediately, there will be two

tunnels dug into the rock on the left, which date back to WWII. When the trail splits, take a left, and within a couple hundred meters you will arrive at the astronomical observatory, and spectacular views of the southern Tuscan coast. From Punta Falcone you can see Monte Argentario (Hike 1), the islands of Giglio, Montecristo, Elba, and Capraia (Hike 10), as well as the city of Piombino. As you continue on the loop toward the tip of Punta Falcone, beautiful tide pools and excellent snorkeling spots become evident. Punta Falcone is made of volcanic pillow basalts, where magma erupted under water at the same time that volcanic activity was creating the islands of Capraia, Montecristo, and Elba.

There are also some old WWII artillery sites with interpretive displays present, that are interesting to look at. The loop will continue north, offering views up the coast where the main route heads. Once you have returned to the parking area, you can begin

Punta Galera

the main segment by walking past the chain and down the old road until the pavement turns into dirt. On a sunny weekend, there may be significant numbers of people near the trailhead and around Punta Falcone, but once you walk about 500 meters down the coast, all evidence of civilization will completely disappear, except for the ferries that are running to Elba just offshore.

Elba dominates the view along this route, with its 1,000 meter summit of Monte Capanne (Hike 7) looking completely out of place surrounded by the sea. Corsica sits behind Elba, extending far to the northwest, with the island of Capraia, a little further north of that. Within 1 kilometer of the parking area, an elbow of coast juts out, providing a great view both north and south along the coast, as well as a myriad of pools and rocks down below in the crystal-clear blue waters. The trail eventually enters a holm oak and strawberry tree woodland. At approximately 2 kilometers from the parking area, a

dirt track will branch off to the right, climbing steeply up the ridge. This route climbs to the summit of the ridge toward Monte Massoncello, and eventually all the way to Populonia. There are virtually no views from up there because of the dense forest; this route is mostly used by woodcutters and hunters. Instead, continue straight along the smaller trail past tree heather and mastic trees, to more open views of the sea. After crossing a pig fence, you will encounter a trail intersection under a dense canopy, with one trail dropping down to the left, to the beach at Fosso alle Canne. The trail to the right eventually dead ends in the brush. As you descend toward the beach, the trail branches again near a picnic bench, where you will again turn left and continue down to the beach.

Fosso alle Canne, located 3 kilometers from the trailhead, is a small isolated cove with excellent snorkeling opportunities. There is a small bar that is open in summer to serve snacks and drinks. For many local visitors, this is where they will take lunch before heading back. But, if you want to eat lunch in isolation, with a spectacular view of the sea, there is a much more interesting spot further north up the coast. To continue past the beach, either return to the picnic bench and turn left, or look for a small way-trail at north end of the beach, next to the bar, which climbs up the slope and eventually meets up with the main trail again. Turn left, and continue on the main trail as it heads in and out of the woods, offering great views along the way. After about 500 meters, the trail will split. To the right, and up the slope, the trail continues for another 4 kilometers or so to Populonia. However, the trail enters a dense thicket of vegetation that offers no further views until the end. Instead, it is recommended that you take the trail to the left, as it will soon come across the ruins of a medieval farmhouse and then the trail will end at a spectacular bluff looking north to Punta Galera. This is where you should eat lunch! If you are even more adventurous, back about 50 meters from where the trail ended there is a small way-trail dropping very steeply to the rocks below, with access to the small beach that is visible from the top of the cliff. The end of the trail is 4.2 kilometers from the parking area. To return, hike back the way you came, following the main trail all the way and bypassing Fosso alle Canne.

10

Island of Capraia

Loop from the harbor to the summit of Monte delle Penne through rare island ecosystems.

Round trip: 14 kilometers (8.7 miles)

Elevation: Sea level–400 meters (1,312 feet)

Hiking time: 4–5 hours

Park: Parco Nazionale dell'Arcipelago Toscana

Difficulty: Moderate

Time to visit: Year round; avoid midday on hot summer days

The island of Capraia sits 68 kilometers off the coast from Livorno and is much closer to Corsica than to mainland Italy. Part of the Parco Nazionale dell'Arcipelago Toscano, this island offers some of the most beautiful wilderness left in Europe. The island only supports one small village with a little over 300 summertime residents. Other than this village and the occasional 1,000-year-old watchtower or 2nd-century church, the island remains wild and untamed. The island is of volcanic origin, and the pillars of andesite are obvious as you arrive by ferry and while climbing Monte delle Penne (Mountain of the Pens). Within the matrix of Mediterranean scrub and on the 300 meter high sheer cliffs of the coast are endemic species of plants, the northernmost population of Mediterranean fan palms in the world, unusual salt-spray grasslands, and the only freshwater marsh in the archipelago. The rare Corsican finch can be found on the island, as well as colonies of the rare Audouin's gull, yellow-legged gull, Mediterranean shags, and the Manx shearwater. Capraia is the closest island to Corsica, and as such offers spectacular views of the mountains. Snorkeling the crystal-clear blue waters is an incredible experience, and diving into the Neptune grass beds and soft coral reefs is also possible, through local services.

In addition, this island contains an abandoned village, which is the Italian equivalent of an Old West ghost town, and where an agricultural penal colony was once located.

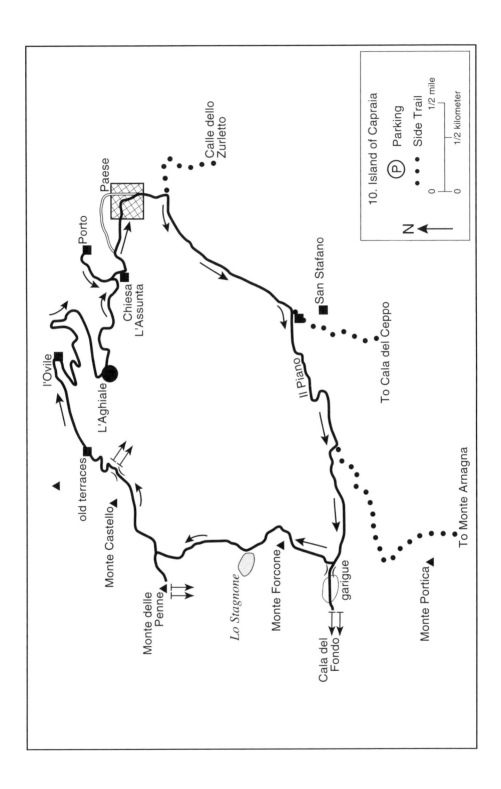

10. Island of Capraia

Ⓟ Parking
••••• Side Trail

N ←

Porto

l'Ovile

old terraces

▲ Monte Castello

Monte delle Penne

Lo Stagnone

Monte Forcone ▲

Cala del Fondo

garigue

Monte Portica ▲

To Monte Arnagna

Paese

Chiesa L'Assunta

L'Aghiale

Calle dello Zurletto

San Stafano

Il Piano

To Cala del Ceppo

0   1/2 mile
0   1/2 kilometer

The Island of Capraia offers some spectacular views.

Capraia has a long and colorful history as a place where people could escape persecution, yet always had to be wary of the Arab invaders or any turf wars among the wealthy Renaissance families on the mainland.

To get to Capraia, the Toremar ferry (www.toremar.it) offers daily service from Livorno. The ride takes about two hours each way. In addition, there are summer ferries that run from Marina di Pisa and other locations which can get you there faster, but this is a trip you need to plan carefully, as lodging on the island is limited. However, if you get an early enough ferry there, you will have time to hike the loop and do a little snorkeling before having to catch a ferry back.

The ferry drops you off at the harbor called Porto. From here you walk along the small harbor and head up into the village of Paese, following the signs for Monte delle Penne, Lo Stagnone, Il Piano, and Chiesa di San Stefano. Once on the other side of the village, you will see these signs again, and soon an old cobblestone route leads away

from the village and into the wilderness. Getting up from Porto and through the village can seem confusing, but do not worry, you will not get lost. Just make sure you do not follow the route to Cala dello Zurletto, unless you want to go swimming.

Once you are on the route leading away from the village, the land will grow increasingly wild, although you will be able to see signs of old rock walls, scattered pine trees, and the occasional terraced slope. After about 15 minutes you will arrive at Il Piano, where you will see a vineyard. This is the site of the first village on the island that dates back to the Roman Empire. The trail splits, with the route to the 2nd-century church of San Stefano—which is one of the oldest churches in Europe—heading left. This church served the village of Il Piano until Saracen raiders destroyed the community in the middle ages.

To the right, the old cobbled path heads up the drainage, climbing to the ridgeline above. At one point, as you wind in and out

Approaching Capraia on the ferry

of lush strawberry tree groves, you will see a grassy saddle that appears to be your goal. While you will reach it eventually, prior to that you will keep climbing up above it to the south. Just as you are approaching the crest of the ridge, a small trail leaves to the right, with a sign that reads MONTE DELLE PENNE and LO STAGNONE. Follow this trail, which is overgrown and not well maintained. If you have those shorts that have zip-on legs, put them on now, because the brush will scratch your legs. You will wind your way through the scrub until you descend to the grassy garigue saddle of Cala del Fondo. The salt grasses and euphorbs are located here because the winds and salt spray that slam against the rocky coast below are forced upslope and find this saddle, nearly 300 meters above the sea, the easiest place to cross the ridge. The winds scour down the shrubs and the salts poison the soil for all but the hardiest, salt-tolerant garigue vegetation. At the saddle, turn left and walk 100 meters to the cliff face, and look down into the beautiful Cala del Fondo for a view across to Corsica, only 30 kilometers off shore.

Once you return to the main trail, continue up the side of Monte Forcone, through more dense *macchia*. Eventually you will descend into another saddle, this one also grassy, but containing a marshy cattail bog known as Lo Stagnone. I saw pictures of it from the past, when it was a beautiful, clear lake reflecting the summit of Monte delle Penne, but when I was there, it was nothing more than an overgrown stagnant cattail marsh. Nonetheless, this is the only freshwater lake on any of the Tuscan islands, and is critical habitat for Sardinian tree frogs, dragonflies, and other aquatic species.

Continue on toward Monte delle Penne, which becomes quite obvious at this point, as a peak with many volcanic columns rising from the summit. This section is probably the most spectacular part of the hike. Below

The Tuscan Coast and Archipelago

are dramatic cliffs, dropping 300–400 meters to the sea. The water is a beautiful blue color and it seems you could just jump off for a little snorkeling, which you will definitely feel like doing on a hot summer day. This section also begins to reveal the entire topography of the island, as you can see all of the mountain tops on the island and the Torre dello Zenebetto, located on the southernmost tip of the island. From the top of Monte delle Penne, you get a 360-degree panorama of the island, including the beautiful northern cliffs and the eroded tuff grottos down below, and the town of Capraia Paese (known locally as Paese) to the east.

According to park maps, the trail ends here and you would have to backtrack the way you came, back to the port. However, from the summit of Monte delle Penne, you can see another small saddle garigue to the north with a trail going through it. It seems as though you could follow that trail back towards Paese, and in fact you can. Follow the trail down the northeast side of Monte delle Penne, walk past the saddle, and then alongside of the ridge of Monte Castello. Once you reach the ridgeline you will come across a very old rock wall some 300 meters above the valley. From here there is a beautiful view of the harbor, as well as the old abandoned vineyards and farms of the penal colony that once occupied the northeast part of the island. The trail descends through the brush toward these terraced slopes, until it reaches a dirt road that has not been driven on in years. Walk between two old abandoned homes, and turn right onto the rough dirt road. This section can be confusing, but keep going east and downhill toward the harbor and you will be headed in the right direction. The roads make long, winding switchbacks, but there are several way-trails that will cut these turns and save you a lot of time.

You will walk by what appears to be an old dairy where you may see some goats grazing, and eventually you will enter the Italian ghost town of L'Aghiale, where the prison guards used to live. The road turns to pavement, but continue descending along the road through the stone arch and past the L'Assunta church. This abandoned road will take you back to the harbor. If you want to snorkel, there is an excellent spot just behind the sea wall that protects the harbor in a cove along the volcanic pillars!

11

Marina di Pisa Loop

Loop through the forests and fields of Marina di Pisa in the Arno River floodplain.

Round trip: 7.3 kilometers (4.5 miles)

Elevation: Sea level

Hiking time: 1.5 hours

Park: Parco di Migliarino–San Rossore–Massaciuccoli

Difficulty: Easy

Time to visit: Year round

The Parco di Migliarino–San Rossore–Massaciuccoli is a conglomerate of pine forests, coastal dunes, wetlands, fields, and a large lake along the Versilia coast and Pisa plain–Tuscany's resort and industrial centers. This area, in the flood plain of the Arno River, was protected for centuries as the exclusive hunting grounds for noblemen. Once full of swamps and marshes, great land reclamation projects in the 19th-century turned this area into flat farmlands intersected with drainage canals and industrial facilities. However, this park has maintained some 24,000 hectares of wild lands within its boundary. Despite being surrounded by about 700,000 people living in the cities of Pisa, Livorno, and the Versilia coastline, the vast majority of this park is completely inaccessible to the public. Much of it is closed off, because the Italian presidential summer villa and the former hunting grounds of the House of Savoy are located within the park at Gombo. Some areas offer occasional guided tours, but few are completely open to the public.

However, in the vicinity of the town of Marina di Pisa, there is a stretch where you can get a nice sense of what these coastal pine forests are like. The Marina di Pisa Loop offers a combination of dense maritime and umbrella pine forests, deciduous ash woodlands, open fields of wheat and sunflowers, and nice views of the surrounding mountains. Along this stretch, the old dilapidated rail line and train station of Marina di Pisa, dating to the Mussolini era, can be found among the pine trees. This rail line

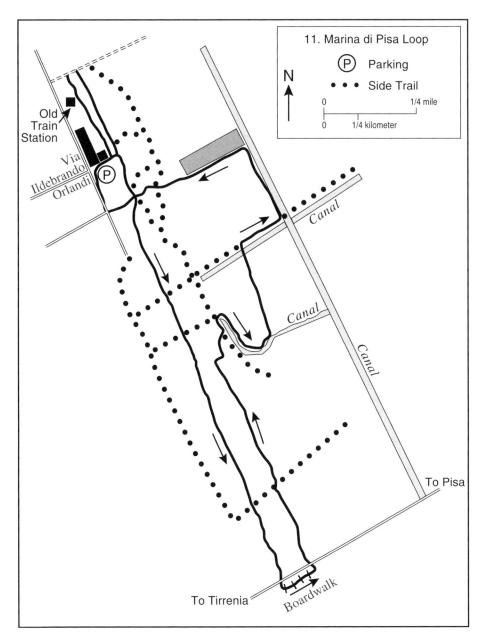

To Pisa

To Tirrenia

took sunbathers to the beach resorts of Marina di Pisa and Tirrenia, while Mussolini used it for his original youth camps in the 1920s and 30s, but today large pine trees grow between the rusty rails.

From Florence or Pisa, take the SGC Fi-Pi-Li highway past the airport to the Marina di Pisa/Tirrenia exit. If you are coming from the north, take the A12 Autostrada to the Pisa Centro exit. Then follow the blue signs

Summer wheat and sunflowers

for Marina di Pisa and Tirrenia, which merges onto the same exit as the Fi-Pi-Li (Firenze-Pisa-Livorno) exit. Either way, when you get to a fork in the road, stay right and enter the village of San Piero a Grado. This village was where the sea was once located some 2,000 years ago, when Pisa was still a major Roman port. Today it is famous for its 10th-century Romanesque basilica. There will be a tiny sign on your left, just before the village, that says Marina di Pisa. Ignore this sign, as it is a very narrow road, and continue through the village, past the basilica, to an intersection with the Arno River road (SS 224). Turn left, and follow the road into the town of Marina di Pisa. As the road is about to curve left into town, look right for a view of the mouth of the Arno River. You can pull over to the right in the parking area to admire the view out over the river, the fishing platforms, the Tyrrhenian Sea, the San Rossore coast (inaccessible to visitors), and the Alpi Apuane mountains beyond.

Just past the mouth of the river, continue into Marina di Pisa for 400 meters and take the third left. After one block you will take a right onto the diagonal road, rather than the one immediately to the right. This is the Via Milazzo (also known as the Marina di Pisa backroad). Follow this road for 1.6 kilometers until you reach a red brick building on your left, and the Via Ildebrando Orlandi on the right. Turn left into the trail parking lot. As this area contains canals and scattered wetlands, mosquito repellent is advised in summer, and watch for ticks in the spring. It is also possible to reach the trailhead by bus from Pisa or Livorno. It is a major route that runs about twice per hour. Just ask the driver to drop you off at Via Ildebrando Orlandi in Marina di Pisa, and walk one block toward the forest. For more information on bus service, contact Compagnia Pisana Trasporti at www.cpt.pisa.it or 800/012733.

From the parking lot, a small brushy access trail goes about 25 meters in to the

The Tuscan Coast and Archipelago

Open pine woodland

main trail. Turn right onto this trail. However, if you would like to see the old 1920s-era train station of Marina di Pisa, turn left immediately next to a small yard at the parking area, and follow the fenceline. After approximately 200 meters, you will encounter a concrete slab and some old rail lines buried in and among the pine needles. Continue a few more meters, and you will walk up onto the old boarding platform of the Marina di Pisa station. The actual station building is visible behind a fence, and is now a private residence. The platform is in remarkable condition, given 70 years of vegetative growth around it, and the concrete sign posts and electric poles are visible among the tree trunks. Continue to the other side of the platform to the dirt road, turn right, and then turn right again onto the first dirt trail, which is the main route. This route will reconnect with the brushy access point near the parking lot in 300 meters.

From the access trail, follow the main trail 2 kilometers as it heads through a maritime/

umbrella pine and holm oak coastal forest. It is easy to tell that prior to the reclamation and modern housing projects, this was a coastal sand dune ecosystem, as the soil is all sandy. For the entire length of this segment you will see old railroad tracks which date back to the days when Mussolini built a boys' camp in Tirrenia, similar to the Hitler Youth. Along this stretch you may encounter horses pulling carriages from the nearby equestrian center, and local townsfolk walking their dogs. This path will cross several dirt roads and side paths, but continue along until you reach the paved road. Cross the paved road to the other side, and turn left. Here you will follow the path a short distance along a wooden handrail to a boardwalk, where you will cross over a small swamp containing alders, ash, figs, and many aquatic plants. In spring, listen and look for the frogs emerging from their winter slumber.

After approximately 200 meters, look for a red and white NO CAMPING symbol (in Italian) on the other side of the paved road and a yellow sign indicating the PARCO SAN ROSSORE. Cross back over the road and go down this old dirt path. This stretch is more open and a little less sandy, which allows for deciduous trees, such as large ash and poplars and beautiful flowering locust trees, to predominate. Follow this section for 1.2 kilometers until you reach a spot where the path meets an open field. Here the path continues back into the woods; instead, turn right here and follow the edge of the field along a small drainage canal. Along this stretch, frogs may be croaking and poplars dropping their cottony seeds like snow. After only a couple hundred meters, a small access road to the left heads across the fields. Follow this path, until it gets to the main field access road in a short distance. Turn right and walk until you reach the main canal.

In this field, you can look out across the entire Arno floodplain: Monte Pisano stands nearly 900 meters above the plain to the east, the Alpi Apuane loom as rugged crags to the north, while the gentle green Livorno Hills stand to the south. In spring, these fields are filled with wheat and clover, but later in the summer, they are often blooming with sunflowers. At the canal, do not cross the bridge, but instead turn left. However, from the bridge you might be able to see turtles, nutria, and small fish in the water. Follow this access path until the end of the field, and then turn left again onto the dirt road. This road will lead you back into Marina di Pisa. Turn right on the first paved road, and walk two blocks back to the parking lot. After your hike, you can walk three blocks to the Marina di Pisa waterfront, where you can stroll along the promenade and breakwaters, while enjoying a wonderful *gelato* or *café* from one of the numerous little bars and shops along the waterfront.

12

Dunes of Torre del Lago

A visit to a sensitive coastal dune ecosystem and protected pineta *in the heart of the Versilia.*

Distance: Approximately 8 kilometers (5 miles)

Elevation: Sea level

Hiking time: 3 hours

Park: La Riserva Naturale della Lecciona; Parco di Migliarino–San Rossore–Massaciuccoli

Difficulty: Easy

Time to visit: Year round; avoid midday in summer

Recommended time: March to June

Pets: Not allowed

The Versilia Coast between Torre del Lago and Marina di Carrara is the heart of the Tuscan Riviera. Each summer, hundreds of thousands of sun worshippers hit the beaches in a swarm of activity. The soft, sandy beaches, warm Mediterranean waters, magnificent mountain backdrop of the Alpi Apuane, and the excellent food draw visitors from all over Europe. In August, the vacation month for Italians, the beaches are packed shoulder-to-shoulder with suntanned bodies baking in the sun. However, despite this mass of humanity, Tuscany has been able to save a little slice of the once common coastal dune ecosystems that today protect a variety of rare and sensitive plant and animal species. The Riserva Naturale della Lecciona protects the Dunes of Torre del Lago, which stretch from the southern end of Viareggio to Marina di Torre del Lago.

These dunes explode in a vivid display of colors when the lilies, evening primrose, goldenrod, catchflies, strawflowers, and curry plants among many others, coat the sand in spring and early summer. Above the dunes, the Alpi Apuane rise up like giants overlooking the sea. Behind the dunes is the protected forest of the Macchia Lucchese, which is part of the 24,000 hectare Parco di Migliarino–San Rossore–Massaciucolli. The dunes are virtually deserted in fall and winter, while spring is by far the best season for wildflower viewing. A visit in summer should be done very early in the morning, before the crowds arrive and the temperatures heat up, making a visit unbearable.

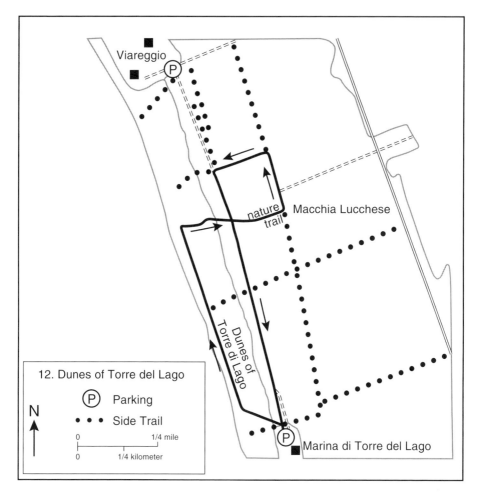

12. Dunes of Torre del Lago

Viareggio

Macchia Lucchese

nature trail

Dunes of Torre di Lago

Marina di Torre del Lago

(P) Parking

• • • Side Trail

N

0 _____ 1/4 mile

0 _____ 1/4 kilometer

Torre del Lago can be a nightmare to visit in summer. Not only is it a hub of beach-going activity, but it is the hometown of Giacomo Puccini, the famous opera composer who wrote such classic works as *Madame Butterfly* and *La Bohéme*. As such, this village becomes overloaded with visitors when his works are performed in town throughout July and August.

To visit the dunes of Torre del Lago, take the SS1 Aurelia north from Pisa towards Viareggio. About 9 kilometers outside of Pisa, after a long stretch through the forest,

look for a left turn into Torre del Lago. There will also be signs for accessing Lago Massaciucolli. Shortly thereafter, the road comes to a traffic light with a sign for Lago Massaciucolli to the right. Instead, turn left and follow the road as it curves under the railroad tracks. Ignore all signs for Viareggio and Mare ("the sea") and continue straight down this narrow road all the way, until you arrive at the beach of Marina di Torre del Lago. Turn right at the traffic circle, and travel past all of the beach resorts until reaching the very end of the parking lot,

Dunes of Torre del Lago

over 1 kilometer down, as the trail begins here. This is a pay parking area, and €2 should be adequate to cover the cost for the time you are there.

This is really an open hike for you to explore on your own terms. The beach be-tween Marina di Torre del Lago and Viareggio is approximately 3.2 kilometers long. Behind the beach, the dune area extends for about 200 meters inland, until reaching the *pineta*. In the transition zone from dunes to forest, junipers and low-growing Aleppo

Lily

pines predominate, in addition to introduced yuccas. Once inside the Macchia Lucchese, maritime pines and stone pines form a typical coastal pine forest.

There are a myriad of way-trails across the dunes, but it is recommended to stay on the main paths, as this fragile ecosystem has a very difficult time reestablishing itself on the unconsolidated loose sand that is created by human paths. One option for the exploration of the area is to start early in the morning before the rush of people arrive, and start out by walking along the edge of the dunes near the beach. At a major access path, walk into the dune ecosystem, until you reach the dirt road that separates the dunes from the *pineta*. Approximately halfway down the coast, a nature trail will head into Macchia Lucchese. This is an interesting path, as it labels the various shrub and tree species that live in the *pineta*. The nature trail arrives at another dirt road that parallels the beach. Turn left, and follow it as far as you feel like going. When you find a path heading back to the beach, or upon reaching the major dirt road that transects the *pineta,* turn left, and follow it back to the dividing road between the two reserves. You may walk the beach back to your car on the dividing road if the loose sand becomes too difficult to walk on.

II

The Tuscan Hill Country

Introduction to the Tuscan Hill Country

Stretching east from the coast to the Apennine mountains, the Tuscan Hill Country occupies all of central and southern Tuscany, and is the quintessential landscape of the region. Most of the valleys at lower elevations contain smooth, rolling hills composed of clays, calcites, and volcanic ash. These clay hills are dominated today by agricultural activity, including wheat, sunflowers, vineyards, and olive groves. This gentle agricultural landscape captures the imagination, and inspires millions to visit Tuscany every year. It is in this region that the fine Italian wines are produced, and where most of the photos for books and calendars are taken.

Geologically, this is a fascinating landscape, as many of the soils in this area are high in heavy metals and volcanic ash, due to the uplift and erosion of the metamorphic Livorno hills and Colline Metallifere, as well as periodic volcanic eruptions in the region. These rolling hills also tend to be very high in a variety of salts, including halite, gypsum, and borates, due to ancient invasions by the sea that resulted in large brackish lagoons. When plowed in late summer, the gray, barren slopes are left containing large, sticky clods of earth, which melt away slowly with the winter rains. Be aware that when wet, walking across these clay hills will leave thick, gooey clumps on your boots.

This is a changing landscape, offering spectacular hues of color throughout the seasons. The barren slopes are gray to buff in winter. They then go through a sequence of varying shades of green, as wheat and clover begin sprouting in the spring. Some fields turn magenta with red clover, while others take on the yellows of mustard, or the tan hues of maturing wheat in early summer. A variety of wildflowers also dot the landscape, including red poppies, orange asters, and purple clover. After the wheat harvest, many of the fields are converted to growing sunflowers, which cover the slopes with a their large, bright yellow flower heads. Many fields will also remain beige with the stubble of wheat, until they are plowed again in the fall.

The higher ridges surrounding these lower valleys are generally rocky, and contain layers of volcanic deposits and marine sediments, including metamorphic serpentines and other metal-bearing rocks, sandstones, and shale. The Colline Metallifere in particular is extremely rich in heavy metals, including iron, copper, silver, lead, nickel, and mercury. In addition, these hills are high in various sulfates, including pyrite, alum, and gypsum. This is particularly noticeable at Larderello, the world's first active geothermal energy site. Here, high-pressure sulfuric and boric acid vents are channeled into electrical generators, supplying energy to over 1 million Italian homes.

These higher ridges tend to be dominated by *macchia* vegetation near the sea, with oak and locust forests dominating inland. These higher ridges are not suitable for agricultural activity, due to their steepness and the high quantities of heavy metals in the serpentine soils. The toxicity of the soil also makes it difficult for the native vegetative communities. Thus, the only plant communities that can thrive in these harsh environments include the *macchia,* stunted pine/oak woodlands, and grassland savannahs. Examples of these serpentine communities can be seen in the Livorno Hills (Hike 13) and in the Colline Metallifere (Hike 16).

The higher, linear ridges separate the valleys and lower rolling hills into several distinct areas. Most visitors to Tuscany are familiar with the Chianti and Siena areas, hills (Colline del Chianti and Colline Senesi) just south of Florence, where most Tuscan tours operate. Most guidebooks for Tuscany focus almost exclusively on these areas. However, there exist several excellent hikes located in other lesser known areas, including the Pisan Hills (Colline Pisane, Hikes 14 and 15), the Vinci area (Colline di Vinci, Hike 20), and the Upper Cecina Valley (Hikes 17 and 18). The Maremma (Hikes 1–5) is covered in the section on the Tuscan Coast and Archipelago.

Also included in the Tuscan Hill Country, are the disjunct lower ridges which geologically are associated with the Apenninic uplift, but ecologically speaking are more similar to the Tuscan Hills. Monte Pisano (Hike 21) is actually associated with the Alpi Apuane, while Monti della Calvana (Hike 19), above the Prato plain near Florence, is associated with the Northern Apennines.

13

Livorno Hills Park and Waterworks of Colognole Loop

A loop to an 18th-century waterworks through the macchia *and pines of the Livorno Hills.*

Distance: 7.5 kilometers (4.7 miles)

Elevation: 182–415 meters (597–1,360 feet)

Hiking time: 2–3 hours

Difficulty: Easy

Park: Parco Provinciale dei Monti Livornesi

Time to visit: Year round; avoid midday in summer

High on the hills above the city of Livorno, beautiful *macchia* and pine woodlands grow on fascinating metamorphic formations of serpentine and gneiss. These woods have supplied the Livorno-Pisa area with wood, mushrooms, hunting, and most importantly with water, for centuries. An 18th-century waterworks and aqueduct was built in a drainage high in the hills, to supply villages and farms with water in the valleys below. Today, the Livorno Hills Park protects these *macchia* and pine woodlands, while providing local residents with a wonderful place to escape the city and commune with nature.

To access the Waterworks of Colognole from Livorno/Pisa, take the SS1 south until the Salivoli/Livorno Sud ("south") exit. After exiting the highway, do not take the first turn towards Livorno Sud, but follow the road over the SS1 and follow signs for Valle Benedetta. You will be on the SP5–Via di Levante. At the first traffic circle, continue straight through, following the signs for Valle Benedetta. After about 7 kilometers, you will reach Valle Benedetta. Take a left into the town, and follow the Via della Sambuca up the hill a few hundred meters. At the corner with the Via del Radar, park in the lot behind a concrete wall on the right. There is a red/white blaze on the pole at this intersection. You can also reach Valle Benedetta by bus from Livorno, using ATL. Contact ATL at www.atl.livorno.it or 800/317709 for more information.

The itinerary begins by walking up the Via del Radar past some apartment complexes, and up the hill towards the radar tower at

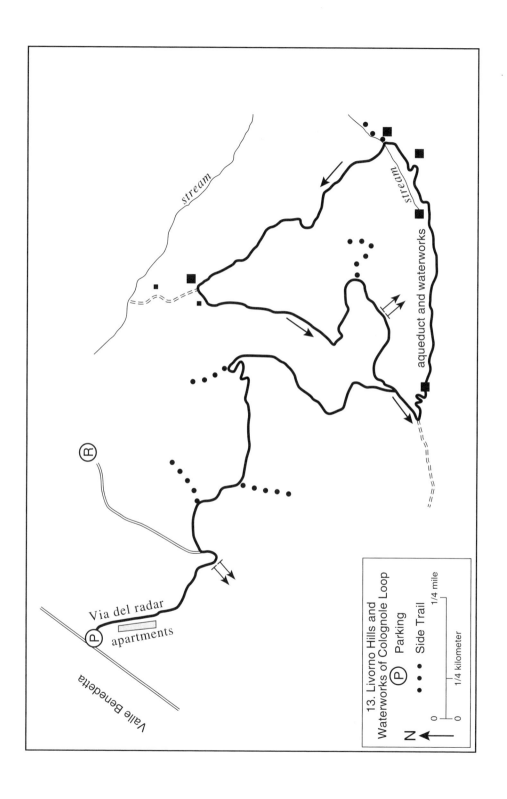

N

13. Livorno Hills and
Waterworks of Colognole Loop

Ⓟ Parking

• • • Side Trail

0   1/4 kilometer

0   1/4 mile

stream

stream

aqueduct and waterworks

Ⓡ

Via del radar

Ⓟ apartments

Valle Benedetta

Strawberry tree

the top of the hill. After approximately 560 meters, just before reaching the radar station, turn right on the dirt track heading to the right. After 180 meters, stay right where the trail appears to split. Then, after 130 meters more, stay left when the trail splits again. After an additional 450 meters, the track arrives at an intersection, where you turn right. At this stage, you have left the pine forest and entered into an open *macchia* woodland on top of greenish metamorphic serpentine rock. Follow the track downslope for approximately 700 meters, until an intersection with a significant dirt road. Stay to the right, and then after walking another 110 meters, look to the left for a trail that turns back and heads downslope, some 300 degrees behind you. (You may have to look closely, because the trail is sometimes obscured by brush and can be difficult to spot.) This trail has several red/white blazes on the trees and on the ground, indicating that the waterworks are below. However, since the trail branches at such an odd angle, it is still possible to miss.

At the bottom of the stream drainage is a concrete wall and platform that marks the beginning of the 18th-century waterworks of Colognole. From here, water is retained and gathered into a concrete aqueduct, where it is piped down the hills to the valley below. At this point, you simply begin walking on top of the concrete aqueduct down the forested drainage. The woods here are lush and moist, in contrast to the exposed rocky slopes above. The steep slopes shade the drainage from the intense summer sun, as streams flowing alongside of the waterworks create a microclimate quite different than the hot, dry *macchia* above. Along this stretch, riparian trees of maple, ash, and alder can be found.

As you continue down the waterworks for the next 1.2 kilometers, there will be several stretches that may challenge those without sure footing or with a fear of heights. The aqueduct is built up high above the creek in places, and has sections where the slope drops off suddenly, leaving you exposed, with no guardrails, and on a bridge less than 1 meter across, but 5 meters above the ground. In autumn, this is not a safe route if it has rained recently and slick, newly fallen leaves cover the stonework. If you are visiting during one of these more treacherous times, it is recommended to get off the aqueduct prior to reaching one of these stretches, and climb down the slope along the streambed.

Along the aqueduct, you will encounter several buildings built to channel, pump, or divert water. At one section, a dirt track heads upslope to the right, while you continue to follow the trail as it descends down a staircase, deeper into the ravine. Continue watching for the red/white blazes. About 200 meters after the staircase, there is a trail which crosses the stream to the left, next to a building on the right side of the trail. Here is where you will cross the stream and head away from the waterworks. If you continued down the aqueduct, it would eventually descend into the valley below.

This stretch of trail is wide and easy, but can get very muddy in autumn. Continue up this same trail for nearly 1 kilometer, to an

Livorno from Valle Benedetta

old stone house at the top of the hill. Here, you will meet up with a dirt track. To the right is a wood house, and about 100 meters or so further is another nice streambed. However, to continue on the loop, turn left, and follow this dirt track for 800 meters through a pine forest. Along this stretch there are some beautiful strawberry trees, whose red fruits are edible in autumn. In spring, this place will be fragrant with flowers, and you will hear the hum of bees. At the next intersection, stay right and follow the path 460 meters to the intersection with the original path down. Turn right, and retrace your steps back up to the Via del Radar, and return to your car.

Introduction to Hikes 14 & 15

Lago di Santa Luce Loops

The Tuscan hill country is a world-famous area of rolling hills, farmland, vivid and constantly changing colors, and quaint medieval villages. It is a dreamland visited by thousands each year for biking, horseback riding, or automobile tours. It is in this area that celebrated wines are produced, extra-virgin olive oil is pressed, wheat and artichokes are grown, and sunflowers color the landscape as far as the eye can see. The senses are awakened by the sights, smells, and warmth of this place, particularly in the early spring. The eastern Tuscan hills near Chianti and Siena are crowded with tourists, and there are many tour operators who pack people onto buses or take them on biking trips by the dozen, but in the western Tuscan hills it is also possible to walk along the many peaceful farm roads, and experience Tuscany in wonderful solitude. Outside of the peak season of July to September, this area is quiet and nearly empty for eight months a year, allowing the visitor to experience the Tuscany of the locals, and to search the soul.

One of the most beautiful and accessible areas in Tuscany for hikers is in the vicinity of Santa Luce, a small medieval village tucked in against a wooded ridge. The ridge itself offers almost unlimited trail options and is nice for the shade the oaks provide in the heat of summer. But for panoramic views of farmland and distant mountains, and for the full use of all your senses, you will want to do the Loops of the Lago di Santa Luce. These loops also virtually guarantee solitude, as I have traveled them a half dozen times, and never once seen another hiker. The northern loop provides opportunities to see wildflowers, pastoral agricultural landscapes, as well as panoramic views of the mountains and hills of the area. The southern loop is one of the best places in Tuscany to observe wildlife, especially for bird watchers, and offers dramatic views of a Tuscan lake, Lago di Santa Luce. It is an artificial lake made in a natural swampy basin that is ringed by reeds and wetland plants, and supports dozens of bird species, and is protected as a nature reserve by the Provincia di Pisa.

In addition, since they begin at the same location, it is also possible to do both loops on the same day, especially by bike. These hikes are accessible any time of year, but if you are going there in summer, only do them in the early morning or near dusk, as the summer heat and humidity can be relentless and there is no shade on either of these routes.

14

Lago di Santa Luce Loop–North

Loop hike from Lago di Santa Luce to Pieve di Santa Luce.

Distance: 10.4 kilometers (6.45 miles)

Elevation: 40–100 meters (130–328 feet)

Hiking time: 3 hours

Park: Riserva Naturale Provinciale Lago di Santa Luce

Difficulty: Easy

Time to visit: Year round; avoid midday in summer

To get there from Florence, take the S.G.C. (Fi-Pi-Li highway) until you reach the SS206 exit at Collesalvetti, and head south toward Cecina. From Pisa, follow the A12 Autostrada south, and take the Collesalvetti exit. Then look for signs for the SS206 south to Cecina. From the south, take the SS1 north, until you reach the SS206 exit for Pisa, and head north. On the SS206, turn east on the SP51 marked Santa Luce and Lago di Santa Luce, and drive 3.6 kilometers just past the bridge over an arm of the lake, then turn right at Colombaie where you will see some buildings and a parking area. Unfortunately, there is no bus service to Lago di Santa Luce. The closest bus service goes to Orciano Pisano (or Orciano) via the CPT bus service approximately 6 kilometers away. Contact CPT (Companie Pisana Trasporti) at www.cpt.pisa.it or 800/012773 for more information.

To hike, cross back over the bridge and turn right at the dirt road immediately on the other side. There will be a placard that says LORENZANA-CASTELLINA 8, indicating that Orciano is 5.5 kilometers away. Walk down this dirt road, which parallels the arm of the lake, and then follow the drainage, where you can see a small stream and riparian trees down below. From here, there are fantastic views of the village of Santa Luce and the wooded hills to the east. To the north, you will see the Alpi Apuane and the Apennines, and if it is winter, they will be snow-capped. As you continue along this route, you will see beautiful fields that will rotate their appearance throughout the seasons.

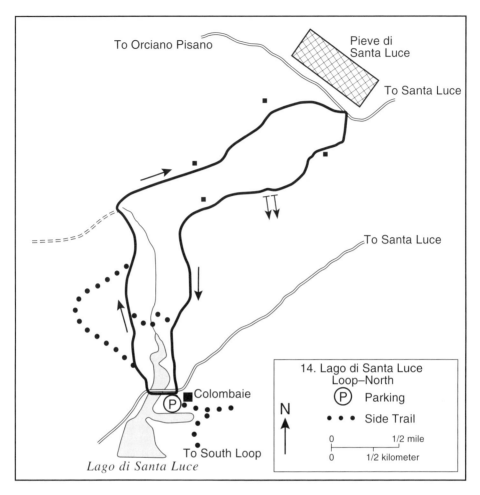

To Orciano Pisano

Pieve di
Santa Luce

To Santa Luce

To Santa Luce

To Santa Luce

14. Lago di Santa Luce
Loop–North

P Parking

N

• • • Side Trail

0   1/2 mile

0   1/2 kilometer

Colombaie

P

To South Loop

Lago di Santa Luce

In winter they will be bare and the gray clay soil will be visible. If it has rained, the route will be muddy, with the sticky clay attaching to your boots. In early spring, the fields turn bright green with young wheat and clover. By late spring, these fields turn beautiful hues of red with clover, and gold with wheat.

After 1.4 kilometers, the main road curves left, and a small dirt track goes straight; stay to the right and continue heading north on this smaller track. Along this stretch, you will continue to follow the wooded stream below. Several small roads will join this track, but continue straight until you descend to the bottom of that drainage and reach a significant four-way intersection near the stream, at 2.9 kilometers from the lake. Turn right, and after 150 meters the road will become paved. Although paved, it will be obvious from the condition of it that this is a seldom-traveled road, so you should expect little or no traffic. Stay on this paved section for 2.9 kilometers, as it passes farmhouses and fields and climbs a slope, until it reaches the village of Pieve di Santa Luce across a major road to the left, which you do not cross.

At this intersection, there is a parking area and a placard. Turn right, and look for a dirt

Santa Luce in early spring

road heading more or less back toward the lake. You will walk along the edge of several fields and past a couple of farmhouses. To the south, you can look across the Tuscan hill country, and will catch glimpses of the lake. To the west are the Livorno Hills, while the village of Santa Luce remains visible to the east. Here, the route continues for about 3 kilometers along the hillcrest. The route will slowly start to descend heading toward the lake. At the bottom of the hill, you will pass a small wooded brook and shortly thereafter, 4.5 kilometers from the start of this section, you will arrive back at the lake.

Santa Luce farmlands in summer

Lago di Santa Luce Loop—North

15

Lago di Santa Luce Loop–South

Loop hike around the Lago di Santa Luce.

Distance: 6.3 km (3.9 miles) or 8.7 km (5.4 miles) with nature walk at the lake

Elevation: 40–100 meters (130–328 feet)

Hiking time: 3 hours

Park: Riserva Naturale Provinciale Lago di Santa Luce

Difficulty: Easy

Time to visit: Year round; avoid midday in summer

At Colombaie, along the side edge of Lago di Santa Luce, continue past the building and soccer field for 1.1 kilometers, to a four-way intersection of dirt roads. You will see a small wooden post with several signs on it. Follow the sign for ROUTE #8 SAN ANDREA, 0.6 KM. As you follow this dirt road, it will lead to the hill top of San Andrea, where there is an *agriturismo* to the left, and a track going straight down the hill ahead, to a dead end and several abandoned buildings. Head down this hill and, at the bottom, turn right and follow the faint track toward the riparian woods along the lake. Along this stretch is a great opportunity to look for birds in the brush. When you cross a small brook, you can follow the streambed to the edge of the lake to look for wading birds such as egrets, herons, and rails among the reeds and mud-flats.

After a couple hundred meters, the track turns left and climbs straight up through a field to the hillcrest. At the top there will be a dirt road and wooden sign that says #89 DIGA, 2.8 KM. Turn right and follow this dirt road along the hillcrest, heading west. This will offer spectacular views out over the Lago di Santa Luce, the Alpi Apuane mountains in the distance, and the Livorno Hills to the west. After only 0.3 kilometer, there will be another sign saying DIGA ("dam") 2.5 KM, in the direction you were traveling, and AN-GELORI to the left. Stay straight, and this track will eventually begin descending to-ward and then past the dam that holds the lake. Near the brook that drains out of the dam is another riparian woodland, and an

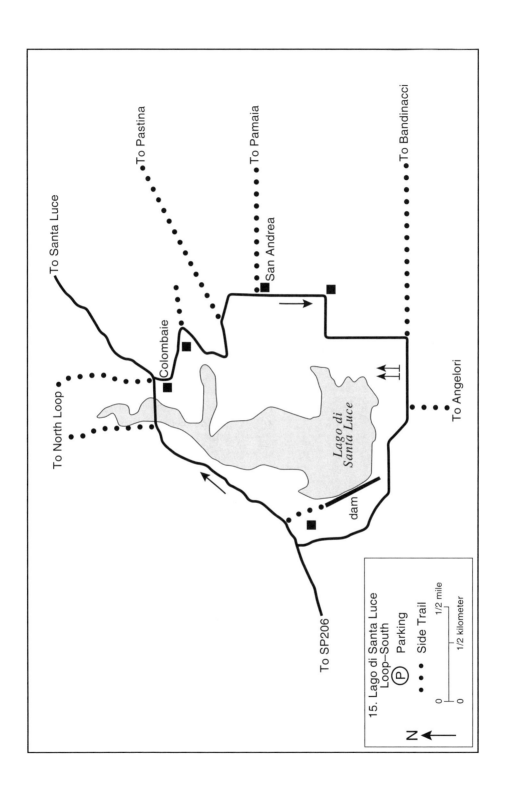

To Santa Luce

To Pastina

To Pamaia

To Bandinacci

San Andrea

Colombaie

To North Loop

To Angelori

Lago di Santa Luce

dam

To SP206

15. Lago di Santa Luce Loop—South

(P) Parking

• • • Side Trail

0   1/2 mile

0   1/2 kilometer

N

Pastina near Lago di Santa Luce

opportunity to do more birdwatching. Continue on the track as it turns to the north and heads out to a paved road. You may recognize that this is the paved road you originally drove in on. There will be a large placard that indicates DIGA 0.5 KM to the right. Turn right here, and walk along the paved road 300 meters to the entrance of the Riserva Naturale Provinciale Lago di Santa Luce. If it is a Saturday or Sunday, you may wish to go into the reserve, purchase a ticket for (€2.60 per person), and walk out over the dam to do the 2 kilometer nature walk. This is the best location to look for wildlife,

Lago di Santa Luce

The Tuscan Hill Country

especially for birdwatchers trying to see herons and bitterns, because you can walk right out along the lake and near the reeds and shrubs. To return to Colombaie from the entrance of the reserve, continue on the paved road, which will work its way up a hillcrest, along the fields, and then descend to the lake and bridge 2.3 kilometers later.

16

Archeomineralogical Park of San Silvestro

A loop through the ancient Estruscan mines and an abandoned medieval village, in southern Tuscany.

Distance: 9 kilometers (5.6 miles)

Elevation: 280–395 meters (918–1,295 feet)

Hiking time: 3–4 hours

Park: Parco Archeominerario di San Silvestro (Val di Cornia)

Difficulty: Moderately easy

Time to visit: Year round

The Colline Metallifere is a range of metamorphic hills in western Tuscany, rich in mineral deposits, that have been exploited for thousands of years. These hills contains copper, iron, lead, manganese, silver, mercury, and even boric acid geysers. Mining activity in this area dates back to the Etruscans of the 7th century BC. The Parco Archeominerario di San Silvestro is a unique kind of park in Italy. It is dedicated to the mining and mineralogical history of the area, as well as the archeological and natural treasures that occur in these beautiful *macchia* and oak-covered hills near the sea. Within San Silvestro, one can walk past dozens of mine shafts dating from Etruscan times up until the early 20th century. The trails snake their way through beautiful cork oak woodlands and *macchia* vegetation. The very ground sparkles with crystals of garnet and quartz, and there is a virtual rainbow of colors painted on the rocks from the precipitates of dissolved copper, iron, manganese, and other deposits. But one of the true highlights in the park is the abandoned 10th-century white village of Rocca di San Silvestro, perched high on a hill above the surrounding mines. This village was abandoned after only some 300 years, due to the lack of water for developing hydraulogical smelting technology, and also the discovery of extensive mineral deposits in Sardinia.

To get to the Parco Archeominerario di San Silvestro from Pisa, take the A12 Autostrada south toward Rosignano Maitimmo, and then merge onto the SS1 south, headed

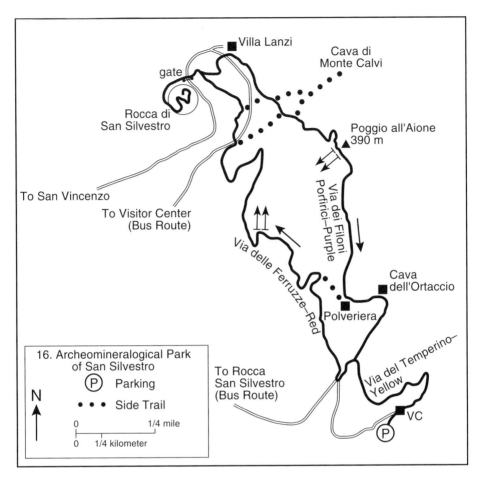

16. Archeomineralogical Park
of San Silvestro

(P) Parking

• • • Side Trail

N

0   1/4 mile
0   1/4 kilometer

towards Cecina and Grosseto. Drive approx-imately 35 kilometers south, until the San Vincenzo Sud ("south") exit. Follow signs for Campiglia Marittima and the Parco Archeominerario di San Silvestro. After about 4 kilometers, look for signs on the left for the park. Trenitalia offers train and bus service to Campiglia Marittima. Contact Trenitalia at www.trenitalia.com for more information.

The trail begins at the park visitor center, located at the Miniera del Temperino. The entrance fee, which can be paid at the visitor center, is €3 per person, not counting any guided tours. You can take a guided tour of the mine shaft of Miniera del Temperino for about €9. The park has several itineraries which are color coded. For the first segment, look for the yellow signs labeled VIA DEL TEMPERINO. After about 1 kilometer, there is an intersection with a road to the left, and red signs labeled VIA DELLE FERRUZZE. Get on the red trail and follow it up the hill. The red trail is moderately steep in the beginning, as it climbs the hill through a nice oak woodland. Along the way there are mine shafts of various ages, labeled with signs. The trail surface itself will sparkle with a variety of minerals, including green copper

Rocca di San Silvestro

oxides, orange iron oxides, red-colored garnet crystals, as well as grey/silver mangenese oxides and white quartz crystals and calcium deposits.

After 1 kilometer of climbing, at the top of the hill the view opens up to a beautiful panorama which includes a view of the sea to the west. Shortly thereafter, the first glimpses of the 10th-century village of Rocca di San Silvestro appear. As the trail descends down the other side of the hill, look to the northwest and you will notice some recent mining activity, including open-pit mines excavated by a British company in the early 20th century. At 3.2 kilometers from the start, you reach the bottom of the hill, where you meet a paved road and blue signs for the Via dei Lanzi.

Turn right, and follow the blue signs for Rocca di San Silvestro, which will now be directly above to the left, on the hilltop. As you climb the hill, there are several trail intersections with blue signs, but continue fol-

lowing the signs to Rocca di San Silvestro. Eventually, you arrive at a paved road at the base of the village, and a metal overpass that crosses the road; cross this road, either on the overpass or, if the gate is locked, through a small wooden opening in the fence directly below. On the other side of the road, the blue trail continues west around the northern base of the village, and eventually wraps around, up to the entrance.

There are guided tours of the village offered for €9 each (including bus ride from the visitor center), but there are no indications that you cannot just walk right in and see it for yourself. There are interpretative signs in English and Italian pertaining to the significant sights of the village. Some of the highlights include the old church, the millstone for pressing olives, the small cemetery, cisterns used to store water, and the tall guard tower. The view from the village is panoramic, and you can see why people here would have thrived in this environ-

Pit mine

ment—rich in minerals, close to the sea, and protected from invaders and disease by their isolation and position in the hills.

After leaving the village, cross back over the paved road and return downslope, the way you came. Make a left turn at the first trail you see, and head toward the Villa Lanzi. This building was originally built in the 16th century to house Tyrolean miners, and was rebuilt in the 19th century by the Eng-

lish mining company that took over operations in the area. Continue on until you see the purple sign for the Via dei Filoni Porfirici. The purple trail enters into a moist woodland protected from the sun by its northern exposure. This trail climbs back up the hill for about 1 kilometer, until it reaches the high point of the day at 395 meters, at the summit of Poggio all'Aione. From the top of the hill, there is a nice view in all directions.

The purple trail begins to descend down the other side, and continues to do so until it reachs an intersection and a small brick structure called the Polveriera. At this point, stay left, walk over the small chain crossing the trail, and continue downslope on the red trail (Via delle Ferruzze).

Soon you arrive at one of the most interesting mine shafts that this itinerary passes, at Cava dell'Ortaccio. The deep hole has streaks of red, yellow, orange, grey, blue, and white from the various minerals leaching out of the rocks. Beyond this shaft, the trail reaches the intersection with the yellow trail you passed earlier in the hike. At this stage, you may return the way you came, on the yellow trail, or just walk straight down the road. When the road reaches a junction after a couple hundred meters, turn left, and you will be back at the parking area shortly.

17

Forests and Canyon of Tatti-Berignone Loop

A loop hike in the wild forests and down a rugged canyon of Tatti-Berignone near Volterra.

Distance: Approximately 15 kilometers (9.3 miles); 17.5 kilometers (10.9 miles) with spur to picnic area and botanical trail

Elevation: 134–518 meters (440–1,700 feet)

Hiking time: 6–7 hours

Park: Riserva Naturale Provinciale Foreste di Berignone

Difficulty: Moderately strenuous— for adventure seekers only

Time to visit: Year round; avoid heat of summer, and rainy season when creek is swollen

Just southeast of Volterra, in the heart of Tuscan hill country, is a forested mountain called Monte Soldano. This ridge and the woodlands on its slopes contain some of the last vestiges of wild Tuscan hill country remaining. Hiking and climbing through the dense oak-macchia thickets along these slopes takes one back thousands of years, to a time when the region was not intensively farmed. On these slopes, there is a terrific opportunity to see wild boar and mouflon, watch birds of prey soar overhead, and descend into a steep-sided canyon. The wild forests and the canyon of Tatti-Berignone are among the few places in Tuscany where one can look out across a panorama and not see any signs of human development and intervention. The only building along this loop is a castle on the cliffs above the canyon, which was abandoned in the 16th century. This area has remained wild because it was set aside long ago as a forest preserve to assure a continuous supply of firewood to Volterra and the salt works of Saline di Volterra.

This hike is challenging, both in terms of the terrain and orienteering. The trails are muddy and uneven due to the constant rooting of wild boar, the dense thicket can make turns hard to see, and the walk along the streambed at the bottom of the canyon is difficult due to the uneven, rocky terrain and the thick, viney vegetation. This place gets very hot in summer, and in the rainy season, the mud and high stream flow can make it quite unsafe, so do not enter this wild land lightly. However, if you really want to experience "wild Tuscany," to take a step back in time,

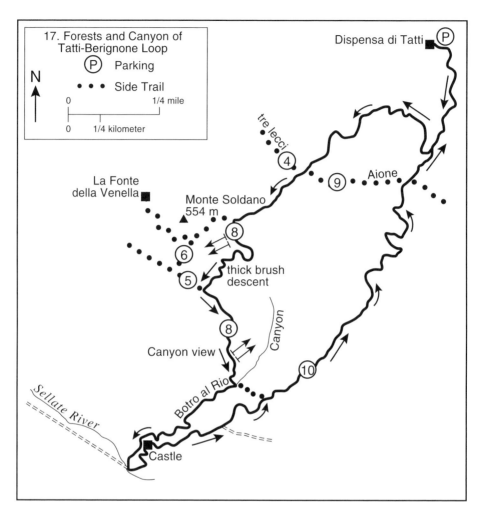

17. Forests and Canyon of Tatti-Berignone Loop

Ⓟ Parking
• • • Side Trail

N

0 _____ 1/4 mile
0 ___ 1/4 kilometer

Dispensa di Tatti ■ Ⓟ

tre lecci

④

⑨ Aione

La Fonte della Venella ■

Monte Soldano
▲ 554 m

⑧

⑥

⑤ thick brush descent

⑧

Canyon view Canyon

Botro al Rio

⑩

Sellate River

■ Castle

this is the place to immerse yourself. You may curse yourself in places, but at the end of this loop, the satisfaction felt will be more than worth the energy you put in getting there.

If you feel like you are ready for a challenge, then from Florence or Pisa, drive to Volterra. At Volterra, take the SS68 east toward Val d'Elsa for 13 kilometers, then take a right on the SP52 toward Casole d'Elsa. After a couple of kilometers, look for the small road to the right, headed toward Ponsano. Follow this road all the way to the end, where there is a building marked DIS-PENSA DI TATTI. There is no public bus service to the trailhead. The closest service is along the Volterra-Val d'Elsa line offered by CPT Pisa, which can be contacted at www.cpt.pisa.it or 800/012773.

The route begins by following a dirt road behind a gate and a picnic area. This dirt road will go through an ash-oak forest for about 1.2 kilometers, before reaching a trail intersection and the beginning of the loop. To the left is a trail sign marked TORRACCIA and this will be where you will return. Stay to the right as the dirt road descends into a

Berignone landscape

drainage and then climbs slowly up the slopes of Monte Soldano. This is a pleasant path through the forest, with buckthorn, laurel, and myrtle found scattered among the taller oak and ash trees. It continues for about 2.6 kilometers up the slope, passing a couple of trails leaving in each direction, until you reach a sign on the left, labeled 8 BOTRO AL RIO.

At this point, the route heads directly into the dense thicket and downslope. However, as an additional side option, you may continue on the dirt road for 1.1 kilometers further, as it rounds the summit of Monte Soldano and descends toward the picnic area of La Fonte della Venella, where a short botanical interpretive trail is located. Unfortunately, you never do get a view out across the landscape from here, even if you scale the slope to the summit of Monte Soldano.

When you turn down Trail 8 for the Botro al Rio, the challenge is about to begin. The trail through the *macchia* thicket is low, narrow, and heavily rooted by wild boar. While nocturnal and very shy in nature, if you listen carefully you may be able to hear them in the distance. About 200 meters down the trail there will be a small way-trail to the right, which will take you immediately to a steep, precarious overlook across the landscape. This way-trail may be hard to see, but if you find it, it is definitely worth the peek.

Occasionally along this route you will see green markers painted on the trees, but this is by no means a sure thing when multiple pig trails crisscross the route. Just try and stay on what seems like the widest and most logical route downslope. About 400 meters down the slope from the road, the trail will take a sharp turn to the right. Now comes the "fun" part. As the trail descends, you will see a tree with green, red, and orange paint on it. Stay right here, and continue down across a dry streambed, where fallen trees can make crossing the drainage somewhat tricky, and keep trying to follow the

The ruined castle as seen from the canyon

main route. This half kilometer stretch is where it is easiest to get lost, but just keep following the semblance of a trail and the occasional green paint. Eventually, some 600 meters after that sharp right turn, you will come across an actual trail intersection, where Trail 8 heads left and Trail 5 heads right. Turn left and follow Trail 8 down the slope, on a wider and more obvious route. The *macchia* will begin to open up a little bit, providing a few views, including the densely forested slope you came down, now behind you, and then you will emerge onto the side of the steep and slick, red-rock canyon of the Botro al Rio.

This canyon overlook is an excellent place to stop for lunch, after the scramble down through the forest thickets. From this vantage point, you can see virtually no signs of human activity. No farms, no roads, no houses; just forests, and a canyon below. This is a Tuscan hill wilderness, and shows what the entire area would have looked like thousands of years ago. The trail will continue down toward the canyon bottom, and as it does, the abandoned castle will come into view across the river. As you get close to the streambed, a couple of different options seem to open up to get down to the bottom. Each one will work, but it is recommended to stay left whenever possible. Do be careful to avoid accidentally coming out onto a steep bank right above the stream.

Once at the stream bottom, there is supposedly a trail route heading directly up the slope on the other side; that would connect up with the loop back; however, I did not find this route. Even if you do, it is worth the experience and the scenery to simply walk down the streambed the additional 1.5 kilometers, until you reach the confluence of the Botro al Rio and the Sellate River, provided conditions are safe. This section along the streambed is rough. The rocks are large and loose, and tough on the ankles, there are patches of blackberries and shrubs that are difficult to maneuver around or through, and flowing water can make certain places difficult to traverse, but it is in this canyon bottom that you are most likely to see wildlife. Deer, boar, and badger can be found here, and I watched a herd of mouflon climb up some 200 meters of loose, almost vertical rock in seconds, as I approached. As you approach the lower reaches of the stream, the castle will again come into view directly above. The stream will curl around the castle cliff and then back, with the canyon opening up as the stream empties into the Sellate River.

It is possible to cross the Sellate River by jumping over rocks near the confluence. In addition, if you stay on the left side of the Botro al Rio, you will notice a concrete bridge over the river, meaning you do not even need to cross, but you will have to work your way through some brush to reach that bridge. At the confluence, there is a dirt road ascending the hill up to the castle. Take this road, a welcome relief for fatigued ankles. The route climbs slowly for the next 600 meters, and it can be quite hot here during the summer.

Once you reach the overlook across the canyon you just came down, look up behind you for another excellent view of the castle. Continue on the road a half kilometer further, until you reach a small dirt track headed left. There should be a sign for Trail 10 here, but it was broken and laying on the ground at the time I saw it. The road continues to the right, but follow Trail 10 left into the woods. After another half kilometer, you will see a sign for Trail 8 on the left, which would have been the way up, had you found the trail climbing up from the creek bed. Instead, stay right, unless you want to go back into the canyon! Keep on Trail 10, as it will provide a leisurely stroll for 3.4 kilometers through oak and ash forests on its way back to the trailhead. The trail may be muddy from boars rooting, but it is level and wide. There is one additional trail intersection about 300 meters before the loop ends, where you will stay left. Once back onto the dirt road, head right and walk back to your car.

18

Ruins of Castelvecchio

A short hike to the ruins of the 13th-century village of Castelvecchio near San Gimignano.

Round trip: 5 kilometers (3.1 miles)

Elevation: 337–383 meters (1,106–1,256 feet)

Hiking Time: 1.5 hours

Park: Riserva Naturale Castelvecchio

Difficulty: Easy

Time to visit: Year round

Castelvecchio is located on the hill of Cornocchio, very close to the city of San Gimignano. This site dates back more than 2,000 years, to the time of the ancient Etruscans. However, it was in the 12th century that the village of Castelvecchio was built as a protectorate of the city of San Gimignano. In the 14th century, San Gimignano was a city of some importance, with some twenty fortified villages under the dominion of San Gimignano, which provided protection from neighboring armies. But as the bubonic plague raged across Italy, the balance of power changed among the Italian city-states. When the plague reached Castelvecchio in 1348, the village was blockaded by San Gimignano's army in an attempt to prevent the further spread of the plague. Within weeks, the village was empty, as the entire population apparently sneaked out past the guards during the night. Except for occasional families of woodsmen over the centuries, the village has never been occupied again. So, during a visit to the ruins of Castelvecchio, one can see the remains of structures and artifacts that are over 700 years old. Millstones and clay jars are still present, showing articles of the daily life of the residents. The church is perhaps the most fascinating structure on the site, with pieces of fresco still clinging to the apse.

To get to Castelvecchio, travel first to San Gimignano, which can be reached from Florence, about 31 kilometers south on the FI-SI Superstrada, headed to Siena. From San Gimignano, get on the SP47 headed

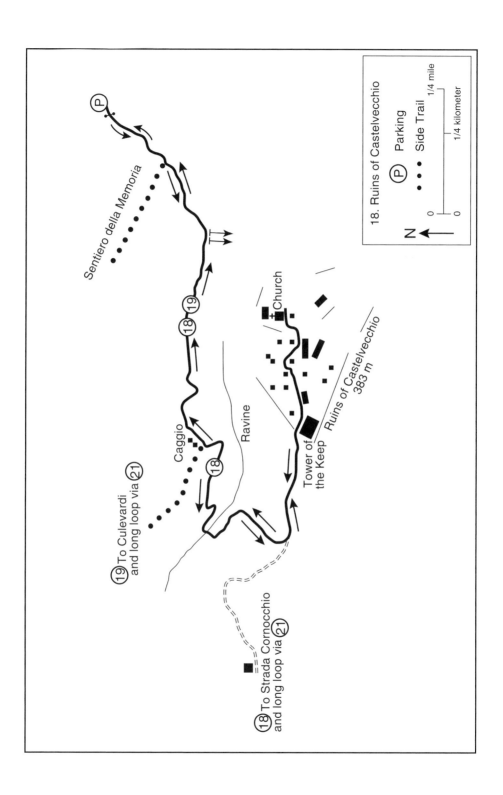

Sentiero della Memoria

P

19 To Culevardi and long loop via 21

18

Caggio

19
18

Ravine

18 To Strada Cornocchio and long loop via 21

Church
✝

Tower of the Keep

Ruins of Castelvecchio
383 m

18. Ruins of Castelvecchio

P Parking
•••• Side Trail

N

0   1/4 kilometer
0   1/4 mile

Castelvecchio

south, toward Volterra. After 6 kilometers, look for the signs for Caggio, and turn right. This is a dirt road and after about 500 meters, there is a red circular sign labeled EC-CETTO AUTORIZZATI, which means "Cars do not enter, except with authorization." Here, to the right of the road, is a parking area. There is no direct bus service to the trailhead. However, a bus does go to San Gimignano from Volterra and Val d'Elsa. Contact CPT Pisa at www.cpt. pisa.it or 800/012773 for more information.

The route to Castelvecchio begins by following this dirt road toward Caggio, which is nothing more than a couple of farmhouses. Shortly after beginning your walk, you will see signs indicating you are now entering the Riserva Naturale Castelvecchio, which protects the beautiful mixed oak woodlands and strawberry tree-juniper *macchia* vegetation on this ridge. Approximately 400 meters down the road, there is a break in the trees with a view across a

ravine, toward the hill of Cornocchio, and on the top of this hill you can see two of the towers of Castelvecchio reaching above the trees. This is the first of several glimpses toward your destination. There will be a few dirt roads which branch off in places, but for the first kilometer, continue on the road toward Caggio.

At Caggio, you will come across a trail intersection sign. Take a left here on Trail 18, which descends into the ravine below. Trail 19, straight ahead, continues back toward San Gimignano approximately 8 kilometers away. As the trail descends into the ravine, the oak woodland thickens. The trail will then climb back up the other side of the ravine, and two kilometers from the start of the trail you will reach another trail junction, with numerous signs. Turn right, following the sign for Castelvecchio as the route heads downhill. There are several signs that indicate no entry for vehicles, and another showing the layout of all the buildings of the ruins. After

The Tuscan Hill Country

The tower of the keep at Castelvecchio

500 meters, you will reach the Tower of the Keep, which was the primary guard tower for the village. You have now reached your destination, which means you are free to explore however you wish. There are at least 25 separate structures, although there may be others still buried under the soil and hidden among the trees. It is fascinating to look at how the trees have overgrown many of the homes, how low the windows are in some of the structures, and to see the mill-stones used for grinding grain or pressing olives. But, by far, the most impressive structure in the complex is the church of San Frediano near the far end of the ruins. This beautiful structure, made of soft white tufa blocks and darker basalt, is held together by restraints to prevent it from collapsing. The apse of the church still has pieces of the original frescoes on it. It is also fascinating to see how the builders used the solid, polished stones for the outer and inner layers of

the church, but used random unconsolidated stones and dirt to fill in the middle spaces of the walls.

At this stage, you can walk back to your car and then have lunch in San Gimignano. It is also possible to walk to San Gimignano on Trail 19 from Caggio, or to make a large loop of approximately 17 kilometers, by following the Strada Provinciale Cornocchio. To do this, continue on the dirt road from Castelvecchio on Trail 21. Then, at Trail 18/21 turn right, then turn right again on Trail 18, as it heads toward San Gimignano. At the next intersection with Trail 19, turn right one more time, back toward San Donato and Caggio.

19

Monti della Calvana

A hike to the barren summit of Monti della Calvana high above Florence.

Distance: 13.7 kilometers (8.5 miles); 17.4 km (10.8 miles, with optional trip along ridge crest, to viewpoint at La Retaia)

Elevation: 125–818 meters (410–2,683 feet)

Hiking time: 4–5 hours

Park: Area Naturale Protetta di Interesse Locale (ANPIL) dei Monte delle Calvana

Difficulty: Moderate

Time to visit: March to November (avoid midday in late summer)

The Monti della Calvana is an intriguing, barren, high ridge that rises 700 meters above Florence and the Prato plain. Every visitor to Florence will notice this ridge, seemingly devoid of vegetation north of the city, and for those with an eye for hiking, it is certainly an inspirational place, calling you out of the city. The Monti della Calvana has an extraordinary history, given its strategic location in both ancient and modern times. For centuries, farmers and herders have lived on its slopes, while criminals hid in the caves and forests on the north side of the ridge. During WWII, it was a key defensive position for the Germans, as the American forces attempted to cross the Apennines from Florence. All across its steep slopes, abandoned buildings, and in some cases entire villages, await exploration. The Rio Buti provides an unexpected coolness for the steady climb up. Shaded deep in a ravine, in a fold in the ridge, moss covers rocks along the brook and small waterfalls parade down from up high. With spring comes a plethora of wildflowers, from violets on the forest floor to cherry blossoms along the cool shade of the Rio Buti, to wild roses on the summit.

The view at the summit is the main attraction. From the summit of the ridge, the city of Florence, with its cathedral dome (Il Duomo), the third largest church in Italy, is in plain sight. The city of Prato sits directly at the base of the ridge and Montalbano (Hike 20) can be easily seen across the valley. This hike is recommended for spring or autumn, as the exposed summit can be

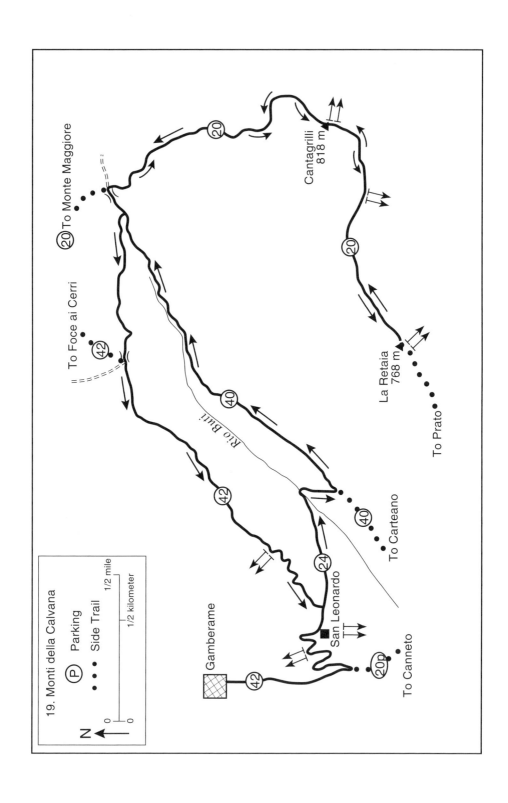

19. Monti della Calvana

Ⓟ Parking
••••• Side Trail

N ←

0 _____ 1/2 mile
0 _____ 1/2 kilometer

Gamberame

San Leonardo

Rio Buti

Cantagrilli
818 m

La Retaia
768 m

To Monte Maggiore
⑳

To Foce ai Cerri
㊷

To Carteano

To Prato

To Canneto

⑳ ㊷ ㊶ ㉔ 20p

View of Prato from Monte della Calvana

scorching hot in midsummer, while wicked winds and ice can hamper a visit in winter.

To get to the trailhead from Florence, take the A1 Autostrade to the A11 headed toward Pisa Nord ("north"). At the first exit, get off at Prato Est ("east"). Look for signs for Vaiano and get on the SS325. This road takes you right through the city of Prato, so keep following signs for Vaiano. Once you cross the river and head out of town you will be riding along the side of the Bisenzio river on your right. Approximately 4 kilometers after having crossed the river, as you enter the village of La Foresta, look for signs for Gamberame. Turn right onto Via di Gamberame, which will descend to the river. Cross the river and drive under the railroad tracks. On the other side of the tracks the road climbs up briefly to an intersection. Follow the road that continues to climb up the hill but, immediately after the intersection, look for a dirt parking area to the right, while the road turns sharply left. This parking area

marks the trailhead and the red/white blazes should be obvious. CAP Autolinee offers bus service to La Foresta from Prato. Contact Cap Autolinee at www.capautolinee.it or 057/46081 for more information.

The trail begins by following a dirt road that parallels the railroad tracks and the Bisenzio River down below. The dirt road continues for about 750 meters before turning sharply left, and steeply uphill. From here, it turns into a medieval stone path that zigzags its way up to an abandoned stone compound called San Leonardo. There may be some ongoing restoration work and signs indicating that you cannot enter. However, just pass on through, with caution, and find the trail on the other side of the compound. The workers are friendly, and should let you pass with no problem.

On the other side of San Leonardo there is a trail intersection. Trail 24 follows the Rio Buti drainage on the right, while Trail 42 climbs steeply up the ridgeline above the

The summit cross at Cantagrilli

drainage. Take Trail 24 and follow the drainage, as the shade and cool waters from the brook will be appreciated on a hot day. Trail 24 works its way toward Rio Buti, while climbing up the drainage. There are two signs along the way, indicating Prato and Filetole to the right. However, ignore both of these, and follow the main path until it crosses the Rio Buti. Once it crosses the brook, the trail will climb again until it meets with Trail 40. Turn left and follow Trail 40 which heads to the top of the ridge. While climbing, Rio Buti comes into view again as a beautiful moss-covered stream in a ravine. There are a couple of access points, but for the most part it is a deep trench. Up on the slope, on the left, is a forest of cypress, which is clearly not natural, but very intriguing. It appears to contain three or four varieties of cypress, some pines, as well as Atlas cedar. You will walk through that forest on the way back.

Once you approach the crest of the ridge, you will see a dirt road headed off on the left, which you will take on your way down. At the ridge crest, there is a junction with Trail 20, which is the summit trail. To the left, the trail climbs to the top of Monte Maggiore, the highest peak on the ridge. However, the peak is not in a good location for views over the plain since its summit is covered with trees. Instead, follow the markers to the right, as the route climbs up to the top of the peak called Cantagrilli, located some 200 meters above. Along the ridge crest, the landscape consists of an open calcareous limestone/sandstone substrate, with scattered wild roses in heavily grazed meadows. You may see sheep and even semi-wild horses on the summit, much as they have been here for hundreds of years. As the trail climbs, the views of Florence and Prato become more and more expansive. Once at the cross of Cantagrilli, the view is incredible. On a clear day, you can see the Apennines headed off to the north and south. Monte Morello, the peak directly above Florence, is directly across the Mugello Valley, and the A1 Autostrada headed to Bologna is directly below.

This is an excellent place to turn around if the weather is very hot, bitterly cold, or appears to be stormy. But, if you have the time and energy, continuing an additional 1.8 kilometers along the ridgeline to the cross at La Retaia is well worth the effort. The terrain is open and gentle at the summit, and the view of Prato and Florence at La Retaia is even more impressive.

On the return trip, backtrack the way you came until the summit ridge junction. Continue back toward the Rio Buti trail. Then follow the dirt road heading off to the right towards the opposite side of the Rio Buti drainage. Follow the dirt road, which is not marked with trail markers, for about 1 kilometer. The road will climb slowly and then, when the road suddenly begins to drop off to the right, you will encounter a trail crossing the road. This is Trail 42, which will lead you back to San Leonardo. Take the trail heading to the left, and follow it through the cypress forest. This trail is initially very gentle, as it follows the ridge crest above the Rio Buti. Eventually, the trail emerges from the forest and begins dropping steeply through oak scrub vegetation. This portion of the trail is rocky, slick, exposed, and hot in summer—which is why you would not want to have climbed it on the way up. The trail will eventually reenter the dense woods, and then emerges at the abandoned buildings of San Leonardo. From here, backtrack down the old stone path, and return to Gamberame.

20

Leonardo da Vinci's Home and Montalbano

A hike from the boyhood home of Leonardo da Vinci to the summit of Montalbano.

Distance: Approximately 11.4 kilometers (7.1 miles)

Elevation: 215–629 meters (705–2,063 feet)

Hiking time: 4–5 hours

Difficulty: Moderate

Time to visit: Year round; not recommended during midday in summer, and there may be snow in winter at the summit.

One of the most interesting historic places to visit in Tuscany is the childhood home of the famous scientist, inventor, and artist Leonardo da Vinci. Leonardo was born on April 15, 1452 just above the village of Vinci on the slopes of Montalbano. He lived near Vinci until he was 15, when his father took him to Florence to be an apprentice painter, and became famous for such works of art as *The Mona Lisa* and *The Last Supper,* as well as his incredible inventions, machine improvements, and drawings that had such remarkable foresight into the future. Many of these inventions, including models of a helicopter, bicycle, parachute, diving apparatuses, weather instruments, early steam devices, and machine tools can be seen at the Museo Leonardiano di Vinci. Besides a recommended visit to the museum, a visit to Vinci also provides insight into his life and environs. It is easy to see from the olive grove-covered slopes near to his boyhood home what living there in the 15th century must have been like. Today, it is possible to hike from his home, past Leonardo's parish church, up to the summit of Montalbano and view out across the Prato plain to Florence, where his future during the Renaissance took shape. This is a hike back through time, to a history we are still discovering!

Along the way, you will walk through olive groves, oak woodlands, a pine and chestnut forest at the summit, and even past some rare white firs that survive in the cool recesses of a ravine. Vinci and Montalbano sit right in the heart of Tuscany, with views of the Tuscan hills, vineyards, olive

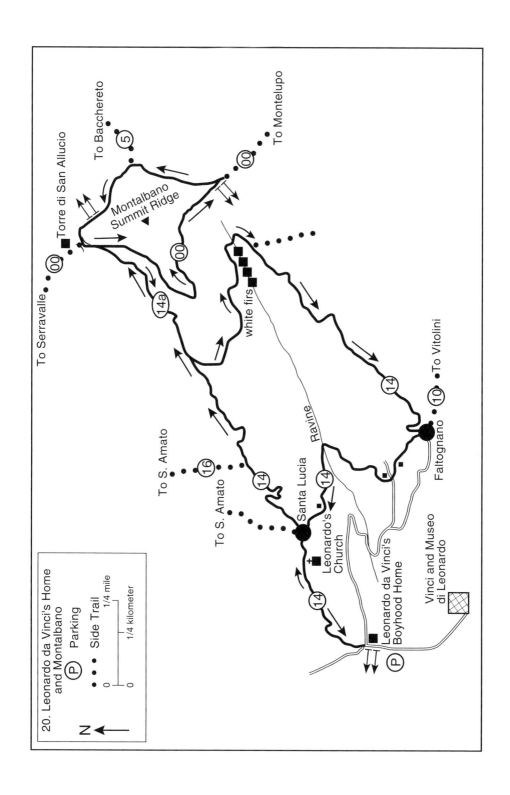

N ←

20. Leonardo da Vinci's Home and Montalbano

Ⓟ Parking

••••• Side Trail

0   1/4 mile
0   1/4 kilometer

To Serravalle
Torre di San Allucio
To Bacchereto
To Montelupo

Montalbano Summit Ridge

white firs

To S. Amato
To S. Amato

Santa Lucia Ravine

Leonardo's Church

Leonardo da Vinci's Boyhood Home

Vinci and Museo di Leonardo

Faltognano
To Vitolini

⓪⓪   ⑤   ⓪⓪   ⑭ₐ   ⓪⓪   ⑯   ⑭   ⑭   ⑭   ⑭   ⑩

Leonardo da Vinci's boyhood home

groves, and fields of wheat as far as the eye can see. Montalbano also sits in the middle of a crescent made by a bend in the Apennines, allowing views of this range that curve nearly 180 degrees around from Monte Giovo (Hike 39) and Corno alle Scale (Hike 40) to the north, Monti della Calvana (Hike 19) over Prato, and Monte Falco (Hike 41) in the south. This hike consists of two loops; the lower loop heads through olive groves, vineyards, and the neighborhoods where Leonardo grew up, while the upper loop heads through beautiful forests atop the summit of Montalbano.

To get to Vinci from Florence or Pisa, take the S.G.C. Fi-Pi-Li highway to the Empoli Ovest ("west") exit. There you will follow the signs for Vinci. The first 2 kilometers from the highway exit is circuitous and can be confusing due to a multitude of traffic circles and the need to circle back to the bridge that crosses the Arno River. Just keep following any and all signs for Vinci, and try to avoid

going into Empoli itself. Once you are on the SP13 heading toward Vinci it is a straight shot into town. To access Leonardo's boyhood home, and the beginning of this hike, drive straight through town and up the hill. About one half kilometer outside of town, the road will branch. The left side heads toward Pistoia, while the right branch heads up to the Casa Natale di Leonardo. Turn right, and in about 5–10 minutes, you will arrive at a parking area on the left, immediately past his home on the right. Empoli can also be easily reached by train from Pisa or Florence and COPIT provides bus service to Vinci from Empoli. Contact COPIT at www.copitspa.it or 057/33630 for more information.

If you have the time or desire, you can also choose to park in Vinci to visit the museum; from there it is possible to walk up the hill to Leonardo's home following the red/white blazes of Trail 14. Walking this stretch will add another 1.2 kilometers each way, and about 1 hour to the hike. One

Vineyards at Montalbano

suggestion is to find lodging in Vinci, use one afternoon to visit the museum and walk up to visit his boyhood home, then, the following morning, drive back up to his home and do the hike to Montalbano.

From the parking area at Leonardo's home, there is a road and trail intersection. Start walking straight up the same road you drove in on; it is marked Trail 14, with a sign indicating Santa Lucia in that direction. In about 700 meters, you will pass the childhood parish church of Leonardo and shortly thereafter you will arrive in the neighborhood of Santa Lucia, where the lower loop begins. Follow the paved road up the hill following Trail 14 toward Torre di San Alluccio. The route climbs up the road a short way, passing two trail branches, and then becomes a dirt road. Continue heading toward Torre di San Alluccio. Eventually, the trail leaves the open olive groves and enters into an oak woodland. About 700 meters after the previous trail junction, you will encounter another trail junction, which will mark where Trail 14

heads downslope, to complete the lower loop. Continue upslope on what is now Trail 14A, which heads up to the summit. Continue up on Trail 14A, toward the upper loop. After another 700 meters, you will reach the summit ridge and the intersection with Trail 00. Torre di San Alluccio is visible above the trees to the left. Continue straight through the intersection towards the powerlines to begin the upper loop.

In early spring and late fall, this stretch will provide views of the Prato plain and Florence, as well as Monte Morello and Monte della Calvana, in the Apennines above the city. In summer, foliage on the trees and shrubs will block most of these views, however you will be relieved by this, as the shade will be most appreciated after the climb to the summit.

Approximately 500 meters from the last intersection, you will arrive at an intersection with Trail 5 that heads down to Bacchereto in the valley below. Stay right and follow the upper trail as it starts heading back up toward the summit ridge. Another half kilometer later you will arrive at Trail 00 again, at the summit. Turn right, and walk 50 meters to a beautiful open view across the Arno valley, and down toward Vinci and Monte Pisano (Hike 21) in the distance. This is a spectacular view across quintessential Tuscan hill country. View the Arno river, snaking its way to the sea, and you can even see Leonardo's house far below, where you started. This is a wonderful place to have lunch, high above the heart of Tuscany.

After lunch, follow Trail 00, back toward the Torre di San Alluccio. Along the way, you will enter an open area with scattered large oaks, that appears to have been opened up by a fire a while ago. Down below, you will see the deep drainage and a line of rare white firs heading down the slope. As you begin the lower loop, you will pass right by these beautiful trees. Once you reach the tower, return down Trail 14A until you reach the intersection you encountered earlier. At this intersection, follow Trail 14 to the left, not the one toward Vinci that you came up along.

Some of the most beautiful sections of this hike are along the next 3 kilometers. The trail descends through an oak/pine woodland, covered in crocuses in early spring. About halfway down, the trail crosses the stream where the beautiful line of white fir sits. White fir generally live at higher elevations and need moisture. In addition, most of the white firs in Italy were harvested over the centuries for wooden ships, thus they are quite rare today. The deep sides of the ridge provide shade, and the water from the brook keeps this small fir population alive.

The trail continues down until it reaches the small community of Faltognano. Here, on a large balcony, sits an enormous holm oak that must be many hundreds of years old. In Faltognano, take a left to head back to Leonardo's house and Vinci following the Trail 14. The trail goes past several homes, and then descends into the deep ravine. Just before entering the woods, you will notice a large amphora (jar), buried in the ground on the left of the trail, that must also be hundreds of years old. The trail descends into the woods, crosses the stream, and the climbs back up through olive groves to the community of Santa Lucia, completing the lower loop. Walk back down the paved road to Leonardo's house, and your car.

21

Monte Pisano Loop

A loop along the ridgeline of Monte Pisano to the summit of Monte Faeta.

Distance: 8.2 kilometers (5.1 miles)

Elevation: 620–830 meters (2,033–2,722 feet)

Hiking time: 3 hours

Park: Area Naturale Protetta di Interesse Locale (ANPIL) "Del Lato"

Difficulty: Moderately easy

Time to visit: March to November

Standing like a great wall, nearly 900 meters above Pisa, is Monte Pisano. This ridge extension of the Alpi Apuane is managed by the Provincia di Pisa, and is easily accessible for hikers and biker alike. There are a series of hiking trails and fire breaks that can be explored, offering panoramic views of the Pisa plain, Lucca, the Tuscan archipelago, the Tuscan hill country, the Alpi Apuane, and the Apennines. Many of these trails descend directly down into the cities of Pisa, Lucca, and Cascina. At the highest point, Monte Serra, are a series of TV and radio towers that are obvious from anywhere in western Tuscany. But there are several other summits on this mountain, including the beautiful Monte Faeta which offers outstanding views across the sea to the islands offshore. Monte Pisano also contains an interesting mix of chestnut, maple, and flowering locust woodlands and Mediterranean scrub, on the rocky exposed outcrops.

To access the Monte Pisano loop from Pisa, take the S.G.C. Fi-Pi-Li highway until you reach the Navacchio exit. Take the SP24 and follow the signs for Navacchio and Calci. You will also see brown signs for Monte Serra. In Calci, the road gets very narrow and steep, so watch out for oncoming traffic and continue up the hill through the town. Upon leaving the town, the road climbs up the sides of Monte Pisano, then reaches a pass with a rifugio on the right.

From Florence, take the S.G.C. Fi-Pi-Li highway towards Pisa, but get off at the Pontadera exit. Take the SS67 into Pontadera, and then look for the SS439

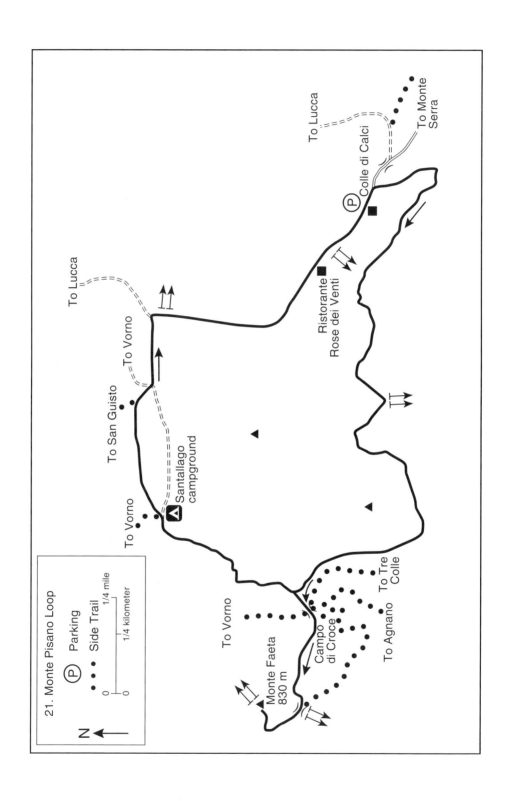

N ←

21. Monte Pisano Loop

Ⓟ Parking
•••• Side Trail

0 ————— 1/4 mile
0 ————— 1/4 kilometer

To Lucca

To Vorno

To San Guisto

To Vorno

Santallago campground

To Vorno

Monte Faeta 830 m

Campo di Croce

To Tre Colle

To Agnano

To Lucca

Colle di Calci

To Lucca

To Monte Serra

Ristorante Rose dei Venti

The Alpi Apuane

toward Bientina, Buti, and Lucca. Follow the SS439 for 7 kilometers, then take a left onto the SS38 that climbs towards Buti. As you enter Buti, the road narrows, so watch for oncoming traffic. Go through Buti, and follow signs for Monte Serra and Calci until you reach the pass.

At the pass, a small road leaves to the north with a sign for Monte Serra. Follow this small road for about 3 kilometers. At one point, you will come to a three-way intersection. To the right is a closed road with a military guard, that goes up to the radio towers of Monte Serra. Straight ahead is a road descending the mountain to the other side. Stay left, and continue a few hundred meters more. When you see a water catchment on the left and red/white trail signs, park on the right side in the spaces under the trees. There is no public bus service to the trailhead.

The trail begins at an intersection of four trails called Colle di Calci. Follow Trail 02 toward Campo di Croce, 3 kilometers away.

It heads down the slope to the south, along an old dirt road. The trail heads through a chestnut/maple woodland, and in the fall this is a great place to collect chestnuts for roasting. In addition, there are locust trees in many openings that have fragrant white flowers in spring. In winter, this section of the trail has magnificent views across the Pisa plain. However, in summer when the trees have their leaves, the views are obscured, although the shade is welcome. After approximately 20 minutes you will come to a rock outcrop that offers a wonderful panoramic view back towards Monte Serra, down to the village of Calci, and across the Pisa plain. Continuing on the road, you will eventually reach a T-junction. Turn left, and within 50 meters you will come to Campo di Croce and a major trail intersection. Here you will see many signs, but look for the Monte Faeta trail marked 00.

This path initially follows a dirt road for about 50 meters uphill, then branches off to the right into the chestnut forest. Look for the red/white blazes headed into the

Monte Pisano in spring

woods. It climbs approximately 220 meters in elevation to the summit of Monte Faeta. If you happen to miss this branch, the road you are on will eventually take you to the summit as well, only it will take a little longer. After a moderately strenuous climb across slippery chestnut leaves, you will reach an incredible 360-degree panorama on the summit of Monte Faeta.

From the summit you can clearly see the Leaning Tower of Pisa and the mouth of the Arno River, as well as the Tuscan Archipelago to the west, the Tuscan hill country to the south, the Alpi Apuane, Cinque Terre, and Lucca to the north. The Northern Apennines, including Monte Giovo (Hike 39) and Corno alle Scale (Hike 40) to the northeast, and the rest of the Monte Pisano to the east/southeast. On an incredibly clear day, particularly in the winter, you can see the snowcapped French Alps across the sea, some 250 kilometers away. Enjoy your lunch here at the summit, then return back down the trail to Campo di Croce. At Campo di Croce, you will follow Trail 00 toward Colle

di Calci, which is the main dirt road headed east. Along this stretch, you will continue to have views down to the walled city of Lucca below and the Alpi Apuane and Appennino Modenese to the north.

After 2 kilometers you will approach a summer campground. At this point there are a series of blue/gold signs for other destinations, but not for the Colle di Calci. Look for the sign for TRAIL 07, SANTALLAGO, which follows the road past the campground and above a large field. After 0.6 kilometers, you will reach another intersection. Turn right here on the dirt road, even though the sign for the Santallago heads left. You will also see the red/white blazes reappear. Follow the dirt road along the east side of the mountain and soon you will reach the Ristorante Rose dei Venti perched on the edge of the cliff, with a magnificent view. This would be a nice place for lunch or dinner after a beautiful hike. The road becomes paved at this point and you follow this paved section a short way back to Colle di Calci, and your car.

III

The Alpi Apuane

Introduction to the Alpi Apuane

The Alpi Apuane are a small but extremely rugged range of mountains located along the northern Tuscan coast from Viareggio to La Spezia. They range in elevation from 1,200 meters to nearly 2,000 meters in height. This mountain range is a metamorphic core complex associated with the Northern Apennines, although it is further west and disconnected from the rest of the Apennine range by the deep valley of Garfagnana. This range is primarily made up of marble, with other metamorphic carbonate rocks and various sedimentary layers also present. Marble is formed when limestone is placed under great pressures and temperatures, causing it to melt and recrystallize. Marble, like limestone, dissolves when it comes into contact with water containing acids. Thus, millennia of rainfall containing weak carbonic acid has caused the marbles of the Alpi Apuane to erode into very deep gorges, steep cliffs, narrow knife-edge ridges, and over 200 known caves. There is even a large, freestanding arch on Monte Forato (Hike 24). These rugged erosional features, and the proximity to the sea, make the range look larger and more mountainous than the relatively low elevations would otherwise indicate. Anyone driving on the A12 Autostrada between Pisa and La Spezia will be in awe at the enormous wall of sheer cliffs rising 1,600 meters above the sea. In fact, the summit of Monte Altissimo (Hike 26), which appears as one of the highest peaks in the range from the coast, is located only 10 kilometers from the beaches. From the north, coming from Parma, the Alpi Apuane are so steep and sharp that they look to be almost overhanging.

The forests of the lower Alpi Apuane consist of chestnuts and holm oak stands. Higher up, the forests change over to scrubby beech woods and scattered white firs. At about 1,500 meters, subalpine grassy meadows and heath moorlands open up toward the mountain summits. The Alpi Apuane get very little snow, despite their high elevations, as their proximity to the sea moderates the temperatures. So, while 1,800 meters in elevation in the Northern Apennines may have two meters of snow on the ground, the same elevation in the Alpi Apuane may only have a dusting. Nonetheless, if you choose to hike in the winter, be aware that ice from melting snow or rain that has frozen overnight may cover the trail, and make already difficult hikes all the more dangerous.

The Alpi Apuane is one of the world's leading sources of high-grade marble. In fact, the quarries *(cave)* of Carrara have been supplying statue-quality white marble to artists and engineers for over 2,000 years. The sculptures of Michelangelo, the marble façades of ancient Roman buildings, and the great cathedrals throughout Europe have all used marble from these quarries. Today, you can hike in and around these active marble quarries (Hikes 25, 26, and 27), as well as on top of the natural exposed substrate, which has not been harvested. From a distance, the tailings from these quarries, such as on Monte Corchia, are so white, they look like glaciers running down the mountain slopes. In fact, the marble is so abundant that the breakwaters and sea walls in Marina di Pisa (Hike 11) are made of huge blocks of lower-quality marble, not considered suitable material for buildings or sculptures.

There are also many other metamorphic and sedimentary layers intermixed with the marble core, and kaleidoscope of colors are present, including silvery schists, green slates, red mudstones, brown shales, white quartz veins, and a variety of multicolored gneisses. This is especially evident on Monte Fiocca (Hike 25).

Hiking in the Alpi Apuane can be an incredible, and sometimes terrifying, experience. The ridgelines are extremely narrow in many locations, and often the footing is not that great. There are places with some exposure that require you to use your hands to climb up. Some trails are labeled EE *("Escursionisti Esperti"),* which means it is a straight drop of several hundred meters, and you should not try here without appropriate climbing gear. But the views are indescribable, and from the summits of many of these peaks you can see the snow-capped Northern Apennines, including Monte Giovo and Monte Rondinaio, Monte Cimone, and Corno alle Scale across the Garfagnana valley. To the west, the islands of the Tuscan archipelago, the Cinque Terre, and if the weather is exceptionally clear, Corsica and the Maritime Alps of Southeast France can be seen across the Tyrrhenian Sea. The hikes in this book are reasonably safe but, if you are afraid of heights, be warned—there are some places that will make you question why you decided to give that particular summit a try!

22

Procinto–Monte Nona Loop

A loop by the free-standing monolith of Procinto and around the rugged peak of Monte Nona, with optional climb to the summit of Monte Matanna.

Distance: 13.1 kilometers (8.1 miles)

Elevation: 527–1,317 meters (1,729–4,320 feet)

Hiking time: 5–6 hours

Park: Parco Naturale di Alpi Apuane

Difficulty: Moderately strenuous

Time to visit: April to October

The southern part of the Alpi Apuane is the most wild area of this range, and is used in its most traditional form by rural Italians. Unlike the heavily excavated marble mines of Carrara and Massa, where the forests are sparse and the earth scarred, the area near Monte Nona and Procinto have extensive and productive forests of chestnuts and beech, rural villages perched on steep cliffs, rocky slopes carved by wind and rain instead of excavators, and beautiful alpine grasslands which seem to have only been visited by a few goats and goatherders.

The fascinating limestone column of Procinto stands besides an incredible 300-meter high rock wall that is Monte Nona. The beech, chestnuts, hop-hornbeam, and maples that adorn the slopes make for wonderful fall colors in October. The sheer quantity of chestnuts that fall to the ground also make for easy and tasty collection on the way down. The views at the top of Monte Nona or Monte Matanna are so expansive, that on a clear day you can see France across the sea. This was the first hike I ever did in Italy, and it sold me to the spectacular potential of hiking in this countryside. From the time I reached the summit of Monte Nona, I knew how truly fortunate I was to be living in Tuscany.

This hike begins right outside of the town of Stazzema. To access Stazzema, take the A12 Autostrada from the Pisa Nord exit north for 25 kilometers, to the Versilia exit. Follow the signs for Seravezza and Stazzema on the SP9. From Seravezza it is approximately 12 kilometers to Stazzema. Just

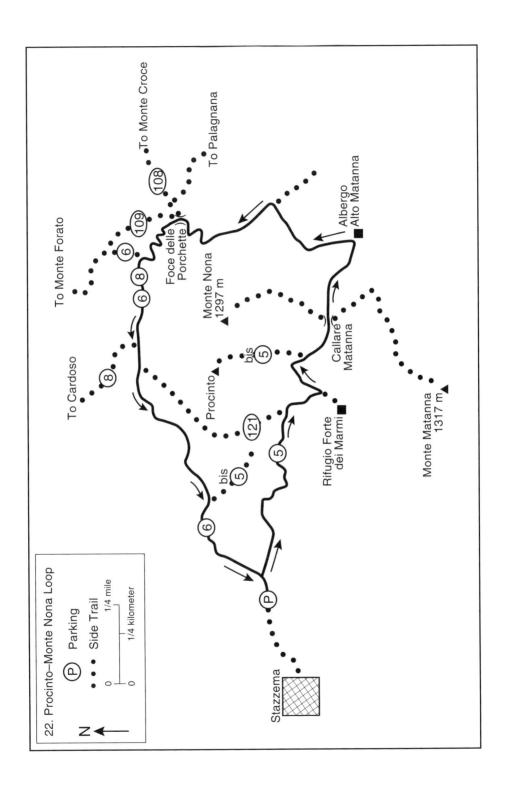

22. Procinto–Monte Nona Loop

- Ⓟ Parking
- ••• Side Trail

0 — 1/4 kilometer
0 — 1/4 mile

N ←

To Monte Croce
To Palagnana
⟨108⟩
⟨109⟩
To Monte Forato
⟨6⟩
⟨8⟩
⟨6⟩
Foce delle Porchette
Monte Nona 1297 m ▲
To Cardoso
⟨8⟩
Procinto ▲
bis ⟨5⟩
⟨121⟩
bis ⟨5⟩
Callare Matanna
⟨5⟩
⟨6⟩
Rifugio Forte dei Marmi ■
Albergo Alto Matanna ■
Monte Matanna 1317 m ▲
Ⓟ
Stazzema

Procinto in autumn

before it reaches Stazzema, the SP9 makes a hairpin turn to the left, and there is a sign for the Chiesa di Santa Maria. At this point, there is an unmarked road going straight ahead. Turn off the SP9 and follow this road up the hill for two kilometers, until you reach the trailhead, which will be marked by a large placard for the Parco Naturale di Alpi Apuane and several red trail markers. If you happen to miss this road turnoff, continue on the SP9 a few hundred meters until the church parking lot and turn around there. The CLAP offers bus service to Stazzema from Querceta/Pietrasanta. Contact CLAP (Consorzio Lucchese Autotrasporti Pubblici) at www.clapspa.it or 058/ 35411 for more information.

Trails 5 and 6 begin together for the first hundred meters, and then split. Take Trail 5 to the right, and follow it up through the extensive chestnut woods. It takes between 60 and 90 minutes to reach the Rifugio Forte dei Marmi. Just before the *rifugio* at a

spring, there is a trail turnoff to the left for Trail 121, heading to Fonte Moscoso. However, stay to the right, continuing on Trail 5. Shortly after that, there is a sign for the *rifugio* to the right, and Trail 5 toward Callare Matanna to the left. You may choose to visit the *rifugio* for some food and drink. Afterward, continue on Trail 5, as it rises above the trees onto a rocky slope towards the base of the Procinto.

Looking up from the base of Procinto at the massive wall of Monte Nona, it seems impossible to scale the summit of that mountain. This part of the trail provides the first expansive views of the area, including Stazzema far below, and the central Apuane peaks. Small hop-hornbeam trees will offer some support for scaling the sometimes loose rocks. The trail follows along the side of the cliff, with the help of some cables. The trail is wide enough through this section, however, that the cables are not really necessary unless the rocks are wet.

The Alpi Apuane

After leaving this exposed stretch, the trail reenters the woods, this time made up mostly of beech and maple. The trail continues climbing for another 15 minutes, until you reach the Callare Matanna at 1,130 meters. This pass occurs at treeline, and offers the first truly panoramic views of the southern Alpi Apuane range. To the north and northwest, you can see the Versilia coast, Cinque Terre, and the central part of the Alpi Apuane. To the northeast is the Pania della Croce, the highest peak visible in this part of the range, the Procinto from above, and the slopes of Monte Nona. To the east are the Northern Apennines in the distance. To the south are the Monte Pisano, the Tuscan hills, the Pisa plain, and mouth of the Arno River.

There will likely be people at the Callare Matanna, because directly below, only a half kilometer away, is the Albergo Alto Matanna, where people can drive up for a quickie hike. To enjoy a quiet lunch, there are two options; both providing extensive and spectacular views of Tuscany. Go north for a 160-meter climb up to the summit of Monte Nona, or go south for a 190-meter climb to the summit of Monte Matanna. Either route takes about 25 minutes each way.

For the Monte Nona summit, there are several way-trails weaving their way around the grassy slopes. Continue on the ridgeline until you reach the large cross. This summit has an incredible view of the Pania della Croce (1859 meters). For Monte Matanna, go through the small metal gate, follow the blue markers up through the woods, then continue up the steep ridgeline until you reach the spectacular false summit. For many, this will be enough, as the views of Pania della Croce, the Procinto, and the Northern Apennines are great. If it is not hazy, continue on the ridgeline until you reach the true summit with the large cross, for the view down to

Viareggio on the coast, and out to the islands of Gorgona and Corsica offshore.

Once back at the Callare Matanna, head down the slope to the Albergo Alto Matanna. Just before reaching the hotel itself, at a fenceline, turn left onto Trail 109. Follow this trail as it works its way along a rocky talus slope scattered with ash and hop-hornbeam trees. The trail on the north side of Monte Nona will then enter a dense hornbeam woodland, later dominated mostly by beech. About halfway across Monte Nona, an unmarked way-trail descends the slope to the right. The red/white blazes that show Trail 109 continuing straight are partially obscured by some large rocks ahead, thus it is easy to mistakenly turn onto this unmarked trail. However, you will realize quickly if you have done this because it descends the wrong direction and you will not see any more blazes. Later, the trail does descend into a steep notch with loose rock and slippery moss, which has visible red/white blazes. At the bottom of the notch, the trail enters an open pasture area, and shortly thereafter, approximately 1 hour from Callare Matanna, you arrive at the all-important pass, at Foce delle Porchette.

This pass is a meeting place of three hikes in this guide, and has provided access to three distinct valleys throughout history. Trail 8, to the right, descends to the village of Palagnana. Trail 108, to the right, heads up to the summit of Monte Croce (Hike 23), above. Trail 6, to the north, heads across the drainage toward the Arch of Monte Forato (Hike 24) and the village of Fornovolasco. However, Trail 8, to the left and headed west down the slope, heads back toward Stazzema. After about 15 minutes, Trail 8 will arrive at a junction. To the right, Trail 6 heads toward Monte Forato, and is heavily marked. To the left, Trails 6 and 8 merge and head back toward Stazzema. But, this junction is

View of Pania delle Croce from the summit of Monte Nona

poorly marked. Turn left, and follow this wide trail all the way around the east side of Monte Nona, through the chestnut woods back toward Stazzema. There will be a couple of significant trail intersections on the route back. The first is where Trail 8 branches right, heading toward Cardoso. Here, you continue straight on Trail 6. Next, Trail 121 appears on the left, from the Procinto and Rifugio Forte dei Marmi. Finally, Trail 5 arrives on the left, also from the Procinto. Ignore these trails and continue straight, past the B&B, until you reunite with Trail 5, where you will turn right and head back to the parking lot.

The Alpi Apuane

23

Monte Croce Loop

A loop to the summit of Monte Croce with views of the Pania della Croce.

Distance: 9 kilometers (5.6 miles)

Elevation: 757–1,314 meters (2,883–4,310 feet)

Hiking time: 4 hours

Park: Parco Naturale di Alpi Apuane

Difficulty: Moderately strenuous

Time to visit: April to October

Monte Croce is one of the southernmost mountains in the Alpi Apuane. It is also on the eastern edge of the range. Thus, by its position, the view at the summit is one of the most expansive in all of Tuscany. From the summit, one can see the Tyrrhenian sea, the Pisa plain, the Northern Apennines, most of the southern and central Alpi Apuane, and the Cinque Terre. Most of the Monte Croce Loop provides a pleasant stroll through beech woods, with plenty of openings offering nice views of the surrounding landscape. There is only one strenuous stretch, on the final grassy ascent to the summit, as well as, an interesting climb up through a narrow, rainwater-cut gorge. Due to the relatively short nature of this hike, it is a very good one to do when short on time, or to include along with the other loops that make up the Grand Loop of the Southern Alpi Apuane (Bonus Hike).

The hike to Monte Croce begins in the village of Palagnana. To get to Palagnana from Pisa or Florence, take the A14 Autostrada to the Lucca Est exit. Look for signs for Abetone and Castelnuovo Garfagnana on the SP2. Take the SP2 for 28 kilometers, until you reach the turn off for Fabbriche di Vallico. It is 7 kilometers on the SP37 to Fabbriche di Vallico and then continue on another 7 kilometers to Palagnana. As you approach Palagnana, the road appears to bend left across a bridge over the stream near some buildings, and then continues uphill. This is the road to the Albergo Alto Matanna, which is discussed in Hike 22. Instead, continue straight another 1 kilometer further, until you reach the actual village of

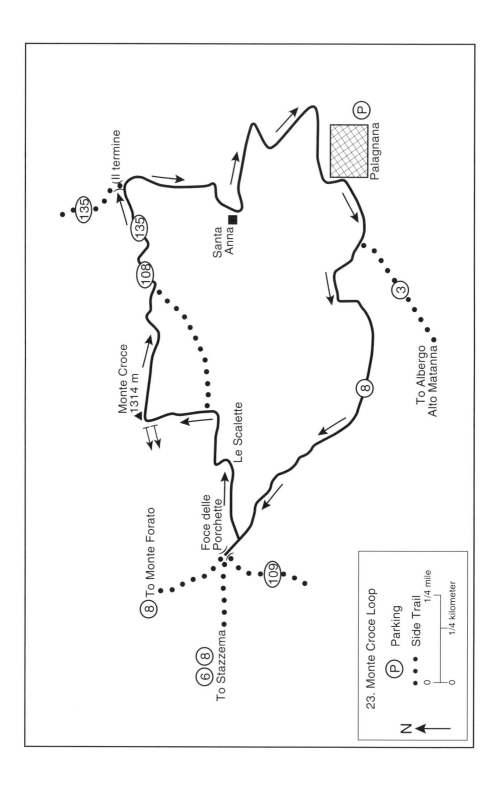

Il termine

135

135

108

Monte Croce
1314 m

Le Scalette

To Monte Forato

Foce delle
Porchette

8

6 8

To Stazzema

109

Santa
Anna

Palagnana

P

3

8

To Albergo
Alto Matanna

N

23. Monte Croce Loop

P   Parking

•••   Side Trail

|0   1/4 mile|
|0   1/4 kilometer|

Monte Croce summit

Palagnana and park at the small bar and *ritorante*. The CLAP offers bus service to Palagnana. Contact them at www. clapspa. it or 058/35411 for more information.

Trails 3 and 8 leave from the bar, initially following the road, which ends at a house. Turn right here, and cross a small field until you reach the woods near an intermittent streambed. When you enter the woods and cross the stream, Trail 3 branches off to the left, while Trail 8 remains on the right side of the streambed. Trail 8 then slowly rises in elevation above the streambed. After about 20 minutes, you will see some structures to the left. As the trail climbs, the forest thins out, and in about 1 hour from Palagnana, you reach the pass of Foce delle Porchette, where several other trails converge. Trail 109 heads to the Albergo Alto Matanna, while Trails 6 and 8 head to Stazzema and Monte Forato, respectively.

At the pass, look for Trail 108 to the right, headed up the side of Monte Croce, which is the summit directly above. The peak to the left is Monte Nona (Hike 22). The peaks across the valley are Monte Forato (Hike 24) and Pania della Croce. Trail 108 reenters the beech woods, and in about 15 minutes arrives at the steep water-cut gorge of Le Scalette. This stretch is narrow and steep, but very interesting. At the top of the gorge, you emerge into a flat, grassy area, where there is an intermittent spring. From here, you will see the summit of Monte Croce above, and the goal is within sight. Continue on the trail as it heads east along the lower slopes of Monte Croce. After about 5–10 minutes, start looking for faint blue markers on the rocks headed up the grassy slopes of Monte Croce. The blue trail heads up to the summit, while Trail 108 continues around to the other side. Once you begin heading upslope on the blue trail, the markers disappear, but the route is obvious. The trail is a deep cut into the dirt of the grassy slopes and the summit is obvious, above. This ascent is by far the most grueling part of the

The summit of Monte Croce offers spectacular vistas.

hike. The summit seems so close, but you must just keep trudging up the slope. This seems especially true when you come to a false summit about halfway up, but the view at the true summit is more than worth it.

From the summit, you appear to be just a stone's throw from the Pania della Croce, the highest peak in this part of the range. The eastern slope of Pania della Croce appears to have a small glacial fold, and it is easy to imagine a small ice field sitting there during the Ice Age. Below this mountain, the ridgeline of Monte Forato (Hike 24) is visible. Looking east, you can view across the Garfagnana valley and see the tilted layers of Monte Giovo (Hike 39) and Corno alle Scale (Hike 40) in the Northern Apennines. The views to the south and west provide opportunities to see the Tuscan hills, Monte Pisano (Hike 21) with its radio towers, the Pisa plain, the mouth of the Arno River, and the Tyrrhenian Sea.

When you are ready to continue, follow the summit ridge to the east until it descends, to reconnect with Trail 108. Continue along the ridgeline east on Trail 108, and soon you will enter the forest. Eventually the main trail will come to an intersection known as Il Termine, where Trail 135 crosses over the pass. Turn right, and follow Trail 135 through thick beech woods. After about 20 minutes the trail emerges onto a paved road. Turn left, and follow the road down as it switchbacks back and forth through farms down toward Palagnana. There are places where red markers shortcut the switchbacks, and this stretch can definitely be confusing, as sometimes it does not seem like you are going in the right direction. Do not fear, though; if you stay on the road, it will take you back to your car in about one hour. You will know everything is fine when you pass the church of Santa Anna on the way down.

24

Arch of Monte Forato Loop

A loop to a natural arch at the summit of Monte Forato.

Distance: 9 kilometers (5.6 miles) for shorter loop; 10.5 kilometers (6.5 miles) for longer loop

Elevation: 757–1,314 meters (2,883–4,310 feet)

Hiking time: 4–5 hours

Park: Parco Naturale di Alpi Apuane

Difficulty: Moderately strenuous

Time to visit: April to October

At the crest of the Alpi Apuane, along the thin ridgeline that separates the coastal Versilia region from the inland Garfagnana valley, there is a large, natural marble arch at the summit of Monte Forato. This arch stands out, high above the valleys below, and is visible from the sea on a clear day. In addition, the summit of Monte Forato provides an extreme closeup view of the most prominent peak in the Alpi Apuane, the Pania della Croce, as well as views out toward the sea, the Northern Apennines, and the Procinto (Hike 22) down below. At the arch, it is common to see rockclimbers swinging from ropes through the arch or people clamboring about on top. In addition to the summit and exposed ridgeline, the hike goes through some very nice stands of beech, and passes several historic abandoned structures that give hints of the rustic life in these mountains before roads and other modern conveniences.

The trail begins in the village of Fornovolasco. To access Fornovolasco from Pisa or Florence, take the A14 Autostrada to the Lucca Est exit. Follow signs for Abetone and Castelnuovo Garfagnana. Take the SP2 out of town, then continue following signs for Castelnuovo Garfagnana on the SP2 for 35 kilometers until you come to the village of Gallicano. Turn left up into the mountains on the SP39 for 9 kilometers until you reach Fornovolasco. The valley you drive through on the way up is quite narrow and beautiful. You will see a small lake behind a dam on the way up, before you reach Fornovolasco. Park in the parking lot near the Rifugio La

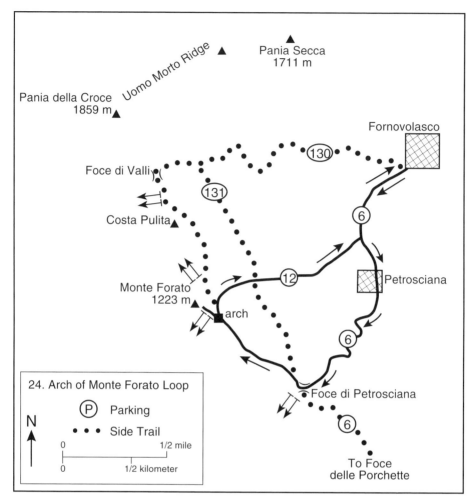

24. Arch of Monte Forato Loop

Pania della Croce 1859 m

Uomo Morto Ridge

Pania Secca 1711 m

Fornovolasco

Foce di Valli

Costa Pulita

Monte Forato 1223 m

arch

Petrosciana

Foce di Petrosciana

To Foce delle Porchette

24. Arch of Monte Forato Loop

P Parking

• • • Side Trail

N

0   1/2 mile

0   1/2 kilometer

Buca. The CLAP offers bus service into Fornovolasco. Contact them at www.clapspa.it or 058/ 35411 for more information.

To access the trail, walk into and through town on Trail 6. Inside the town, Trail 130 takes off to the right, which is where you return if you do the long loop. After leaving the town, the trail passes a few garden plots and then crosses a paved road. Continue across the road and up the valley along the side of the creek, and the trail will eventually enter a chestnut forest. Shortly thereafter, at an overlook of the valley, there is an old structure where Trail 12 branches off to the right; this is the return route for the short loop. Continue straight on Trail 6 as it follows the creek bed. The trail will come to a point where it crosses the creek bed and follows a dirt road up the valley. There are some confusing sections where it appears as if the trail crosses the creek over and over. Do not be concerned; there are parallel trails on each side of the creek. Just continue going uphill, alongside to the creek, until you reach a dirt road which crosses it. Turn right and start up the road, but then

Fornovolasco

immediately turn left at a small track, and continue up the valley. The trail will soon begin to switchback, as it climbs the ridge above. The slope is steep and loose in some places and then the trail enters a nice beech forest. After about 90 minutes of walking, you will reach the pass at Foce di Petrosciana. At 960 meters, this pass represents

---

Arch of Monte Forato Loop

The summit arch

the divide between the Versilia coastal region and the Garfagnana valley. The view here is extensive. To the west one can see the coast, as well as Monte Nona and the column of Procinto. Monte Croce stands directly above, to the left. Back across the valley to the east is a wonderful view of the layered summit of Monte Giovo (Hike 39).

From here, Trail 6 descends along the Versilia side and then across to Foce delle Porchette, to where the trails of Monte Croce (Hike 23) and Monte Nona (Hike 22) are accessible. Trail 131 heads north across the lower slopes of Monte Forato. However, look for the red/white blazed, unnumbered trail that climbs the narrow ridgeline above. It is narrow, and there are some chains and exposed spots in places, but overall this trail is generally quite easy. The trail then enters the forest for a brief time, before emerging at the base of the Arch of Monte Forato. At the arch, the view is incredible as you look through the opening to the Mediterranean. There will likely be rockclimbers on, around, or hanging within the arch if it is a weekend. In fact, on a sunny weekend, there may be dozens of people milling around the arch. But, if you climb up the slope just north of the arch to the summit of Monte Forato, not only will you avoid the crowds, but you will be treated to one of the most spectacular panoramas in all of Tuscany.

The most prominent feature is the spectacular view at the Pania della Croce, so close that you could almost touch it. The arch sits below, while much of the Northern Apennines and the southern Alpi Apuane are easily visible. After lunch at the summit, return to the arch, and then there are two choices for your return loop.

The longer, more strenuous loop leaves following a blue-marked route that follows the ridgeline toward Pania della Croce. It is rough terrain and as it heads up the ridge of Costa Pulita. It can get dicey in spots, particularly when it climbs up the vertical stretch and reaches the narrow summit of the ridge. After almost 1 hour, the trail will reach the Foce di Valli at the base of the Pania della Croce. From here, Trail 130 will descend the steep, rocky slopes to the right. Heading across the steep basin of the mountain, you encounter Trail 131 branching to the right, as it heads to the Foce di Petrosciana. Continue straight on Trail 130 through the woods and past some fields until you reach a dirt road. Turn right on the road and then look for the trail heading into the woods on the other side. Continue on the trail until it reaches the road to Fornovolasco. Trail 130 continues across the street, and emerges in the center of town.

If you feel the summit was enough of an adventure and want to return on the less strenuous shorter loop, look for Trail 12 descending into the forest just below the arch. It switchbacks down steep slopes through mature forests of beech to Fornovolasco below, in about 60 minutes. Along the way, you will pass the old abandoned cottage of Casa Felici, which has no road access—making you think about what life was like in these mountains before roads and modern conveniences were introduced. Trail 12 will come out at Trail 6 not far from Fornovolasco. Turn left and retrace your steps back to your car.

Bonus Hike

The Grand Loop of the Southern Alpi Apuane

A two-day loop across the spectacular southern portion of the Alpi Apuane range.

Distance: *Approximately 29.5 kilometers (18.3 miles)*

Elevation: *440–1,317 meters (1,443–4,320 feet)*

Hiking time: *10–13 hours*

Park: *Parco Naturale di Alpi Apuane*

Difficulty: *Strenuous*

Time to visit: *Late April to October*

The southern part of the Alpi Apuane is a rugged and wild area, where small villages are found nestled among dense forests. High above the bustling Versilia coast and alpine grasslands are incredible exposed marble peaks. While most tourists visit the marble quarries of Carrara, the local villagers gather mushrooms and chestnuts, or hunt wild boar in the forests of the southern part of this range. High above treeline, the gray marble landscape offers impressive panoramas of sheer cliffs and jagged peaks. From the summit of any of these peaks, the view across the Tyrrhenian Sea toward Gorgona and Corsica is awe-inspiring on a clear day, while the late afternoon sun on the Apennines shines golden in spring, when snow is still present. Despite thousands of years of human presence, the southern Alpi Apuane offers a glimpse of an Italian mountain wilderness right in the heart of Tuscany.

If you were to fly over the Alpi Apuane, there are basically two remarkable things you would immediately notice. First, is how incredibly steep these mountains rise above the sea. Second, is how small this range really is. That being said, the range is so rugged that it could definitely take several days to hike across it. Due to the topography of the area, it is difficult to do large loops. However, the Grand Loop of the Southern Alpi Apuane is one excursion that incorporates three other day hikes from this guide (Hikes 22, 23, and 24) to make for one large multiday adventure in the most rugged landscape in Tuscany.

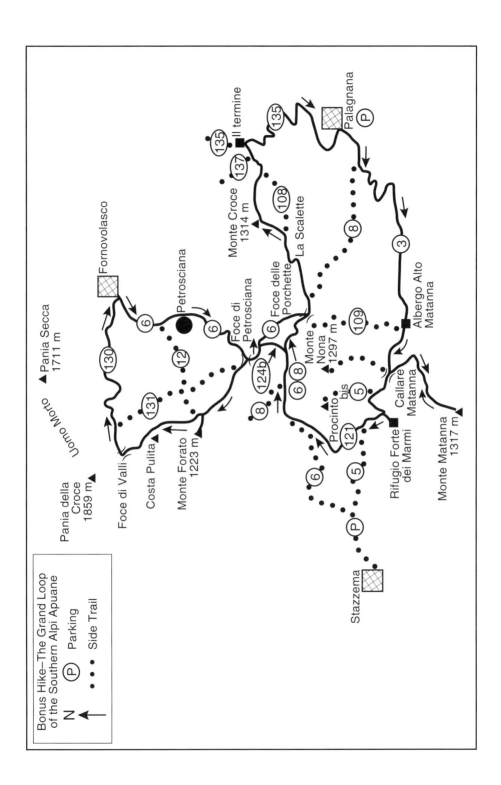

Bonus Hike—The Grand Loop
of the Southern Alpi Apuane

N

Ⓟ Parking

• • Side Trail

Pania della
Croce
1859 m ▲

Pania Secca
1711 m ▲

Uomo Morto

Foce di Valli

Costa Pulita ▲

Monte Forato
1223 m ▲

130

131

12

6

Petrosciana ●

6

Foce di
Petrosciana

Fornovolasco

8

124b

6 8

8

121

6

5

Ⓟ

Stazzema

Procinto ▲

bis

5

Monte
Nona
1297 m ▲

109

Foce delle
Porchette

6

Monte Croce
1314 m ▲

108

137

135

Il termine

135

La Scalette

8

3

Albergo Alto
Matanna

Callare
Matanna

Rifugio Forte
dei Marmi

Monte Matanna
1317 m ▲

Palagnana

Ⓟ

The three smaller loops used in this hike have been connected via a series of shortcut trails, making for one larger loop. There are three possible places for lodging along the way, although it would be possible to do the entire loop in one very long, and strenuous, day. This description will offer basic details, including specific directions for the short-cuts. For more detailed information about each individual segment, go to each individual smaller loop description when directed.

Begin at the village of Palagnana (directions available at Hike 23). Follow the signs for Trails 3 and 8. In the Monte Croce hike, you are advised to follow Trail 8, but instead stay on Trail 3 as it heads toward the Albergo Alto Matanna. The trail will head along the base of Monte Nona, above, and then begins climbing the slope until it reaches the Albergo Alto Matanna, just below the pass of Callare Matanna. At this stage, begin climbing the slope toward the pass and, just as you reach the pass, look left for a trail that ascends to the summit of Monte Matanna. This section is described in more detail in Hike 22. It is a steep climb at first, until you reach the false summit. At the top of the ridge, the view is spectacular, as it is the very first time that you can look out and see the entire Alpi Apuane range. Continue west along the ridgeline, past a small saddle, to the summit of Monte Matanna. From here, you will be at the southwesternmost edge of the range, with sheer drops down to the Versilia coast below. The view across the Tuscan coast and across to the islands offshore, including Corsica, simply do not get any better! To the south, look for the mountain with the radio towers on it—that is Monte Pisano (Hike 21). The hills along the coast further south are the Livorno Hills (Hike 13), while the small peninsula where the Arno River empties into the sea is Marina di Pisa (Hike 11).

When you are ready to continue, back-track until you reach the Callare Matanna. From here, descend along the other side of the pass into the chestnut forests of Stazzema. This section of the trail descends toward the Procinto, the large freestanding cylinder of rock noted in Hike 22. Continue descending past the Procinto access trail, until you reach the Rifugio Forte dei Marmi, which is located just before the intersection with Trail 121. This *rifugio* is the first good opportunity to get some food and drink along this route, especially after having climbed Monte Matanna. Do note that from Callara Matanna to the *rifugio,* the route is heading in the opposite direction as described in Hike 22.

After stopping at the *rifugio,* stay straight at the spring, following Trail 121, as Trail 5 descends steeply through the forest down to Stazzema. Trail 121 will continue along the base of the Procinto, and then will intersect with Trail 6 on the other side. Turn right, and follow Trail 6 until you see Trail 124B. This trail will descend through a deep gash in the cliff, and then meets up with Trail 6 again on the adjacent ridgeline heading toward Monte Forato. If you miss Trail 124B, you may continue on Trail 6 until Foce della Porchette, where many trails conjoin. Here you follow Trail 6 to the left, as it also heads toward the adjacent ridgeline of Monte Forato. Either way, Trail 6 will descend into the forest and then climb back up again to the pass at Foce di Petrosciana. Here you will get spectacular views across to the Apennines, and down the valley of Fornovolasco.

From this pass, follow the details laid out in Hike 24 to reach the Arch of Monte Forato. Follow the unmarked trail onto the rocky ridge, where there are red/white blazes ascending the slope. Continue to follow the red/white blazes until you reach the arch. Just above is the summit of Monte

Approaching the summit of Monte Croce

Forato, with spectacular views of the Pania della Croce. From the arch, there are two options, based on how much time you have and how adventurous you are.

You can take the shorter route to Fornovolasco, by descending the slope on Trail 12, until it meets Trail 6. If you chose this route, you may turn left at Trail 36, and follow it into Fornovolasco for lodging at the Rifugio La Buca. However, if you want more adventure, and even more spectacular views, continue along the ridgeline to the summit of Costa Pulita, then on, to the base of Pania della Croce at Foce di Valli. This route is very steep, as it ascends Costa Pulita, and is sometimes hard to follow, but the views are absolutely outstanding. Once you reach the saddle of Foce di Valli, Pania della Croce literally rises 600 meters straight up! From Foce di Valli, follow the details in Hike 24 back to Fornovolasco, where the Rifugio La Buca is just the place to overnight and have a wonderful Italian dinner.

So far, you have completed over 60 percent of the loop, and a majority of the most rugged terrain. The second stage is gentler, which I am sure will be a relief. From Fornovolasco, take Trail 6 back up to Foce di Petrosciana, as described in Hike 24. After Foce di Petrosciana, continue on Trail 6 until you reach Foce delle Porchette on the opposite saddle. From here, several trails branch out. Follow Trail 108 toward the summit of Monte Croce (Hike 23). The rest of the way back to the town of Palagnana is exactly the same as described in Hike 23. This trail will go along the side of Monte Croce, but does not actually climb to the summit. Once you get into the grassy slopes above treeline, look for the blue markers headed up to the left, and climb the grassy slopes to the summit of Monte Croce for your last spectacular views of the Southern Alpi Apuane, including Pania della Croce, Monte Nona, Monte Matanna, and the Apennines. From here, you follow the ridgeline down, reconnect with Trail 108, and follow the description of Hike 23, all the way until you reach Palagnana. There is a *ristorante* in town to celebrate the completion of this extended loop.

25

Monte Fiocca Geological Tour

A loop around Monte Fiocca, offering a fascinating geological cross-section of an Alpi Apuane peak, and spectacular subalpine heath moorlands.

Distance: 12.4 kilometers (7.7 miles)

Elevation: 920–1,711 meters (3,018–5,612 feet)

Hiking time: 5–6 hours

Park: Parco Naturale di Alpi Apuane

Difficulty: Moderately strenuous

Time to visit: April to October

Located in the heart of the Alpi Apuane, Monte Fiocca provides exceptional views across the entire landscape. In addition to the panoramic views of the Versilia coast, the Garfagnana valley, the Northern Apennines, and nearly all of the Alpi Apuane, this peak offers beautiful alpine grasslands and heath moors, as well as some incredible geological formations, including marble and various other metamorphic and sedimentary rocks that provide a kaleidoscope of color and texture to this steep mountain. Rock collectors are sure to walk off the peak with several specimens in their packs. Perhaps overshadowing Monte Fiocca, are the dramatic sheer cliffs of its slightly higher neighbor, Penna di Sumbra. A hike to the smooth-layered saddle of Passo Fiocca, directly between these two adjacent peaks, offers what is in my opinion the greatest scenery in the Alpi Apuane.

To get to Monte Fiocca from Pisa, take the A14 Autostrade north, to the Versilia exit. Follow the signs for Castelnuovo Garfagnana and Seravezza. Continue following signs for Castelnuovo Garfagnana for 20 kilometers past Seravezza, and head through the Galleria di Cipollaia, a 1.1 kilometer tunnel drilled through the ridge crest of the Alpi Apuane. On the other side, look for a left turn toward Arni, about 2 kilometers after the tunnel. Drive into the small village of Arni, and when you see a blue sign for Massa pointing left, stay straight, and park immediately in the town parking lot on the right.

The route begins by following the signs for Trail 144 and crossing the creek on the

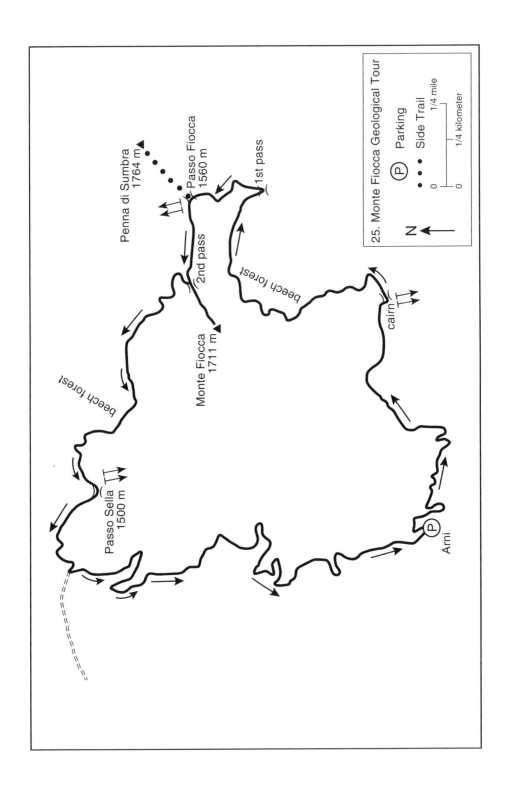

25. Monte Fiocca Geological Tour

Parking ⓅP

Side Trail •••••

0   1/4 kilometer
0   1/4 mile

N ⟵

Penna di Sumbra 1764 m

Passo Fiocca 1560 m

1st pass

2nd pass

beech forest

Monte Fiocca 1711 m

beech forest

Passo Sella 1500 m

cairn

Arni

Passo Fiocca and Penna di Sumbra summit

bridge, just up from the parking lot. After crossing this creek, look for red/white blazes on the right side of the road, which is Trail 144. Here the trail looks like a staircase climbing up the ridge, overgrown by grasses. Follow these blazes, as the trail immediately begins climbing steeply up through grass and small shrub up toward the ridgeline above. The steep ascent to the ridgeline is about 1 kilometer, and climbs about 200 meters in elevation. From the ridgeline, the first expansive views open up, but the climbing is far from done. The trail relentlessly continues to ascend, following the steep ridgeline, with the summit of Monte Fiocca visible high above. Looking left from the summit, you can see Passo Sella, and the marble truck road that you will descend on your return. To the right is a large rock cairn, which is a point you will pass near the top of the ascent.

The trail is well marked, but the terrain is very rugged and steep. The ridgeline is covered with steeply tilted gray limestone layers, which make hiking this stretch difficult, but the higher you climb, the more fabulous the views get. Approximately 1 kilometer after first reaching the ridgeline, you will arrive at the large rock cairn on the west side of Monte Fiocca. At this point, you have ascended 500 meters above the parking area. This spot offers incredible views down the valley, and across to the Pania della Croce and limestone cliffs of Monte Corchia. Looking west, you can see the Versilia Coast. The peninsula sticking out into the sea is the mouth of the Arno River and Marina di Pisa. A smaller peninsula further north is the mouth of the Secchio River, which flows down the length of the Garfagnana valley.

A little way past the cairn, the trail takes a bend, and arrives at what is perhaps the most spectacular view in all of Alpi Apuane. The sight of the sheer rock wall of Penna di Sumbra across the drainage, and the

A cloudy ridgeline at Monte Fiocca

beautiful gray saddle of Passo Fiocca will stop you in your tracks.

The trail soon levels off, but does not yet become easy, as it traverses the southern slopes of the mountain. There are a couple of tricky spots where some rock scrambling is necessary, before you reach the stand of beech in the middle of the drainage. When the trail enters the stand of beech, there appears to be a small trail dropping down; ignore that, and follow the red/white blaze on the rocks above. This stretch through the beech stand is quite easy as it is mostly level and not at all rocky. The shade is also very welcome on a hot summer day.

The trail will eventually emerge from the woods and then curve around through grasslands, until reaching a false pass. From the false pass, the views of the cliffs of Penna di Sumbra are just as dramatic. The trail then climbs up the ridge toward the smooth, gray Passo Fiocca. This stretch has some fascinating rocks, including metamorphosed granite, various schists, and gray limestone. Passo Fiocca sits directly between the summits of Monte Fiocca and Penna di Sumbra. The short summit ascent of Penna di Sumbra is considered an "experts only" trail, and should only be attempted by the most experienced hikers. It has cables to help with the exposed stretches and the cliffs appear to drop off into oblivion, when clouds are covering the summit. A dog should not be taken to this summit, as the footing is not good and its steepness and the ledges also make it difficult to negotiate.

Passo Fiocca is a great place to stop and eat, as it is the halfway point of the loop. The view from the pass includes the Garfagnana valley, a long stretch of the Northern Apennines including Monte Giovo (Hike 39) and Corno alle Scale (Hike 40), the Versilia coast, and most of the southern Alpi Apuane. To continue on, head to the left side of the pass here, and follow the red/white blazes of Trail 144 up the ridge, headed

The Alpi Apuane

north. After about 300 meters of slow climbing, the trail will arrive at a small notch, and a trail intersection. Heading down to the right is Trail 144, on its way to continue the loop around the mountain. Heading up the grassy ridge is the Monte Fiocca summit spur. The spur trail will climb about another 100 meters in elevation, to panoramic views at the summit. The view of Monte Altissimo (Hike 26), directly across the valley from Arni, is particularly fantastic. After returning from the summit back to the notch, head downslope following Trail 144.

Trail 144 now heads along the eastern slopes of the mountain, through raspberry-filled fields, across heather moorlands, and through a small beech stand. The trail will generally maintain its elevation, despite some ups and downs, as it traverses small stream drainages. Trail 144 will continue for the next 1.6 kilometers, until it reaches Passo Sella. Just before the final ascent to Passo Sella, as you are exiting the beech stand, there is a very short, steep rock scramble, with some exposure. As you climb the last stretch to Passo Sella, you will climb on some beautiful maroon mudstones with a waxy texture.

From Passo Sella, views of the marble mines of Arni become visible, as well as Monte Altissimo. The trail will head right from the pass, descend down a soft, gentle, heather moorland, and then arrive at the marble truck road at another lower pass. The marble truck road is the return route all the way down into the village of Arni. The road is very rocky, with a lot of loose material and dust, so do not get complacent. The walk down along the road is 3.5 kilometers long, and descends nearly 600 meters in elevation. The road continually switches back and forth down the flanks of Monte Fiocca, offering some fascinating cross-sections of the mountain. A myriad of colors and textures are there to examine, including green slates, brown shales, red mudstones, white limey sandstone, silvery schists, various gneisses, and several varieties of marble. The layers in the rocks vary in texture from paper-thin to several meters thick, and the tilting and twisting of the layers indicate the great tectonic pressures and temperatures these rocks have endured over the eons. Several sections of marble lower down contain extremely wavy, dark streaks, created as the limestone and shale melted under the intense pressure.

26

Monte Altissimo Loop

A loop to the summit of the most dominant peak as seen from the Versilia through marble quarries and the WWII-era German Gothic Line.

Distance: 9.5 kilometers (5.9 miles)

Elevation: 990–1,589 meters (3,247–5,212 feet)

Hiking time: 4–5 hours

Park: Parco Naturale di Alpi Apuane

Difficulty: Moderately strenuous

Time to visit: April to October

Driving along the Versilia coast from Viareggio to La Spezia, there is one peak that really stands out among the steep Alpi Apuane range rising above; this is Monte Altissimo, a rocky cliff that rises almost completely vertically up from the sea. Although it is not among the highest peaks in the range, it appears that way due to its close proximity to the sea and its sheer steepness. On the southern end of the mountain, there is a small quarry area that is obvious, because it looks like a white castle perched high above the landscape. The mountain is so steep that it is virtually devoid of vegetation, giving the impression that it higher than it really is. A hike to the summit of Monte Altissimo is not long in distance, but it is rough on your knees, and has some very steep sections. However, its central location in the range offers a chance to see nearly every peak in the Alpi Apuane, the Northern Apennines to the east, the entire Versilia coast, the Tuscan Archipelago, and the Pisa plain. This trail also offers hikers an opportunity to hike right through two operating marble quarries, where real statue-quality marble, such as was used for such masterpieces as Michelangelo's *David* and the sculptures of the Roman Empire, can be found.

To access the trailhead for Monte Altissimo from Pisa or La Spezia, take the A12 Autostrada, and use the Versilia exit. Follow signs for Seravezza and Stazzema on the SP9. Continue on the SP9 past Seravezza for 4.5 kilometers and then look for signs for Castelnuovo Garfagnana. Turn left onto the

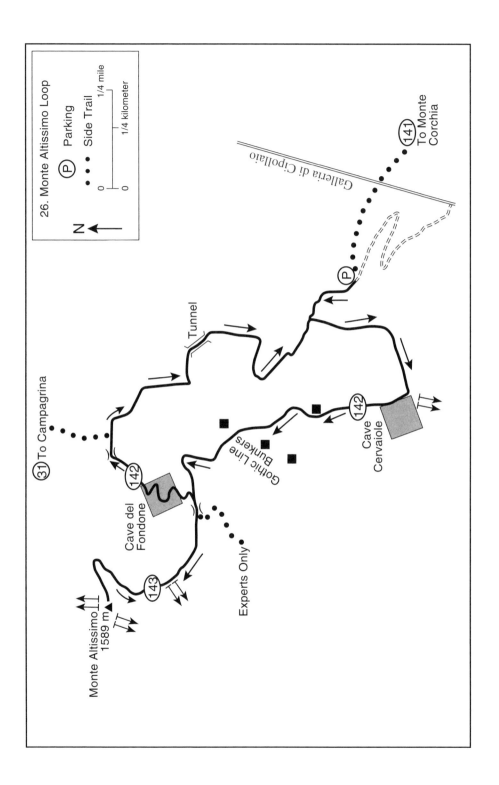

26. Monte Altissimo Loop

Ⓟ Parking
•••• Side Trail

0   1/4 mile
0   1/4 kilometer

N ←

Galleria di Cipollaio

Ⓟ

141
To Monte
Corchia

Tunnel

31 To Campagrina

Cave del
Fondone

142

Gothic Line
Bunkers

142

Cave
Cervaiole

143

Experts Only

Monte Altissimo
1589 m

View from Monte Altissimo

SP10 and drive as the road switchbacks for a little more than 12 kilometers. Just before entering a long tunnel called the Galleria del Cipollaio, there is a turnoff to the left. Take this turn and follow the narrow, paved road up for 2 kilometers until the road ends at a gate, and park here. There is no direct bus service to the trailhead. The closest service offered is by the CLAP on the Pietrasanta–Castelnuovo di Garfagnana line. Contact CLAP at www.clapspa.it or 058/35411 for more information.

Trail 31 starts at the gate and follows the paved road. At the first fork, turn left and follow the paved road up the hill. After a few hundred meters, the road will enter the quarry of Cave Cervaiole. At this spot, there is a spectacular view south toward the Pisa plain and Marina di Pisa. The quarry itself is fascinating, with beautiful, white marble blocks and massive equipment set up around the walls of cut rock. At the first building, the road splits and you will turn

right. Follow the road up, and it will soon turn into dirt. Continue following the red/white blazes as the route becomes Trail 142. The road will end at a building. Go to the left side of the building and walk around to the back. At this stage, the trail becomes difficult to follow. The area is grassy with scattered trees, and the trail is just a faint track through the grass. Look for some scattered red marks on exposed rocks that mark the route. At a patch of trees, the trail will begin climbing the ridgeline fairly steeply. If you lose the trail, do not be concerned; just keep climbing up the ridge on the rough rock and you will encounter the trail again upslope, when it becomes more obvious once more.

You may notice, about halfway to the summit of the ridge, some small walls of stone and other artifacts of the German Gothic Line. The Gothic Line was among the largest and most important battles of WWII in Italy, with over 80,000 deaths. In 1944, after the fall of Rome, the Germans

The Alpi Apuane

Marble quarry

attempted to set up a defensive line here in order to hold onto the important industrial and economic resources of the Po Valley in Northern Italy. The Gothic Line extended across the Alpi Apuane and the Apennines all the way to the Adriatic, and included thousands of gun emplacements. The rugged terrain made it almost impossible to penetrate, which you will easily relate to by hiking this stretch. Great battles were fought along the Versilia plain and in the Garfagnana Valley, as American forces suffered enormous casualties trying to cross the mountains. The British forces and their colonies eventually broke through the line along the gentler Adriatic Coast, allowing them access to the industrial Po Valley. However, these stubborn German defenses in the Apennines near Bologna held off American forces well into the spring of 1945, preventing American forces from joining the British and other allied troops.

Along the ridgeline, the trail will become obvious again as it heads along the side of the ridge. Monte Fiocca and Penna di Sumbra (Hike 25) dominate the view directly across the valley. There are great views of Monte Giovo (Hike 39) across the Garfagnana valley in the Northern Apennines, and Monte Cimone to the left of that (Hike 38). The trail soon enters a beech woodland, and in about 30 minutes you will emerge at a pass sitting above the Cave del Fondone, which has a spectacular view of the summit of Monte Altissimo above the amphitheater below. At this stage, the trail descends steeply to the edge of the quarry, and back up again to the Passo del Vaso Tondo, where there is a view out toward the coast. There is an intersection here, with Trail 142 descending down to the quarry and Trail 143 heading toward the summit of Monte Altissimo. Dropping down the cliff, on the other side, is a tiny trail labeled EE *("Escursionisti Esperti")*

Monte Altissimo Loop

indicating that this route is for experts only. Frankly, I do not even see how experts could do it, because the cliff drops nearly 90 degrees down toward the sea.

Trail 143 follows the knife-edged ridge-line from here to the side of Monte Altissimo, then loops around, and up to the summit. Trail 143 is not for the faint of heart. It is narrow, exposed to steep cliffs, and has loose footing in places. If it is icy, or the weather is inclement, reconsider doing this stretch. However, once you reach the other-side of the knife-edge, and begin ascending along the side of Monte Altissimo, the trail once again feels safe and is reasonably easy up to the summit.

The view at the summit is nothing short of spectacular. There are views across the entire Versilia coast, the Alpi Apuane, and on a really clear day, Corsica and Southern France. Once you have enjoyed lunch at the summit, return back to Passo del Vaso Tondo and take Trail 142 down into the Cave del Fondone. The trail goes into the quarry and has some absolutely beautiful marble. You may see some really interesting equipment as well, such as a giant 2-meter long chainsaw. The trail will descend down the winding dirt road until it reaches the settling ponds at the bottom of the quarry. Follow the road as it loops back towards the beginning of the hike. Trail 31 will branch off to the left, but you should continue straight. The road will go through a tunnel, which if you do it in late fall or winter may be draped with icicles. On the other side, the road continues following the contours of the ridge until it rejoins the original paved road that you started on, and you will return to your car shortly.

Bonus Hike

Marble "Glacier" of Monte Corchia

A hike up a marble quarry road to the marble "glacier" and summit of Monte Corchia.

Distance: Approximately 7.0 kilometers roundtrip (4.3 miles)

Hiking time: 3–4 hours

Elevation: 1,160–1,675 meters (3,804–5,494 feet)

Park: Parco Naturale di Alpi Apuane

Difficulty: Moderately easy

Time to visit: April to October

From Pisa, there is a mountain in the Alpi Apuane that appears to have a glacier coming down its south face. This bright, white mass is actually the marble tailing pile from a quarry high up on the slopes of Monte Corchia. Sitting right in the heart of the Alpi Apuane, it is quite easy to get to the "glacier" to see it up close, as well as explore an incredible cross-section of marble in situ, within the quarry itself. On the north slopes of the mountain, you will see some absolutely outstanding limestone cliffs that rise 500 vertical meters. By hiking up the quarry road as it switchbacks up the south slope of Monte Corchia, it is possible to reach the summit to view out across the entire mountain range. From this summit, every other hike in Alpi Apuane in this book is visible. The view across the valley to Monte Fiocca (Hike 25) and the Penna di Sumbra, with its gray barren saddle, is particularly spectacular.

To get to Monte Corchia, follow directions for Monte Altissimo (Hike 26). About 2 kilometers before reaching the tunnel, and shortly after passing signs for the village of Terrinca, look for a sharp turn to the right, which is virtually unsigned. This narrow, paved road will climb the slope until it reaches Passo di Croce. Continue beyond the pass, and park near where the road turns to a dirt surface, and splits. The upper dirt road is the path to the quarry of Monte Corchia. From this trailhead, the 500 meter limestone cliffs of Monte Corchia dominate the view. From here, it seems impossible that the road will eventually take you to the summit. The road begins by climbing the north slope, before curving around the west-

Marble cliffs at Monte Corchia

ern flanks of the mountain. The road passed through a small tunnel and along the sides of these vertical cliffs. As the road curves around the southern slopes of the mountain, the "glacier" and the quarry become visible.

Be aware that this is an active marble quarry, and heavy machinery may be operating on the site during your visit. While the quarrying activity seemed rare in my previous visits, and many hiking trails crisscross

Marble "glacier" at Monte Corchia

these quarry areas, be prepared for large trucks and falling rocks at any time.

Upon reaching the "glacier" it will become obvious that this "ice" is actually a giant pile of 2–4 meter long slabs of marble that were thrown down from the quarry above. Continue on the road as it switchbacks up the mountain toward the summit. Each time the road branches, stay left. The road ends just below a saddle, between the twin peaks of Monte Corchia. At the end of the road, it is an easy scramble up to the saddle, where the spectacular views begin.

From the saddle, it is just a short way, to the right or left, to the summits of the mountain. The views of Monte Fiocca (Hike 25) and the Penna di Sumbra are incredible, across the valley. The smooth saddle between these peaks and the sheer cliffs of Penna di Sumbra will really draw you to do that hike, as well. Monte Altissimo (Hike 26) and its quarries are visible further west, as well as the entire Versilia coastline. Pania della Croce and Monte Nona (Hike 22) are visible to the south. Retrace your steps back to Passo di Croce.

27

Monte Sagro Loop and the Quarries of Carrara Loop

A loop in the northern Alpi Apuane above the famous marble quarries of Carrara, to the summit of Monte Sagro.

Distance: 8.5 kilometers (5.3 miles)

Elevation: 1,279–1,749 meters (4,195–5,734 feet)

Hiking time: 3–4 hours

Park: Parco Naturale di Alpi Apuane

Difficulty: Moderate

Time to visit: April to October

If you take a drive on the A14 Autostrada south from Parma to La Spezia, there will be a spot where you will see a view so incredible and awe-inspiring that you may have to pull the car over, or risk an accident. It is the first view of the northern Alpi Apuane, which appear like enormous shark's teeth. The northern wall of the range is so steep and rugged that many of the peaks appear to be almost overhanging. These sharp, towering peaks give the impression that only experienced rockclimbers and the more nimble mountain goats could ever explore this terrain. The northern stretch of the Alpi Apuane not only contains the highest and steepest peaks of this range, but also the best and most extensive marble quarries in all of Italy. The famous marble quarries of Carrara have supplied marble for ancient Rome, the great cathedrals of Europe, and Michelangelo. While these rugged peaks may seem impossible to climb, there is a peak, Monte Sagro, that is not only accessible, but actually quite doable. Along the hike and at the summit are spectacular views of nearly vertical cliffs and snow-white marble quarries, the Northern Apennines, the gulf of La Spezia, and the Versilia coast.

To get to Monte Sagro, take the A12 Autostrada from Pisa or La Spezia, and get off on the Carrara exit. Follow signs for Carrara, and once in the city center (CENTRO), look for signs for Campo Cecina and Fosdinovo. The roads can be a little confusing in this winding, urban stretch so just keep following the signs for Campo Cecina, as the roads heads generally north and uphill. The road will then

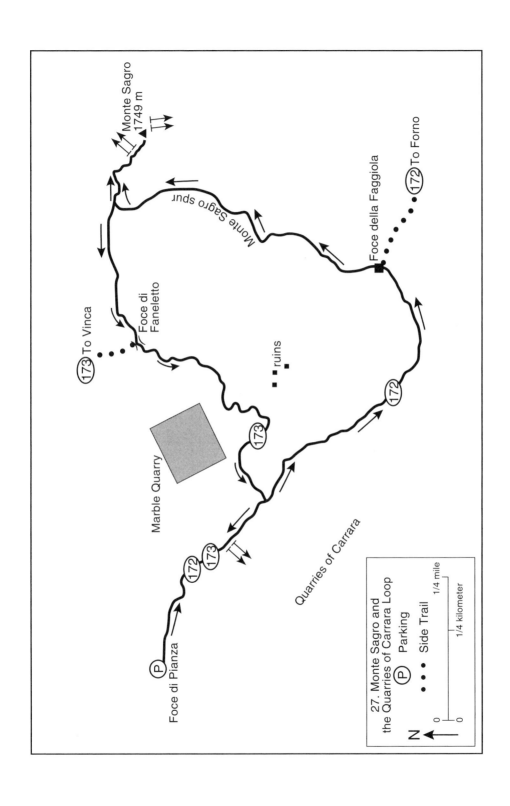

Monte Sagro
1749 m

Monte Sagro spur

Foce della Faggiola

172 To Forno

To Vinca 173

Foce di
Faneletto

ruins

172

173

Quarries of Carrara

Marble Quarry

172 173

Foce di Pianza

P

27. Monte Sagro and
the Quarries of Carrara Loop

P Parking

••• Side Trail

0 ¼ kilometer

0 ¼ mile

N

The Carrara marble quarries

pass through the small village of Gragnana. At 9.5 kilometers up from Carrara, there is a sharp right turn for Campo Cecina. After another 9 kilometers, you will reach an intersection, with the road to the right signed for Cave Cecina and Foce di Pianza. Turn right here and follow the road into the marble quarry, parking where you see red/white blazes on a power pole, with an incredible view of the quarries of Carrara far below. Bus service is available to Campo Cecina via CAT S.p.A. of Carrara. They can be contacted at www.catspa.it or 058/5852125.

Trails 172 and 173 begin at this parking area. They climb up onto a rocky ridge just above and parallel to the dirt road. From here, you can see the summit of Monte Sagro directly across the basin. After about 10 minutes, Trail 173 branches off to the left, but you should continue on Trail 172 straight ahead. The trail goes along the southern slope of a grassy ridge, and slowly rises up toward the ridgetop, all along the

way curving in, toward Monte Sagro. After about an hour you will reach the Foce della Faggiola (Pass of the Beeches), which is situated at the base of Monte Sagro. From here, Trail 172 crosses the ridge and heads south towards the village of Forno, down below. To the left is the Monte Sagro summit trail, which starts by heading north along the grassy slopes, before turning right at a faint intersection and climbing up the eastern face of the mountain. This summit trail is the most challenging part of the route, as it is steep, but fortunately is not very rocky.

At the summit, the view is spectacular. Directly below, you can look down onto the ridgeline you ascended from, and can gaze down onto the 90-degree vertical cliffs that drop off into oblivion. The scene can be particularly eerie if clouds of mist from the sea are streaming up from below. Directly to the northeast are the steep, and almost barren, rocky slopes of the Pizzo d'Uccello and the highest summit in the Alpi Apuane, the 1,947

The Alpi Apuane

The Monte Sagro ridgeline

meter Monte Pisanino, behind it. Some 1,000 meters below, at the base of the Pizzo d'Uccello, is the village of Vinca, with its orange-roofed dwellings perched high on the slopes above the Torrente Lucido. As steep as the slopes are in that direction, you may be amazed to know that Trail 173 actually continues on, down to Vinca. There is a large plaque at the summit, with arrows to show the summits and significant features that are visible in all directions. To the north lays the rock wall of the Northern Apennines, including the tilted sandstone layers of the high crest of Monte Sillara (Hike 34), rise nearly 2,000 meters above the Magra valley.

On the way back down, you descend the same way you came up, until reaching the trail intersection where you turned to head up the summit. Continue heading down the east slope, until you come to the Foce di Faneletto, where Trail 173 comes up from Vinca. Turn left, and follow Trail 173 as it winds down the steep, rocky slope to the southwest. On a hot day, this stretch can be unbearable, and there is no shade except for a few scattered bushes. Directly below is a small quarry, and if you look toward the center of the basin, you will see some scattered ruins. Trail 173 will drop down across very rocky terrain, until it reaches the low point at a dry streambed at the bottom of the basin. At this point, the trail crosses the stream and turns right, climbing the small ridgeline, and returns back to the intersection with Trail 172. Turn right, and in about 10 minutes you will return to the parking area.

IV

The Ligurian Coast and the Cinque Terre

Introduction to
the Ligurian Coast and the Cinque Terre

The Cinque Terre (meaning "Five-Lands") was once an isolated strip of rugged coastline that was disconnected from the rest of the world. In fact, until the train line was built here in the 1870s to connect La Spezia and Genoa by tunneling through the high cliffs, the only way to reach any of the five villages was to hike in or travel by boat. This isolation resulted in unique cuisines and customs. As the land was so steep, keeping animals was very difficult, therefore most of the cuisine was seafood based. Pesto and *focaccia* are also local specialities. Even after the train line was put in, driving was still impossible until the very narrow and winding roads were built in the 1960s.

Today, the Cinque Terre has been discovered as one of the premier visitor destinations in all of Europe. Flocks of Germans, Americans, Dutch, and just about everyone else, come to experience the spectacular cliffs, beautiful little fishing villages, and azure blue waters. Despite the boon of tourism, the villages still maintain their old-world charm, while a stroll through the terraced olive groves and vineyards takes you back to the middle ages. While the crowds may have increased, it is still possible to hike much of the area relatively undisturbed, if you come in the off-season. In fact, during our visits in the winter and early spring we found virtually no hikers on the trails. In addition, the mild climate of the region in winter allows hikers to climb the steep cliffs in cool, refreshing air, rather than sweating profusely as one would in summer.

In addition to the five main villages, there are lesser known routes leading to Portovenere and Levanto on the fringes of the Cinque Terre that see far less traffic, but provide even more spectacular scenery! The Cinque Terre can be traversed in two major routes: the coastal stretch and the ridgetop. To do the whole thing from Portovenere to Levanto in one day would be suicide. Instead, this guide has broken it up into three coastal segments for your convenience. However, there are a multitude of side routes and other options, should you wish to combine or alter any of these routes.

One major recommendation: *Do not drive here!* The roads are ridiculously narrow, the curves sharp, and parking is virtually nonexistent. The best way to visit the this region is to park your car in one of the cities outside of the Cinque Terre along the rail line such as La Spezia, Massa, or Sestri Levante, and take the train in. One of the best places for getting to and from the area is to park at the train station in Viareggio, because it is a relatively small city with an adequate amount of parking. Of course, if you don't have a car, you can also take the train from Pisa or Genoa.

A common way to visit the Cinque Terre is to establish a home base in one of the villages, where you have a room for a couple of nights. Then, you can hike down the coast to another village and take the train back. The next morning, you can take the train back to where you ended the day before, hike further, and take the train back again! The trains generally run once an hour, but be aware that not every train stops at every village, so check the schedule ahead of time. In summer, there are also ferries that run from La Spezia and Viareggio that stop at all of the coastal villages, except Corniglia. This is a spectacular way to see the cliffs and villages from a completely different perspective than the trails provide.

Although the Cinque Terre gets much of the fame, other spectacular hikes await you throughout the Ligurian coast. Portofino, just a short way from Genoa, is also famous with tourists and celebrities, both for its beautiful harbor and its spectacular sea cliffs. However, in winter and early spring, this area is free from crowds, and solitude is easy to find. For those who wish get off the beaten track and see sights similar to the Cinque Terre, the hikes of Montemarcello to Monte Murlo, and the Amphitheater of Moneglia, are excellent choices. The cliffs are just as dramatic, the vegetation similar, and traditional quaint villages are still available at the end of the walk. The Amphitheater of Moneglia also offers visitors an opportunity to study the natural regeneration of the coastal pine forests and *macchia,* following the catastrophic fires that burned the area in 2003. Rock roses and other wildflowers are spectacular along this route in spring, and the opening of the canopy has exposed incredible views of the entire Ligurian coast.

28

Montemarcello to Monte Murlo Loop

Loop hike from the village of Montemarcello along sea cliffs to the summit of Monte Murlo.

Distance: Tellaro Option: 9 kilometers (5.6 miles); Ameglia Option: 10.5 kilometers (6.5 miles)

Elevation: 280–361 meters (918–1,184 feet)

Park: Parco Naturale Regionale di Montemarcello–Magra

Hiking time: 3–4 hours

Difficulty: Moderately easy

Time to visit: Year round

The Parco Naturale Regionale di Montemarcello–Magra, located on a promontory on the southern boundary of Liguria, which separates the Gulf of La Spezia from Carrara, contains a combination of pine woodlands, *macchia* vegetation, steep rocky cliffs, medieval villages, and terraced farms. Generally overlooked due to its more famous neighbor to the north—the Cinque Terre—this park offers outstanding views out onto the Mediterranean sea, north toward the peninsula of Portovenere, east down to the fertile valley at the mouth of the Magra River, and across to the marble quarries of Carrara in the Alpi Apuane. This park also offers relaxing strolls through ancient olive groves and picturesque villages. The loop trail begins in the village of Montemarcello near the top of the promontory. At the far end of the loop, there are two options, depending on your desire for distance and sights. One spur heads down to the beautiful village of Tellaro, perched on a rocky bluff above the crashing waves of the sea. The other loops up into the hills and then down to the wonderful village of Ameglia, overlooking the Magra valley and the Alpi Apuane.

From Pisa, take the A12 Autostrada to the Carrara exit and follow signs for Marina di Carrara. Once at the waterfront of Marina di Carrara, turn right onto the SS432 (via Genova), and follow this north until you cross the Magra River. Just 200 meters after crossing the river, turn left onto the SP30 where you will see signs for Montemarcello. Drive on the switchbacks up the ridge,

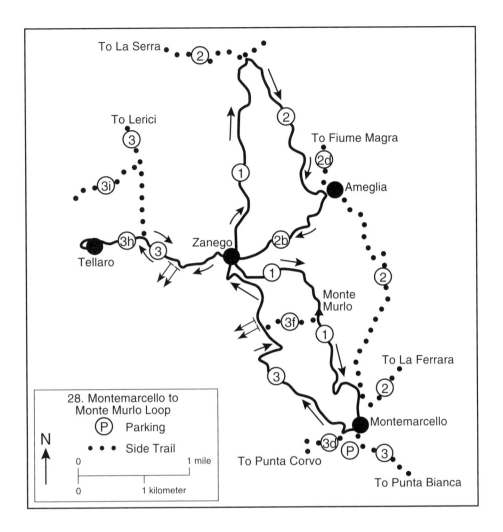

To La Serra

To Lerici

To Fiume Magra

Ameglia

Zanego

Tellaro

Monte
Murlo

To La Ferrara

28. Montemarcello to
Monte Murlo Loop

Ⓟ Parking

• • • Side Trail

N

0   1 mile

0   1 kilometer

Montemarcello

To Punta Corvo

To Punta Bianca

watching for signs for Montemarcello. Once you enter the town, look for the free parking lot on your left. From the north, take the A15 Autostrada south, almost all the way to La Spezia, then transfer onto the A12 south. Take the Sarzana exit after 7 kilometers. Follow the signs for Bocca di Magra and Marina di Carrara. Follow the SS432 south until you reach the SP30 and see the signs for Montemarcello. ATC La Spezia offers bus service to Montemarcello from Sarzana.

Contact them at www.atclaspezia.it or 018/7522511 for more information.

The trail begins directly in the medieval village of Montemarcello. This old village has marvelous views of the sea and the valley below. Follow the red/white blazes through town. Initially, you will follow Trail 3 out of the village and into some farming areas, but eventually Trail 3 descends into an old terraced farm, that is now overgrown with large cypress trees. When the trail meets an open

The Versilia coast from Monte Murlo

field, turn left and shortly you will encounter a paved road. Turn right at the road, and follow it for 100 meters, then turn right again as the path heads back into the woods. Where Trail 3F leaves to the right, to the summit of Monte Murlo, look for a clearing on the left, for a spectacular overlook at the edge of a cliff that is nearly 300 meters above the sea. From this panoramic spot you can see Portovenere, the Cinque Terre, and the Gulf of La Spezia to the north. Continuing along the trail, you will eventually enter the village of Zanego. First, you will see an intersection with a trail that cuts back behind and to the right, where Trail 1 heads up to Monte Murlo. This will be the return route, regardless of the route option you choose next. Shortly thereafter, you will reach a paved intersection which is the crossroads for several trails. Here is where the two options come into play. The Tellaro loop option follows Trail 3 down the slope. The Ameglia loop option follows Trail 1, toward Trebiano. Trail 2B leaves for Ameglia to the right (you would return on this trail, if you do the Ameglia option), and

Trail 4 is a dangerous trail, which is sometimes closed, that heads down the cliff to the left.

If you choose to do the Tellaro option down to the sea, the route will be about 1.5 kilometers and 30 minutes each way. Trail 3 descends down an old stone path, passing olive groves and houses until it reaches the cliffs. These sheer cliffs may make those who are nervous of heights a little jittery, but a protective wall makes viewing safe. At one of the overlooks, you can see Tellaro far below, perched on the rocks above the crashing waves. At this angle, it looks a lot like Vernazza in the Cinque Terre. Soon the trail will branch, with Trail 3H heading downslope to Tellaro, and Trail 3 continuing on to Lerici. Take Trail 3H, as it descends into the village and follows a very narrow corridor through town, until it reaches the small harbor. If you follow the steps to the left, the route will loop around to the other side where you can look out across the cliffs that line the promontory. Looking at the view from Tellaro, there is no way to tell that you

The Ligurian Coast and the Cinque Terre

Tellaro cliff

are not in the Cinque Terre. Return the way that you came, until you reach Zanego and the main intersection.

If you chose to do the Ameglia loop option instead, follow Trail 1 up the hill from Zanego, toward Trebiano. This trail starts out steep, going past a field with donkeys and into some oak woodlands. The trail then becomes a dirt road, and continues for the next hour through woodlands and past summer homes until it reaches another intersection, in a clearing which is full of wild daffodils in spring and has views of a radio tower on a hill above. Here it can be a little confusing, as there is a trail marked #2 LA SERRA that leaves from the left, and a small dirt road with a gate leaving to the right. Do not take Trail 2 or this road, which dead ends at a yard. Instead, continue down the main path you were on, and shortly you will reach a paved road and signs indicating the "real" intersection with Trail 2. Turn right, following Trail 2 down a paved road toward Ameglia. After passing several farms, the trail leaves the road and enters a steep ravine area and forest. This

stretch is quite beautiful, offering glimpses of the Alpi Apuane and the Magra valley below. After about 45 minutes the trail emerges into the quaint village of Ameglia. Once you reach the paved road in town, turn right and climb back out of the village on Trail 2B. This trail climbs along some old fields and into a drainage until it reaches Zanego again.

From the main intersection, look for Trail 1, headed toward Monte Murlo. The trail quickly enters a pine woodland, then climbs up the slope of the ridge, until you reach the summit of Monte Murlo. There is a botanical garden here that offers a sampling of typical Mediterranean vegetation, and there is a wonderful overlook of the Alpi Apuane and the Versilia coast. From Monte Murlo, Trail 1 descends along the mountain until it reaches a paved road. Cross the road, and rejoin the trail on the other side of the cemetery. The trail will climb through some trees and rejoin the road near the village of Montemarcello. From here the trail follows the pavement into the village, and back to the parking area.

29

Cinque Terre–Portovenere to Riomaggiore

Hike from the pastel village of Portovenere along towering sea cliffs, to the first village of the Cinque Terre.

Distance: 13.5 kilometers (8.4 miles)

Time: 5–6 hours

Elevation: Sea level to 515 meters (1,690 feet)

Park: Parco Nazionale delle Cinque Terre

Difficulty: Moderate

Time to visit: Year round; avoid midday in summer

While the stretch between Riomaggiore and Monterosso is more famous and far more popular with visitors, the trail from Portovenere to Riomaggiore offers the most spectacular scenery and dramatic cliffs of the Cinque Terre. This five-hour segment is the most physically demanding, and offers some solitude from the crowds. While the five villages themselves get all of the attention, the Cinque Terre truly begins at Portovenere, at the entrance to the Gulf of La Spezia. From this small, pastel-colored village, enormous limestone cliffs rise directly out of the water, creating a magnificent and inaccessible wall that has virtually isolated the rest of the villages from the world.

A hike along the top of this ridge and eventually along the sides of these cliffs offers a splendid introduction as to why this region remained secluded for so long. However, as you reach the crest at Telegrafo and begin the long descent toward Riomaggiore, you will begin to see an amazing site. Even on these remote stretches, where no roads go, olives and grapes are being grown on terraces. Small hamlets are perched precariously on the cliffs above the azure-blue waters of the Mediterranean. You start to realize that the Cinque Terre is not just five villages, but dozens of tiny communities, that for centuries have struggled to survive in this harsh and hostile environment. While thousands of tourists pour into the primary villages, along this stretch you will readily see what the real Cinque Terre was all about before trains and automobiles connected these lands with the modern world.

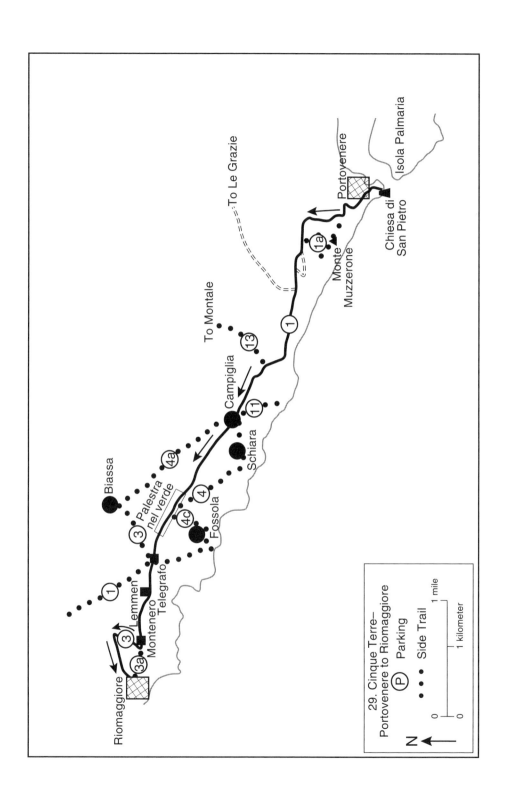

29. Cinque Terre—
Portovenere to Riomaggiore

Ⓟ Parking

•••• Side Trail

0   1 mile

0   1 kilometer

N

To Le Grazie

Portovenere

Isola Palmaria

Chiesa di
San Pietro

Monte
Muzzerone

1a

1

To Montale

13

Campiglia

11

Schiara

4a

Biassa

Palestra
nel verde

3

4

4c

Fossola

1

Lemmen

Montenero
Telegrafo

3

3a

Riomaggiore

San Pictro church in Portovenere

The trail can be done in either direction, but the lighting is better on the cliffs if you begin from Portovenere, and hike north. Once you get to Riomaggiore, you may choose to continue on the next segment discussed in Hike 30, or take the train back to La Spezia.

To get to Portovenere, there are several options. Parking is difficult, so it is recommended that you either park in or take the train to La Spezia. From La Spezia, you can catch the #11 bus to Portovenere. The bus stop is located approximately 10 minutes from La Spezia Centrale train station, near the corner of Corso Cavour and Viale Giuseppe Garibaldi. Contact ATC La Spezia at www.atclaspezia.it or 018/7522511, for more information. You can also take the ferry to Portovenere from the waterfront in La Spezia. Contact Consorzio Marittimo Touristico 5 Terre–Golfo dei Poeti, at www.nav igazionegolfodeipoeti.it for more information and scheduled departures.

Once in Portovenere, walk out to the very tip of the peninsula, where the striped 12th-century stone church of San Pietro, built of bands of black and white stone and black marble, sits perched on a rocky outcrop directly across the small channel from the island of Palmaria. Besides the interesting Gothic architecture of this beautiful chapel, the views down the limestone cliffs of the Cinque Terre are absolutely breaktaking. On the cliffs just below the 13th-century fortress on the hill, twisted and mangled layers of sedimentary rock alternate in patterns of beige, white, gray, and black. Once you have soaked in the splendor of these magnificent 300 meter high cliffs, it is time to ascend them.

From town, look for the red/white blazes heading up a staircase, toward the fortress above. This is Trail 1, the Cinque Terre "high" trail. It continues on the highest ridges nearly all the way to Levanto, and is estimated to take about 12 hours. You will

View from the Portovenere Trail

follow this segment for about 9 kilometers to Telegrafo. As you approach the top of the fortress, you will notice a cemetery below, to the left. Continue following the path upslope, which is the steepest portion of the entire journey. As you climb, you will pass a rock wall, behind which are wind-blasted olive trees, with their flagging branches just barely peaking above the protection of the wall. Below, you will see San Pietro and the Island of Palmaria in spectacular detail.

Near the top of the initial climb, a small branch heads left from the trail, called Trail 1A. It is considered an experts-only trail, as it clings to the dramatic cliffs and climbs up to the summit of Monte Muzzerone, before rejoining Trail 1 approximately 2 kilometers later. This is the trail route that rock climbers will use. Continuing on Trail 1, it will flatten out after the 1A trail leaves, and enters into a nice pine forest. The trail will eventually emerge onto a road that makes a hairpin turn. This can be a confusing spot, because there will be red/white blazes in both directions. The segment going uphill is where Trail 1A trail rejoins the path. Instead, follow the road downslope, even though this may seem counterintuitive. After a short time of walking down the road, the trail will briefly leave the road to cut a switchback, then rejoins the road again, before finally branching off to the left for good.

For the next 2 kilometers or so, the trail reaches its absolute pinnacle of spectacular scenery. Behind you are the amazing white cliffs of Monte Muzzerone dropping down to the sea. Tiny San Pietro appears as a speck compared to the island of Palmaria beyond, while the tiny island of Tino is visible even further out. The trail will eventually reenter a pine forest, and then generally parallels a paved road heading to the village of Campiglia, 5.5 kilometers from Portovenere. In Campiglia there is a major trail intersection, with various trails heading downslope that connect to the farming terraces and hamlets on the exposed slopes below. The most significant route is Trail 4, heading to Schiara.

However, stay on Trail 1, which is well-marked. From Campiglia, the trail climbs the spine of the ridge through pine forest, until reaching a high point in the Palestra Nel Verde, where a variety of exercise stations are placed along a 2 kilometer stretch. Additional trails also branch off to the left, to access the hamlets of Fossola and Colombaie. Shortly after Trail 4 rejoins the route, you will reach the high point at Telegrafo, where a road intersection also occurs. At Telegrafo, look for Trail 3 heading downslope toward Riomaggiore. Trail 1 will continue to climb up and above the Cinque Terre, eventually reaching a high point of 780 meters. Trail 3A will follow the paved road downslope, and then rejoin Trail 3 lower down. First, you will pass the hamlet of Lemmen, then the Santuario Madonna di Montenero, at 350 meters above the sea. Montenero is now a restaurant, hotel, and meeting center, which dates back to 1335. It is located just upslope from the road that heads down to Riomaggiore, and which continues across the entire Cinque Terre. Trail 3 will then turn away from the coast, as it descends through olive groves and terraced fields down into the stream valley below, before following the stream right into the heart of Riomaggiore itself. However, it is also possible to follow Trail 3A trail from Montenero more directly into town, although the route is quite steep.

From Riomaggiore, it is easy to catch the train back to La Spezia Centrale train station, as that is its next stop. If you wish to do a little bit more walking closer to the sea, the beautiful, short, and easy 1 kilometer Via dell'Amore provides a gentle walk along the cliffs above the beautiful blue waters to the next village of Manarola, from which you can also take the train back.

30

Cinque Terre–Riomaggiore to Vernazza

Hike from the first village of the Cinque Terre to the fourth, along spectacular rugged sea cliffs.

Distance: 9.8 kilometers (6 miles)

Time: 4–5 hours

Elevation: Sea level to 300 meters (984 feet)

Difficulty: Moderate

Park: Parco Nazionale delle Cinque Terre

Time to visit: Year round; avoid midday in summer

Recommended: Early spring

Most hiking information in guides and on the internet recommend doing all five villages of the Cinque Terre, from Riomaggiore to Monterosso, in one day and list it as being a 12 kilometer hike. However, the hike is often longer and more difficult due to a section of the trail between Manarola and Corniglia that is often closed, and a long, steep detour necessary to get around it. Besides, why feel rushed in such an incredible landscape? Vernazza is arguably the crown jewel of the Cinque Terre, with its buildings hanging over the cliff, and a spectacular view over the entire length of the Cinque Terre. This medieval village, with its narrow alleys and beautiful harbor, is also a great place to end a hike, due to the many wonderful restaurants where you may enjoy a meal before catching the train back.

To get to Riomaggiore, take the train from La Spezia or Genoa and stop at the Riomaggiore station. From here, look for the red/white blazes on the walls that say SEN-TIERO #2. Trail 2 is the main coastal route. There will be a booth along the trail, open in spring and summer, where you must purchase tickets for the route. The cost is €3 per person, for a day pass without train fare. The first segment, which is only 1 kilometer long, is called the Via dell'Amore ("The Way of Love"). It is a wide, paved path to Manarola. It hangs out over the sea in places, and is very beautiful, although perhaps too easy and too crowded for some tastes. For wilderness enthusiasts, do not fret—the trail will get wild soon enough.

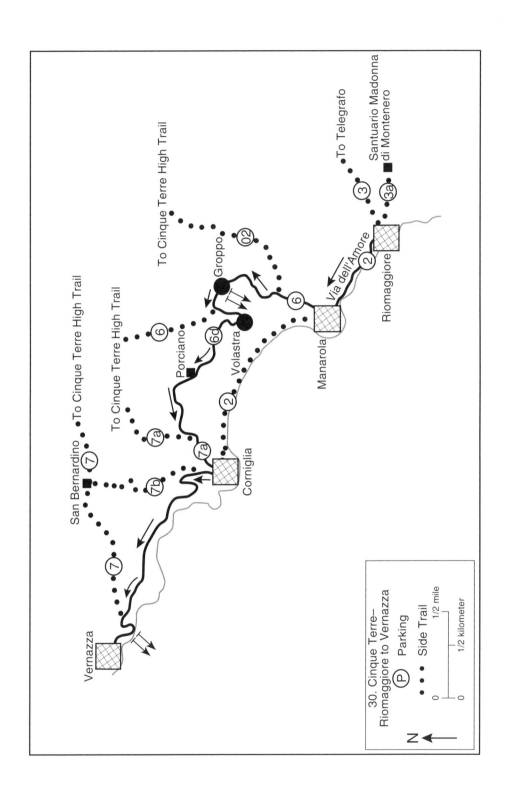

30. Cinque Terre—
Riomaggiore to Vernazza

P Parking
• • • Side Trail

0   1/2 kilometer
0   1/2 mile

N

To Telegrafo

Santuario Madonna
di Montenero

3a

3

Riomaggiore

2

Via dell'Amore

Manarola

6

02

Groppo

II

To Cinque Terre High Trail

Porciano

6

6d

Volastra

2

7a

7a

To Cinque Terre High Trail

7b

Corniglia

San Bernardino

To Cinque Terre High Trail

7

7

To Cinque Terre High Trail

Vernazza

II

The Cinque Terre coastline

In 1995 and again in 2002, the lower Trail 2, from Manarola to Corniglia, was closed, due to landslides. This 3 kilometer segment was finally reopened in 2006, but this stretch still contains very unstable terrain, and is suseptible to additional landslides in the future. Even if it happens to be open when you visit, this guide suggests you take the detour route, going past Volastra on Trail 6. The detour climbs up to 340 meters above the sea, offering you a chance to see some nice pine forests perched above the beautiful blue waters, and the view from Volastra will make this detour well worth it, despite the extra work!

Locating this detour can be a little confusing at first. Look for signs for Trail 6, headed toward Groppo. The trail climbs through narrow alleys and along drainage channels, through some vineyards, goes along the paved road, and continues uphill, some 200 meters in elevation. The trail will enter the tiny village of Groppo after about

45 minutes, then continues on to the village of Volastra. Keep following the red/white blazes on Trail 6 as it climbs into a pine wood. At one point, you can see Volastra directly below, and you may start worrying about whether it is really going to you there; rest assured, it will. The view from here, with Manarola and Volastra below you, and the sea below them, is incredible. When you reach about 300 meters in elevation and you are in the pine trees, you will come across a paved road. This paved road descends down to Volastra. You may choose follow the road down, or cross the road and follow the trail, which before long will come down to the road anyway. In Volastra, look for Trail 6D which heads out on the ridge through pine forests. This is a comfortable, relatively level trail. If it is sunny, you will appreciate the shade. After 20 minutes, you will come across Trail 7A, which will descend to Corniglia. It is a 200 meter descent and quite steep in places, so do be

Vernazza

careful, but the view upon descend into Corniglia is excellent.

In Corniglia, you will reconnect with Trail 2 to continue north. The Corniglia to Vernazza section is probably the best section of trail in the entire Cinque Terre. The cliffs are spectacular, the vegetation, wildflowers, and rocks are beautiful, and it has the most wild feeling of anywhere along this coastline. Introduced agave, with their enormous flower stalks, and an interesting tree, the euphorb *(Euphorbia arborea)* with its milky sap, are among the more interesting plants along this 4 kilometer stretch. When you reach the point where you can first see Vernazza, it will literally stop you in your tracks. The view looking straight down onto this medieval village, sitting out by itself, perched high on the rock cliff, is stunning. Once in Vernazza, there are many places to eat and a visit to the little harbor is a must. There is a lookout tower that you can climb, for a small fee. Since Vernazza is out on a promontory, from the top of the tower you can look back across the entire village and down the coastline. From Vernazza, you can catch the train back to your point of departure.

31

Cinque Terre–Vernazza to Levanto

Hike from the fourth village of the Cinque Terre over the promontory of Punta Mesco to the village of Levanto.

Distance: 12.1 kilometers (7.5 miles)

Elevation: Sea level to 150 meters (492 feet)

Difficulty: Moderate

Park: Parco Nazionale delle Cinque Terre

Time to visit: Year round; avoid midday in summer

Recommended: Early spring

The stretch from Vernazza to Levanto is not nearly as crowded as the Riomaggiore to Vernazza stretch, perhaps because it is not advertised as much. This trail will take you out of the Cinque Terre proper, over the promontory of Punta Mesco, then north along the Ligurian coast. If you are looking for a home base village to take the train to and from for several days, Levanto may be your spot, since it is not as busy as the villages of the Cinque Terre during high season. If you made Levanto your home base, then by taking the train to Vernazza first, you could simply walk "home."

From Vernazza, look for the red/white blazes designated SENTIERO #2, headed toward Monterosso. Located just 4 kilometers away, this is the last village of the Cinque Terre and probably the largest in terms of population and development. The initial stretch is beautiful, as you head up and over the ridge that separates these two villages. Once on the other side of the ridge, Monterosso and its sandy beaches become evident, as well as the large promontory of Punta Mesco. This entire stretch hangs on cliffs above the sea, and azure blue coves lure you to explore underwater sights as well. All along this stretch, you will also see tilted layers of rock twisting into the sea.

Once you approach Monterosso, the trail levels out and parallels the sandy beaches into the village. There are many places to stop for *gelato* or a refreshing drink in Monterosso, however, the village seems more built up than one would expect, knowing the isolated history of this place. It

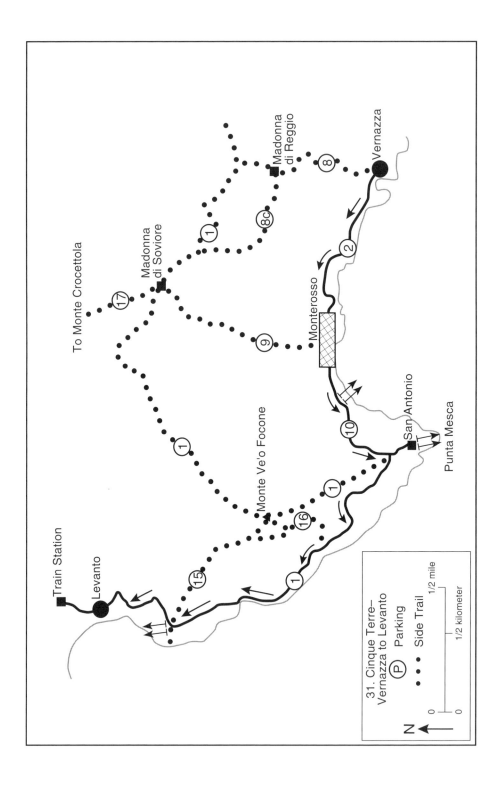

Train Station

Levanto

To Monte Crocettola

Madonna
di Soviore

Madonna
di Reggio

Vernazza

Monte Ve'o Focone

Monterosso

San Antonio

Punta Mesca

⑰

①

⑮

⑯

①

⑨

⑧C

①

⑧

②

⑩

①

31. Cinque Terre—
Vernazza to Levanto
Ⓟ Parking
••• Side Trail

0   1/2 mile
0   1/2 kilometer

N

Steps built into a stone wall

On the Levanto Trail

seems to take some time to walk through the village, as it is almost 1.5 kilometers long.

Trail 2 officially ends at the train station, but the red/white blazes continue to the other side of the village in what becomes Trail 10, which starts out by slowly climbing along the promontory on a paved path. As you climb, you can look south along the entire stretch of the Cinque Terre. Eventually, the trail climbs steeply up and over the promontory, and into a pine forest. Once you approach the crest, you will see a small trail heading left, out to the Punta Mesca overlook and the ruins of San Antonio church.

After soaking in the panorama, return back to Trail 10, which will shortly meet up with an intersection with the Trail 1, the high trail that travels on the high ridge, from Portovenere all the way to Levanto. If you turn right, you will climb to the summit of Monte Ve' (486 meters). If you turn left here, you will continue on your way to Levanto. This stretch of the trail is quite pleasant, with nice views of the cliffs and coastline, as it gradually descends. The trails goes through patches of thick pine woods and open Mediterranean scrub. Soon, as you approach the other side of the promontory, the trail starts descending steeply down steps, with views of the Gulf of Levanto. After a long descent, you emerge at an alley at the edge of town. Turn left and follow the streets into the heart of the city.

If you used this as a home base, you are back. If you need to find the train station to get back to Vernazza, head inland. The train station is just out of town, toward the back of the valley and up on a small hill. Keep heading away from the water, up the valley and you should see the train station above, once you leave the narrow alleyways.

32

Amphitheater of Monte Moneglia

A loop hike from the coast to the summit of Monte Moneglia: A lesson in fire regeneration.

Distance: 7.6 kilometers (4.7 miles)

Elevation: Sea level to 520 meters (1,705 feet)

Hiking time: 4 hours

Park: Area Protetta Punta Manara–Punta Moneglia

Difficulty: Moderate

Time to visit: September through June (avoid heat of summer)

Along the Ligurian coast, in between the Cinque Terre and Portofino, sits a little-known and hardly visited section of rugged coastline shaped much like an amphitheater, with the stage being the sea. This loop hike starts at the sea, climbs the ridgeline, and follows it around this amphitheater until the summit of Monte Moneglia at 520 meters elevation, before returning back down to the coastline. Besides spectacular views along the Ligurian coast and across to the Ligurian Apennines, this hike also provides a wonderful lesson on the ecology and regeneration of Mediterranean vegetation after catastrophic fire. Once a mature pine-oak woodland, the entire watershed was consumed by fire in September 2004. Virtually eliminating every mature pine and oak tree in the area, this fire left behind only standing trunks and barren sandstone rock.

However, this is a resilient ecosystem adapted to fire, and the recovery has been remarkable. In just two years, strawberry trees and tree heather have re-sprouted from the roots up, and grown up to two meters tall, while rock roses, lavender, asters, and brooms bloom in a dense carpet on the formerly scorched earth. The area is alive, and this hike provides a wonderful opportunity to watch nature's rebirth in action, while admiring spectacular views across the landscape and sea that have been opened up by the elimination of the tree canopy. In addition, there are small pockets of vegetation that did not burn completely, which are full of chestnuts, aspens, and deciduous oaks, offering a reminder of what this watershed looked like previously, while providing a

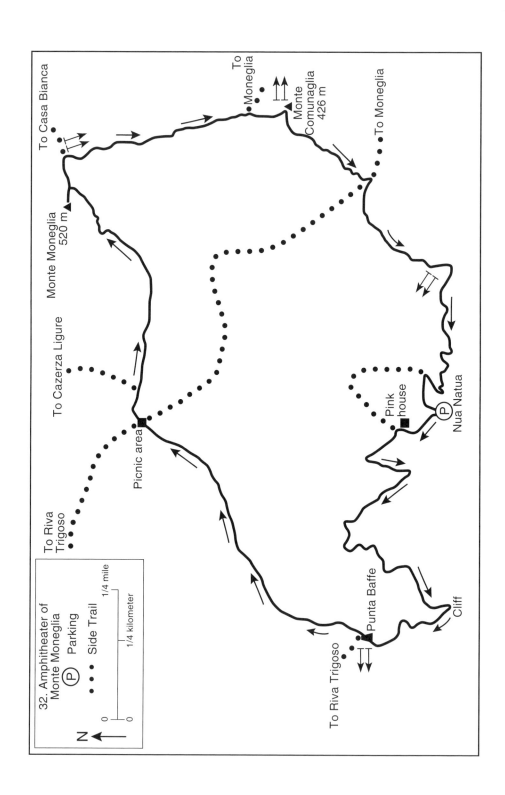

32. Amphitheater of
Monte Moneglia
Ⓟ Parking
•••• Side Trail

N

0   1/4 kilometer
0   1/4 mile

To Casa Bianca

Monte Moneglia
520 m

To Cazerza Ligure

To Riva
Trigoso

Picnic area

To Riva Trigoso

Punta Baffe

Cliff

Nua Natua

Ⓟ

Pink
house

To
Moneglia

Monte
Comunaglia
426 m

To Moneglia

To Moneglia

The Monte Moneglia forest is recovering from fire.

valuable seed source for the regeneration of the burned area.

Accessing the amphitheater of Monte Moneglia from Genova or Pisa by automobile is extremely easy, unlike the dangerous roads that lead to the Cinque Terre or Portofino. Just take the A12 Autostrada until the Deiva Marina exit, approximately 12 kilometers south of Sestri Levante. This exit will also have Moneglia listed on a blue sign, along with several other villages. Once off the Autostrada, follow the road as it winds its way downhill. At the first intersection, turn right and continue down to the sea to Deiva Marina. Once in town, there will be an intersection with La Spezia to the left, and Genova to the right. Turn right, and leave town. The road will follow the sea, and will go through a series of very narrow one-way tunnels, that have traffic lights to indicate when it is safe to enter. Once at the town of Moneglia, continue past the town center and through another tunnel. There is one opening in the tunnel, then a left turn that is actually inside the tunnel and into a campground.

Then, approximately 4 kilometers after Moneglia, there will be another break in the tunnel and a large blue/white sign for Nūa Natūa, and a parking area on the right. This is where the hike begins. It is also possible to take the train to Moneglia from La Spezia or Genoa. Then bus service to Nūa Natūa a is available from Tigullio Trasporti. Contact them at www.tigulliotrasporti.it or 018/53731 for more information.

The hike begins at a creek that flows down the heart of the amphitheater. Directly above and slightly to the right is the 520 meter Monte Moneglia. There is a sign for Punta Baffe at the base of the stairs to the left. Follow the stairs up to the highest building. Go around the back of the building and up to a metal pole with a burned and faded sign, and the words PUNTA BAFFE barely visible. Follow the trail to the left.

This first 2.5 kilometers to the tower at Punta Baffe is by far the most challenging section of the hike. As of the time of the writing of this book, trail crews had not yet cleared the trail or replaced the faded signs and blazes, so you will have to walk up through some thick brush, as spiny brooms, tall grasses, and rock roses reach across the trail. However, this is also an intimate opportunity to see regeneration in action. The brush is thickest as you cross the first creek, where shade and water have resulted in massive regrowth. Keep your eyes open for the trail, as it can seem to disappear in places; however just remember to keep working your way north, toward the sea, and higher in elevation. In places, you can see the faded red marks painted on the rocks to indicate the trail. At one point, far above the sea, you will come to sheer cliff where the trail seems to end. Look hard to the right and above, and you will see the trail climb directly up the spine of the ridge, and a faded trail marker on the rocks. Soon thereafter, you will arrive at the old tower atop Punta Baffe.

From the tower, you get your first views across to Riva Trigoso and Sestri Levante below. Along the coast you can see the promontory of Portofino (Hike 33). Below, inside the amphitheater, you can see the pink house of Nūa Natūa where you started, the entire watershed, and the summit of Monte Moneglia. Beyond, you can see the promontory of Punta Mesco near Levanto, where the Cinque Terre begins (Hike 31).

At the tower, there is a trail intersection. Stay right and follow the ridgeline toward Monte Moneglia. After the tower, the trail has been repaired, and there should be no additional thick brush or other hindrances. The rest of the hike is pleasant, although steep in places. From this ridgeline, great views of the Ligurian Apennines open up. Continue along the ridge, until you reach a picnic area where several trails intersect. Here, there is a sign that is scorched on its backside, that predates the latest large fire,

but discusses a fire that scorched the area 20 years earlier. At this intersection, there is a trail that heads left down toward Riva Trigoso. There is a trail that heads right down, toward both Nūa Natūa and Moneglia. Continue straight ahead, toward the summit of Monte Moneglia. Shortly thereafter, there is another branch to the left for Casarza Ligure. The trail to the summit of Monte Moneglia goes past regenerating chestnuts and oaks, and a few surviving pine trees. The last stretch is somewhat steep and ends at a picnic table at the wooded summit of Monte Moneglia, just a few meters left of the summit trail intersection. At the summit, mature oak and pine trees are joined by aspen, hornbeam, and chestnuts.

From the picnic area, follow the summit ridge south until you reach an opening, where you'll find great views of the surrounding area. Here the trail branches; left heads to Casa Bianca, but stay right and follow the descending ridgeline toward the lower Monte Comuniglia. This stretch of trail is quite beautiful. It was singed, but not destroyed, by the fire and contains Hungarian oaks, with their tiny leaves, strawberry trees, and many more flowering shrubs. Just below the summit of Monte Comuniglia, a trail branches left towards the village of Moneglia. Stay right for the summit, where the best views of the entire day are located. From Monte Comuniglia, you can see the entire amphitheater, the village of Moneglia below, Punta Mesco and the Cinque Terre beyond, as well as north along the Italian Riviera.

From here, a trail descends the slope to the right to return you to Nūa Natūa. The trail is steep and slick in places and fallen trees over the trail can make it confusing at times, but the red dashes and dots visible on the rocks should make finding your way down

The coastline at Monte Moneglia

easier. Just keep heading down toward the pink house (if the color changes, it is the only house in the drainage!), and you will be fine. There will be a trail intersection halfway down where you stay right. Once you reach the bottom of the drainage near the creek, there is one more left turn that is not signed, where you return to the car.

You can also hike in from Moneglia, by looking for the trail markers leaving the village toward Monte Comunaglia. From Monte Comunaglia, follow the trail down to Nūa Natūa and then complete the loop. Hiking from the train station in Moneglia will add approximately 5–6 kilometers roundtrip to the route.

33

Promontory of Portofino

Hike along the high cliffs of the Portofino Coast to an isolated cove.

Distance: 8 kilometers (5 miles)

Elevation: Sea level to 250 meters (820 feet)

Hiking time: 4 hours

Park: Parco Naturale Regionale di Portofino

Difficulty: Moderately easy

Time to visit: Year round; avoid midday in summer

The Promontory of Portofino, along the Ligurian Riviera, is a jewel of the northern Italian coast, rivaling the famed Cinque Terre in awe-inspiring scenery. The cliffs stand 200 meters above the azure-blue waters of the Mediterranean, amid *macchia* and shady pine woodlands. The trail to San Fruttuoso is not long or overly strenuous, which allows the visitor to fully appreciate the surroundings, while escaping the massive crowds that flock to the beaches and tourist towns of this area.

Like the Cinque Terre, if you are visiting in summer, it is advisable to take the train and bus to Portofino. Parking in Portofino is notoriously difficult. To arrive by train, get off at Santa Margherita on the La Spezia/Genoa line. Then, take the bus from the Santa Margherita train station to Portofino. Contact Tigullio Trasporti at www.tigulliotrasporti.it or 0185/3731 for more information.

However, if you choose to drive from either Pisa or Genoa, take the A12 Autostrada to the Rapallo/Santa Margherita exit. Follow signs through Santa Margherita toward Portofino. There is a small underground parking garage in Portofino, if you arrive early in the morning in summer or during the off-season.

Portofino is a very narrow village tucked into a steep ravine. The trail begins at the back of the village, and continues up along the stream that flows through the ravine, marked by red/white blazes. The trail starts by climbing up the ravine, then enters olive groves and small farms on the hillsides.

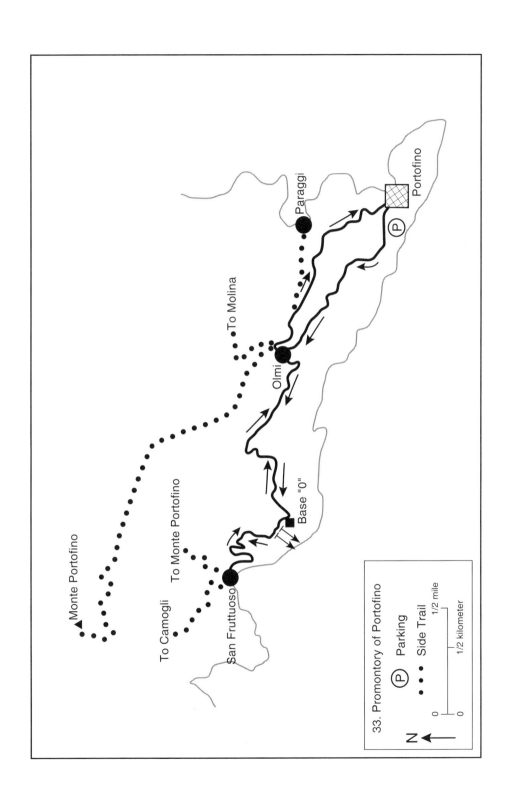

Monte Portofino

To Camogli

To Monte Portofino

San Fruttuoso

Paraggi

To Molina

Olmi

Base "0"

Portofino

P

N

33. Promontory of Portofino

P Parking

••• Side Trail

0 ———————— 1/2 mile
0 ———————— 1/2 kilometer

The coastline seen from the Portofino Trail

Follow the signs for Olmi. For the first 30 minutes, the route follows old paths around terraced slopes of olives and fruit trees, and generally heads uphill. However, it will not be until you reach the small housing area of Olmi that the first views of the coast will be visible. At Olmi, notice the road branching off to the right, signed PORTOFINO, as this will be your return route. From the last house, which has a spectacular view and garden perched on the cliff, the route is completely undeveloped, providing spectacular views of the wild Italian Riviera. The trail stays approximately 200 meters above the water. In spring, the *macchia* is in bloom, and the perfume of rosemary and the flowers of strawberry trees fills the senses, while the views just continue to amaze visitors. For the next hour, you will hike through patches of pine forest and open scrub along the steep cliffs. As you approach the cove of San Fruttuoso, you will reach the ultimate panoramic point at Base "0".

From this point, the trail begins to drop rapidly down to the hamlet of San Fruttuoso, located at the back of the cove. This community is located in an unbelievable setting. It is at the bottom of a steep cliff at the end of a turquoise-blue cove, and there are no roads heading into it. The primary features you will notice right away are the 13th-century monastery and the 10th-century church. If it is late spring or summer, the other thing you will notice is the beach covered with sunbathing bodies. This seems shocking, given how few people you have encountered on the trail, until you notice the ferry pulling into the cove. So, while you have trekked over 200 meters up and down for the last two hours to get to this remote cove, everyone else has ridden the boat just to lie stretched out on the beach. Nonetheless, a trip into the village is well worth it. There are several small restaurants that are perfect for getting lunch. The traditional Ligurian pesto is excellent, and taking in the views over the

The Portofino Trail offers spectacular views of the rugged Ligwian coastline.

cove while sipping the local wines makes for a wonderful break, before trekking back up the cliff for the return hike to Portofino.

For an extended adventure, you can continue north from San Fruttuoso towards Camogli. This route climbs the cliffs using chains in exposed sections, to provide extra safety and aid in climbing. The total distance from Portofino to Camogli is 15 kilometers, and is considered strenuous. From Camogli, you can take the train back to Santa Margherita, where you can take the bus back to Portofino, if you drove in. It is also possible here to climb up to the summit of Monte Portofino (610 meters) from San Fruttuoso or Olmi.

If you are interested in seeing the coast from a different perspective, or feel you have exerted yourself enough today, you can also elect to take the ferry back to Portofino. However, the return trip is only 4 kilometers, and the hike back is equally spectacular, especially in the afternoon light. Just be prepared for the summer heat, and be sure to let the effects of the wine wear off a little, before making the 200 meter climb back up.

If you hike back, upon your return to Olmi, turn left following signs for Portofino. You will follow small roads among olive groves and traditional-style homes. From this route, you can look out across the Bay of Santa Margherita and down the Italian Riviera, towards Chiavari and Sestri Levante, and can see Monte Moneglia (Hike 32) in the distance. This view is great, but if it is summer, expect to see a swath of umbrellas and sunbathing bodies strewn as far as the eye can see along the beaches, even from so many kilometers away.

V

The Northern Apennines

Introduction to the Northern Apennines

From the French border in Liguria, to the tip of the boot in Calabria, the Apennines form the backbone of Italy. Formed by tectonic processes, this range has been uplifting for the past 5 million years, as the African plate slams into the Eurasian plate, closing off the Mediterranean Sea by a few millimeters each year. The Apennines are uplifting at a rate of between 0.5 and 1 millimeter per year while, at the same time, the entire Italian peninsula is slowly rotating counterclockwise, closing off the Adriatic Sea as the Italian peninsula merges with the Dalmatian coast. In addition, this rotation forces the Apennine chain to bend eastward, adding particular stresses to the northern and central portions of this range. The actual tectonic processes that contribute to the formation of this range, as well as the many volcanoes in Italy, are not well understood. However, it appears to be an extremely complex combination of plate convergence where the oceanic crust of the ancient Tethys Sea is subducting, the continental collision of the African and Eurasian plates, and possibly some oceanic tectonic rifting near Mount Etna.

One thing is clear, however: that there are some locations where the compression and uplift of the peninsula is more dramatic than on average. Where these high ridgelines form and rise above the treeline, alpine ecosystems and fascinating Ice Age glacial features occur. The Northern Apennines are one of the highest segments on the Italian peninsula extending all the way from the Ligurian coast near La Spezia, south to just beyond Florence.

Many of the peaks of the Northern Apennines exceed 1,500 meters (5,000 feet), with Monte Cimone (Hike 38) being the highest at 2,163 meters (7,094 feet) and Monte Cusna (Hike 37) ranking second at 2,110 meters (6,921 feet). Most of the high ridges above treeline offer beautiful alpine meadows, and spectacular views of the surrounding landscape.

The range consists primarily of sandstones, clays, and other sedimentary rock that formed along the shores of the ancient Tethys Sea, some 200 million years ago. In places, sandstone has been metamorphosed into quartzite due to intense tectonic stresses. The action of the current tectonic uplift is extremely evident within this range, as the tilted and twisted layers of sandstone can easily be seen throughout the range. The southwestern faces of the range are lifted dramatically upwards as spectacular cliffs rising 1,000 meters or more above the deep valleys below, while the northeastern side descends more gently toward the Po Valley. This pattern indicates that the direction of the tensional strains are from the southwest. These thrust blocks are particularly evident from the A15 Autostrada from La Spezia to Parma, when you look at the cliffs of the Appennino Parmenese (Hike 34).

In addition to its more ancient past, the Apennine chain has been sculpted more recently by Ice Age glaciers, particularly in the north. The gentle northeastern slopes collect and retain more snow than the exposed southwestern cliffs, primarily because these slopes have more shade, less wind exposure, and fewer avalanches. Thus, the ancient glaciers generally ran to the north or northeast, and most of the glacial cirques are oriented in that direction. Glacial tarn lakes spot the high ridges within these cirques. At the upper end of these cirques, high glacial headwalls rise dramatically up to the narrow arête ridgelines. These features are all particularly evident at Monte Giovo (Hike 39), Monte Sillara (Hike 34), and Corno alle Scale (Hike 40). At some locations glacial scrape marks can be seen, where ice and rock slowly sliced into the bedrock.

Today, beautiful alpine meadows and grasslands provide critical habitat to endemic wildflowers, Alpine marmots, and the rare Apennine wolf. Covered in snow during the winter, the meadows come alive in May and June with spectacular displays of wildflowers. In early fall, the blueberry shrubs turn to magnificent hues of red and orange, while foxes and deer can be seen eating the ripe berries.

Administratively, the crest of the Northern Apennines forms the boundary between Tuscany and Emilia-Romagna. Thus, when you hike in the range, you will often be crossing in and out of Tuscany. Emilia-Romagna names the segments of this range based on the city and province in which they fall and, more historically speaking, where the source of each city's water comes from. The primary mountain segments are the Appennino Parmense (Parma), Appennino Reggiano (Reggio Emilia), Appennino Modenese (Modena), and Appennino Bolognese (Bologna), among others. Much of the Northern Apennines are protected within the Parco Nazionale dell'Appennino Tosco-Emiliano, a loose conglomerate of several regional and provincial parks, which are managed by the regional governments of Emilia-Romagna and Tuscany.

Crossing the entire length of the Northern Apennines is the Grande Escursione Appenninica (GEA), which is a trail that goes for over 400 kilometers, from north of La Spezia south, to just east of Arezzo. It is said to take 25 days to complete the entire excursion, requiring one to stay at various mountain huts *(rifugi)* along the way. Several of the hikes in this section use parts of the GEA, while others access mountain peaks that are not on that route. But, the primary focus of the Northern Apennines section of this book is to provide hikers with an opportunity to see what the Apennines have to offer along the crest of this beautiful mountain range.

34

High Crest–Monte Sillara Loop

Loop along the high crest of the Appennino Parmenese to the summit of Monte Sillara.

Distance: Approximately 10 kilometers (6 miles)

Elevation: 1,320–1,859 meters (4,330–6,098 feet)

Hiking time: 6 hours

Park: Parco dei Cento Laghi

Difficulty: Moderately strenuous

Time to visit: April to October

Parco dei Cento Laghi, which when translated means "Park of 100 Lakes," is one of several regional parks that follows the crest of the Northern Apennines. All together, they make up the *Parco Nazionale dell' Appennino Tosco-Emiliano.* There are several clearly identifiable Northern Apennine ridges that head in a generally northwest to southeast direction. One of the northernmost stretches and perhaps the most spectacular of these ridges, is the Appennino Parmenese, located within the Parco dei Cento Laghi. This park contains open beech forests, high-elevation heath moors full of blueberries, alpine wildflowers, and of course, wonderful alpine lakes. From the Magra valley below, you can clearly see the layers of quartzite and sandstone, as this large fault block was lifted and tilted by the same tectonic processes that produced the Alps. Upward tilting resulted in extremely steep, almost vertical cliffs to the southwest, and the more gentle, glacially eroded basins to the northeast. These northern-facing glacial cirques contain dozens of small tarns that dot this magnificent landscape. A great trail, called the Grande Escursione Appenninica (GEA), travels along the crest of this range, and the views along this trail are unbelievable. This hike follows one portion of the GEA and climbs to the summits of three peaks in the park, including the highest, Monte Sillara at 1,859 meters.

In order to access the trailhead at Lago Lagoni, coming from Pisa or Florence, take the A12 Autostrada to La Spezia then take the A15 Autostrada (the Parma–La Spezia

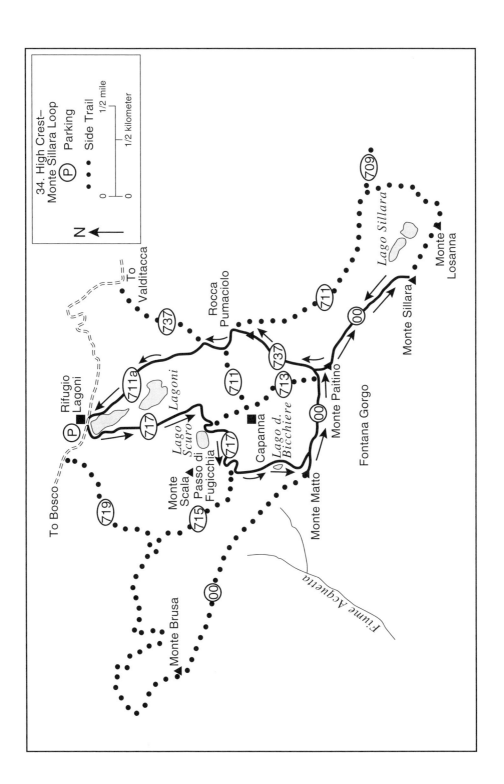

N

34. High Crest–
Monte Sillara Loop

Ⓟ Parking

•••• Side Trail

0 ————— 1/2 mile
0 ————— 1/2 kilometer

To Valditacca

737

Rocca Pumaciolo

711

Lago Sillara

709

Monte Losanna

711

00

Monte Sillara

737

713

711a

717

Lagoni

Lagoni

Rifugio Lagoni

Ⓟ

To Bosco

719

Lago Scuro

Monte Scala

Passo di Fugicchia

715

717

Capanna

Lago d. Bicchiere

00

Monte Paitino

Fontana Gorgo

Monte Matto

Fiume Acquetta

00

Monte Brusa

Looking south from the summit of Monte Matto

highway) north 10 kilometers, to the Aulla exit. Follow signs for the SS665 Statale Massese, for Passo del Lagastrello. After crossing the pass, follow the road until Rimagna, then start looking for a left to Trefiume and Valditacca, on the SP86. Almost immediately after turning onto this small road, there is a fork. To the left is a road headed to Lago Ballano. Stay right, head past the community of Trefiume, and up toward Valditacca. At Valditacca, the road comes to a T-junction. Left is a dead end into the center of the village. Turn right here, and then almost immediately turn left at the Lagoni sign. Continue as it climbs up toward the mountains, and after about 10 minutes the road will turn to gravel. The road will climb to the edge of the treeline, offering beautiful views of the ridgeline above, before descending back into the forest. Once you reach the lake at Lagoni, park at the *rifugio* on the right.

Start the hike by crossing the dam (1,320 meters) and look for red/white blazes indicating the start of Trails 717 and 715, which begin together, separating at Lago Scuro. The trail begins by climbing slowly through a dense beech forest above the shores of I Lagoni ("the little lakes"). From rocky outcrops, views open up across the lake. The hike through the forest to reach Lago Scuro (1,526 meters) should take about 20 minutes. From Lago Scuro, the trail will climb more steeply as it approaches the treeline. Continue following the red/white blazes and when you see some small wooden signs, stay on Trail 717. After an additional 15 minutes, you will reach the Passo di Fugicchia (1,669 meters). Although you are not yet at the crest of the ridgeline, wonderful views will open up across the area. At the pass, continue up higher on Trail 717, headed for Lago Bicchiere (Lake of Glass), a small pond at the base of Monte Matto. As the trail climbs the ridge further, you will be treated to ever more impressive views as here the heath landscape is full of blueberries and alpine wildflowers.

There is a sign at the lake indicating that the Monte Matto summit trail (Trail 00) is straight upslope. It may have been at one time, but since seems to have grown over. Instead, continue on Trail 717 for a short way up the ridge, until it reaches the ridge crest at Quota (1,807 meters). At this point, you have met up with the 00 GEA trail. While the view here is breathtaking, it will only get better by turning right and hiking five more minutes up to the summit of Monte Matto (1,837 meters). From this summit, you can see the Gulf of La Spezia and the Cinque Terre to the west. To the south, you can look along the ridgeline to the highest peak in the Appennino Parmenese, Monte Sillara. Further on, the summit of Alpe di Succiso in the Appennino Reggiano (Hike 35) and the peaks of the Appennino Modenese are visible, while the Alpi Apuane are visible across the Garfagnana valley to the southwest. To the north, are the Ligurian Apennines. Directly below you is a small glacial cirque and its incredible hanging valley. The cliffs here are almost vertical and the tilted and uplifted rock strata are a geological sight to behold.

From Monte Matto, it is possible to hike north along the 00 GEA to Monte Brusa and then descend down on Trail 719, leading almost all the way back at Lagoni, but it is recommended you return by way of Quota, then continue south on the 00 GEA, toward Monte Paitino and Monte Sillara. This crest trail just continues to impress, as there are basins and tarns below on the left, and a vertical cliff descending on the right. After 10 minutes or so, you will approach the summit of Monte Paitino.

However, at a north-facing cliff just the summit, there is a stretch that can be tricky as even into spring, patches of snow will still linger here. If you do come across snow, the slope is extremely steep and the melting snow will be very slick. Take great precaution in passing this short stretch of no more than 30 meters, as it can be dangerous. Directly after this stretch, you will come to a trail intersection with Trail 713, heading down toward Lagoni via Lago Scuro, while the 00 GEA trail will head up to the summit of Monte Paitino. In addition, the recommended return route to Lagoni, on Trail 737, also leaves from here. However, there is no sign for Trail 737, only paint on a large rocky outcrop.

Continue on the 00 GEA to the summit of Monte Paitino (1,815 meters). Then continue an additional 15 minutes, to the summit of Monte Sillara (1,861 meters). Once you reach the summit of Monte Sillara, there is a spectacular scene of a beautiful glacial basin below. There is a series of beautiful blue tarn lakes in this basin. At the summit, you may also get a chance to see paragliders lifting off the mountain, using the thermals like hawks, to soar high above the mountains.

From this point, you have a choice for your return to Lagoni. The longer option is to continue along the 00 GEA trail south for 20 minutes until Monti Losanna, then after another 5 minutes, turn left onto Trail 711, which heads back across the basin off the Sillara lakes toward Rocca Pumaciolo. Follow Trail 711 to a saddle at the base of Rocca Pumaciolo, until it intersects with Trail 737.

The recommended shorter option is to turn around and return to the intersection you came across, just below the summit of Monte Paitino, where Trail 737 also heads down to Rocca Pumaciolo, and will follow a

A paraglider sails above the basin at Monte Sillara.

perpendicular ridge downward, toward this rocky pinnacle. This trail is somewhat brushy, as it goes through juniper and blueberries. Just before reaching Rocca Pumaciolo, the trail become quite steep, difficult to follow, and very brushy. Your instincts are to head down toward the Lagoni below you, however, you will need to stay higher on the trail, as you will have to climb to the summit of the Rocca Pumaciolo (at 1,711 meters) before you can start descending for good. This rocky summit, in the middle of the basin, provides the last great views of the high crest ridgeline and you can see the Lagoni clearly below you. The trail then descends through brushy beech trees, until reaching an intersection with Trail 711 at the saddle.

From the saddle, follow Trail 711 as it descends down toward Lagoni. Next, when you reach an intersection that says 711 LAGONI to the right and 737 to the left, stay on Trail 737. The 711 option is a longer route back, through the middle of the cirque. Following 737, you will reach an intersection for Trail 711A shortly, which will take you back to Lagoni significantly faster than Trail 711 would have done.

35

Springs of the Secchia River

Passo del Cerreto to the source of the Secchia River located in the glacial cirque of the Alpe di Succiso.

Distance: Approximately 8 kilometers (5 miles) round trip; approximately 12 kilometers (7.5 miles) with Alpi di Succiso summit

Elevation: 1,261–1,779 meters (4,136–5,835 feet), or 2,017 meter (6,616 feet) at Alpi di Succiso summit

Hiking time: 3–4 hours; or add 2 additional hours for Alpi di Succiso summit

Park: Parco del Gigante

Difficulty: Moderate (strenuous, with Alpi di Succiso summit climb)

Time to visit: April to October

The springs of the Secchia River originate high in the Appennino Reggiano. The Secchia River flows down into the Po Valley through Modena, and enters the Po River near Mantova. The Northern Apennines are an impressive sight to behold while driving on the *autostrada* between Parma and La Spezia. The springs are located in a beautiful hanging valley, carved by the glaciers in the last Ice Age, with an amphitheater of cliffs and ridges ringing the meadows and inviting you upward. The meadow is so picturesque and seemingly so perfect, that it seems almost unnatural. From the back of this glacial cirque, one can climb up to a bench high above this arena, to marvel at the scenery and contemplate the somewhat technical climb onto the Pietra Tagliata above. Another option, to the north of the basin, is a trail that will lead you up to the top of the Alpe di Succiso (2,017 meters), one of only four peaks in the Northern Apennines over 2,000 meters high.

From Pisa, take the A12 Autostrada to La Spezia and then get on the A15 Autostrada north. Take the Aulla exit and get on the SS63 headed north. Look for brown signs indicating the Passo del Cerreto. Follow the SS63 for 35 kilometers until the Passo del Cerreto. From Milan, take the A1 Autostrada to Reggio Emilia and then get on the SS63 headed south, until you reach the Passo del Cerreto in 70 kilometers. Park at the pass, near the buildings. CAT S.p.A. offers bus service to Passo del Cerreto from Aulla, which can be reached

The Northern Apennines

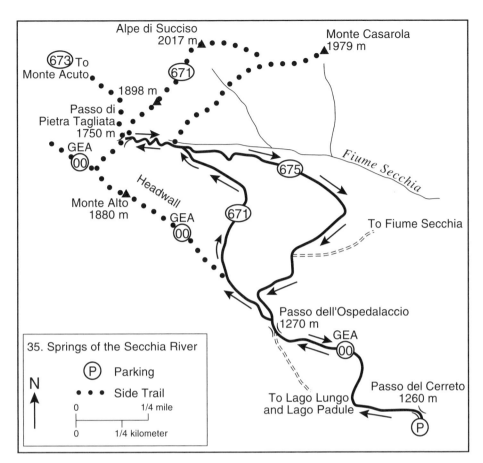

by train from La Spezia. Contact them at www.catspa.it or 0585/852125 for more information.

From the pass, follow the red/white blazed Trail 671 to the northwest, as it heads through open meadows and stands of beech. Approximately 1.5 kilometers from the pass, you will arrive at a saddle called the Passo dell'Ospedalaccio. This was an important pass across the Apennines and a station for medical care and rations for centuries until the road was built in modern times. From here, the view looking down into the Secchia Valley is superb. This is also a major trail intersection. A red/white

painted arrow points west for Sassalbo. Instead, follow the dirt road to the right and continue straight ahead, until it comes to a large map and sign, about 100 meters away. Look for the large stone monument near the sign, indicating the boundary marker for the French Empire, during the reign of Napoleon.

From the sign and stone monument, take the trail that leaves from the left side of the road and heads up the hill. This trail is somewhat steep and the soil is loose. This ascent, up the slopes of Monte Alto into open meadows, offers magnificent views. After a couple hundred meters the trail

The cliffs of Monte Alto

starts to level out a bit, as it goes along the side of the mountain. After a few short, steep sections, you will arrive at a small pass with the last open views for a while.

Once you have caught your breath, the trail enters a dense beech forest. For a few hundred meters, it is very dark and there are no views. But, shortly thereafter, you emerge out into a beautiful alpine meadow located at 1,510 meters. A small stream flows through the meadow; this is the Secchia River at its headwaters. This glacial cirque is rimmed by magnificent rock cliffs, especially the magnificent headwall of Monte Alto, on the left. In the back of the valley, the springs of the Secchia River cascade down from the rocky pinnacle of Pietra Tagliata (1,898 meters). To the right of the pinnacle are the slopes of the Alpe di Succiso (2,016 meters), the fourth highest peak in the Northern Apennines. Further right are the slopes of Monte Casarola (1,979 meters).

The meadows are a great place to rest and enjoy lunch. After lunch, you have a couple of options. To get a wonderful view of the hanging valley from above, continue along to the back of the meadow, toward the springs of the Secchia River, following the red/white blazes, and begin climbing. The trail will take you up to a bench, from where you can look back onto the meadows below. From here, you can clearly see this is a hanging valley. In addition, you will likely see climbers on the Pietra Tagliata above, which is a semi-technical climb. If you are adventurous, then continue further until you reach the Passo di Pietra Tagliata (1,779 meters), which offers spectacular views to the north. Expert climbers can then follow the rugged ridge-line up to the top of the Pietra Tagliata or to the summit of Monte Alto.

Another option from the cirque is to take Trail 675 leaving from the north side of the meadows toward Monte Casarola. This trail

Looking down into the hanging valley

enters the beech woods and gradually climbs the steep slopes until it reaches the Sella del Casarola. From here, take Trail 671 left to the summit of Alpi di Succiso, which should take approximately one hour more.

Once you have returned to the meadows, back-track into the forest a short way and start looking for a trail to the left. Follow Trail 675 through the dense beech forest back to the Passo dell'Ospedalaccio. It is more gradual, and easier on your knees than descending the slope that you climbed on the way up. While it offers no views, this is one of the more impressive beech stands I have seen in Italy. When the trail reaches the dirt road, turn right and follow it back to the Passo dell'Ospedalaccio and then back to Passo del Cerreto.

36

Monte Sillano Loop

*Loop around Monte Sillano in the
Appennino Reggiano.*

*Round Trip: 15 kilometers (9.3 miles); add
1.6 kilometer roundtrip and 150 meter
climb for the Monte Sillano summit spur*

*Elevation: 1,575–1,810 meters
(5,166–5,937 feet), or 1,824 meters
(5,983 feet) at Monte Sillano summit*

Hiking time: 4–5 hours

Park: Parco del Gigante

Difficulty: Moderate

Time to visit: May to October

Monte Sillano is located in the heart of the
Northern Apennines within the Parco del
Gigante. Along the top of this long ridge,
the Grande Escursione Appenninica (GEA)
works its way north to south. In places, the
ridgeline of Monte Sillano follows a narrow
hogback that drops steeply down into the
valley below, offering incredible views some
1,000 meters above the surrounding landscape. The views along this trail, as in virtually every other location in the Apennines,
are spectacular. On a clear day, the rugged
grandeur of the Alpi Apuane can be seen
across the Garfagnana valley, as well as
most of the Northern Apennines. Across the
deep valley of the Ozola to the north is the
isolated Monte Cusna, which stands over
2,100 meters high. In early fall, when the
blueberry leaves are turning color, the hillsides are ablaze with brilliant shades of orange and red. Fall is also the season of
mushroom hunting, and if you go in late
September, expect to see dozens of locals
in the beech woods, looking for porcini and
chanterelles. Once above treeline however,
expect to be alone on the trail, save for the
occasional fox or deer munching on blueberries. Of course, if you arrive in early summer, a multitude of wildflowers will catch
your eyes in the alpine meadows.

The trailhead for the Monte Sillano loop
begins at Passo di Pradarena. To get there,
take the A11 Autostrada from Pisa or Florence to Lucca, and take the Lucca Est exit.
Passo di Pradarena is 79 kilometers from
Lucca and will take about 1.5 hours. Follow
signs for Abetone and Castelnuovo Garfag-

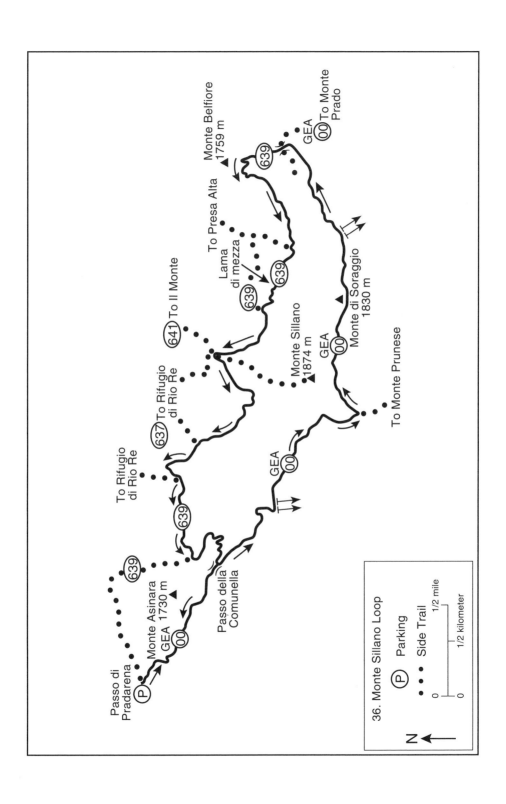

Passo di Pradarena

Monte Asinara 1730 m
GEA
00

To Rifugio
di Rio Re

637 To Rifugio di Rio Re

641 To Il Monte

639
639

Monte Belfiore
1759 m

To Presa Alta

Lama
di mezza

639

GEA
00 To Monte
Prado

639

Monte di Soraggio
1830 m

Monte Sillano
1874 m

GEA
00

To Monte Prunese

639

GEA
00

Passo della
Comunella

36. Monte Sillano Loop

P Parking

Side Trail

0 1/2 kilometer
0 1/2 mile

N

The Monte Sillano basin an autumn

nana, as the road wraps around and eventually away from Lucca. Stay on the SS12 for 6 kilometers, and then get onto the SP2 following signs for Castelnuovo Garfagnana.

The roads along the Garfagnana valley weave back and forth across the Fiume Serchio like a braid, and the numbers will change from SP2 to SP20 to SS445 to SR445, but always keep following the signs for Castelnuovo (or Aulla, if that is given) and you will be fine. Watch for very slow traffic along these roads, particularly tractors. After passing through Castelnuovo Garfagnana, follow signs for Aulla, until you reach the village of Piazza al Serchio. From here, get onto the SP12 toward Reggio Emilia for 20 kilometers, to Passo di Pradarena. At the pass, park on the pullouts near the Albergo, and the trail is on the right-hand side of the road. Unfortunately, there is no bus service to Passo di Pradarena. The closest bus service is to the village of Sillano, about 13 kilometers from the pass.

Contact Vai-Bus at www.vaibus.it for more information.

There is a sign at the trailhead showing Monte Sillano on the 00 trail, to the right, and Presa Alta on Trail 639 to the left. Get onto the 00 trail, following an old dirt road. The 00 trail is the Grande Escursione Appenninica (GEA) that is also followed on several other trails in this book, as it works its way down the backbone of the Northern Apennines. The trail and the road follow each other up the slope, with the trail cutting across switchbacks that the dirt road takes in several places. The red/white blazes make the way obvious, but if there are any doubts, the dirt road will take you in the right direction. After about 15 minutes you will emerge above treeline, into open grassy meadows.

For the next 30 minutes or so, the trail and road slowly wind their way uphill, with Monte Sillano visible above and to the left. The route will slowly turn southeast, and

The Northern Apennines

The ridgeline of Monte Sillano

eventually descends into the beech forest below. After another 400 meters in the woods, the trail will clearly branch sharply left marked, with red/white blazes, while the road continues downhill. After emerging from the woods, the most spectacular stretch of the hike begins to open up. As the 00 GEA travels just below the summit of Monte Sillano, the views across the Garfagnana to the Alpi Apuane are spectacular.

The trail slowly climbs up as it runs along the side of the mountain, and in about 2 kilometers you will reach the top of the ridgeline, for views in all directions. From the top of the ridgeline, look down on the left into a steep glacial cirque that will be bright-red with the leaves of blueberries in the fall, and there will be two small ponds. After about 15 minutes or so along the ridgetop, at 6.6 kilometers from the start you will reach a poorly marked intersection. At the time of this writing, the signs were so decrepit that one could not even read them. To the right is the 00 GEA trail. The trail you will take is the 639 trail, which branches left, continuing along the ridgeline. There is also a faint way-trail descending straight down the slope, which is a dead end, so ignore it. Continue straight along the ridge top for about five more minutes, and then the 639 trail will descend down the slope to the bottom of the ridge where it will reenter the beech forest.

From this point on, the 639 trail remains at the bottom of the slope, going into and out of the beech forest and several times into meadows, with marvelous glimpses of the ridgeline above. The 639 trail will take you back to Passo di Pradarena in about 2 hours. There will be several trail intersections along the way. The first and second intersections are other branches of the 639, headed toward Presa Alta. These trails branch back in the opposite direction, so just keep going the way you were headed. Next, is the major intersection with the 641 and 637 trails. To the right, the 641 heads north to Il Monte, while to the left it heads up to the summit of Monte Sillano. This summit spur is optional, if you want to get to the top and see what is up there. It is about 800 meters long, and climbs another 150 meters. If you chose to skip the summit, the views are not significantly better than what you have already seen.

The 637 heads off to the right, toward the Rifugio di Rio Re, and is one of three trails to the right you will encounter headed in that direction. Just keep headed on the 639 towards Passo di Pradarena, and you will be fine. The final trail intersection you will encounter is where the 639 branches into two again. To the right, the trail heads back to the trailhead through the woods in about 45 minutes. To the left, it heads towards Passo di Comunella, which you passed earlier in this hike when you emerged into the meadows for the first time. My personal suggestion is to take the route to Passo di Comunella because it is a little faster and more interesting. When you reach the road, turn right and you will be back to the pass in no time.

37

Monte Cusna Loop

Distance: Approximately 14.5 kilometers (9 miles)

Elevation: 1,150–2,120 meters (3,772–6,954 feet)

Hiking Time: 4–5 hours

Park: Parco Regionale Alto Appennino Reggiano (Parco del Gigante)

Difficulty: Strenuous

Time to visit: May to October

Monte Cusna is the second highest peak in the Northern Apennines. It also happens to be one of the most remote and difficult to get to. However, despite the long journey, this mountain offers hikers some of the most expansive panoramas in all of Italy. Monte Cusna sits on a back ridge, further east than the rest of the Northern Apennine crest, and thus offers a different perspective than most of the other hikes in this area. From its towering summit, the Northern Apennine crest passes by from north to south, offering 180-degree views of these mountainous peaks, including Monte Sillara (Hike 34), Alpe di Succiso (Hike 35), Monte Sillano (Hike 36), Monte Cimone (Hike 38), and Monte Giovo (Hike 39). The long ridgeline and glacially carved basins provide extensive stretches of alpine meadows, which are home to numerous colonies of alpine marmots that provide habitat for the rare and elusive Apennine wolf. Looking north and east across the Po Valley, you will be able to see the Alps on a clear day. There is a strenuous climb, of nearly 1,000 meters in only 4 kilometers, but the views from the summit ridge make this climb a worthwhile experience.

Monte Cusna is located near the ski area of Febbio in Emilia-Romagna. Getting to Febbio can be a real chore, as it is in an isolated location, requiring the traversing of many long and winding roads to reach it. It is easiest to reach from Reggio Emilia, by taking the SS63 towards Casina, then getting onto the SP9 to Villa Minozzo, and then following the brown signs towards the ski area of Febbio.

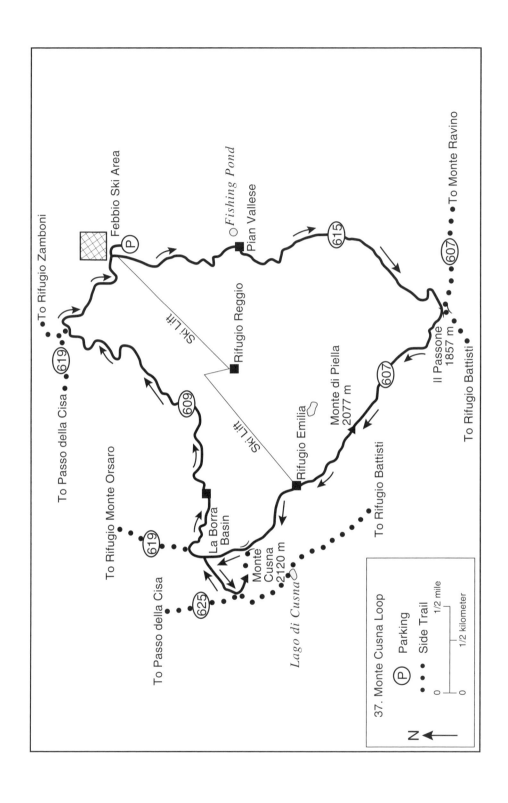

To Rifugio Zamboni

Febbio Ski Area

Fishing Pond

Pian Vallese

615

To Monte Ravino

607

To Passo della Cisa

619

Ski Lift

Rifugio Reggio

607

Il Passone
1857 m

To Rifugio Battisti

To Rifugio Monte Orsaro

609

Ski Lift

Rifugio Emilia

Monte di Piella
2077 m

607

To Rifugio Battisti

To Rifugio Monte Orsaro

619

La Borra
Basin

Monte
Cusna
2120 m

Lago di Cusna

To Passo della Cisa

625

37. Monte Cusna Loop

Ⓟ Parking

••• Side Trail

| 0 | 1/2 mile |
| 0 | 1/2 kilometer |

N

Monte Cusna

From Florence or Pisa, follow directions for Monte Giovo (Hike 39). Once the village of Pievepelago, turn left following the signs for Passo del Radici. At Passo delle Radici, turn right onto the SS486 toward Piandelagotti. At Piandelagotti, turn right on the SP 38, toward Civago. At Civago, look for brown signs for Febbio ski area. Continue to follow these brown signs. Once in Febbio, follow the signs toward the ski lifts and the Centro Visita (visitors center).

The ski lifts of Febbio operate in the summer up to Rifugio Emilia, along the summit ridge. Taking the lifts up makes for a very short hike to the summit of Monte Cusna. To do the full loop, follow the road past the ski lifts, heading toward Pian Vallese. The road climbs slowly uphill, while the ski lifts are on the right. After a short way, turn right onto Trail 615 and follow it up through the moist beech forest for about 800 meters. The trail will then rejoin with the same road near the camping area of Pian Vallese, where there is a small donut-shaped fishing pond. Pian Vallese is the upper trailhead and many people will park here for the climb up to Rifugio Battisti. However, as this is a loop hike, driving up to this upper trailhead would make no sense for you. Continue on Trail 615 as it climbs through the beech forest, until it emerges above treeline at approximately 1,600 meters elevation. From here, there is a spectacular view up the steep basin to Il Passone at the top of the ridgeline. This arduous climb up the steep headwall will be by far the most strenuous part of the hike, as it climbs 300 meters in elevation in only 1 kilometer. As you approach the top, listen for the whistles of the marmot colony located on the left.

As tough as this climb is, the views at Il Passone are more than rewarding enough. Il Passone is at the intersection of several trails; however, the majority of the people you see here are heading straight down the other side about 1 kilometer further, to

Monte Cusna Loop

The summit of Monte Cusna from La Piella

Rifugio Battisti. This large hotel and restaurant can be seen once you begin climbing the ridgeline toward Monte Cusna.

From Il Passone, catch your breath, because the trail will follow the ridgeline for the next 1,500 meters upward, gaining another 200 meters in elevation, until you reach the summit of Monte la Piella. The trail is not always completely obvious in the soft, grassy meadows, but just keep heading along the ridgeline and you will be fine. Below and to your left are the alpine meadows and hummocks of the Costa delle Veline, while on your right is the Emilian hill country expanding out to the flat Po Valley in the distance. Once at the summit of Monte la Piella, the views become truly panoramic in all directions. It is from here that the first glimpses of the summit of Monte Cusna come into view. From this vantage, the summit rises nearly vertically on its western slope, with distinct sedimentary layers being evident, and a large cross placed on

the top. Up ahead, the small Rifugio Emilia and the top of the ski lifts are visible. Febbio also comes into view some 900 meters below. Looking west, the long ridgeline of Monte Sillano (Hike 36) looks much smaller and lower than it seems when you are actually hiking there.

Another 700 meters along the more gently rolling ridgeline, you will arrive at Rifugio Emilia, which also happens to be at about the halfway point of the hike. If open, this small hut offers beverages and some packaged snack items. Most of the people you will see here have ridden the ski lifts to the top, however, it certainly gets much less traffic than Rifugio Battisti, and is a nice place to rest and get some fluids. If thunderstorms threaten, you are fatigued, or are just looking for a gentle way back to your car, it is possible to ride the ski lift back down to Febbio from here, if it is operating.

Continuing past the ski lifts, the trail continues to follow the ridgeline, slowly descending until it reaches the base of Monte Cusna, about 800 meters later. From the small pass, the sheer rocky summit rises 200 meters above, while the small tarn of Lago di Cusna can be seen 200 meters below. A rocky scramble to the summit leaves from here, although it should be left to those who are experienced climbers. Instead, follow the main trail to the right as it goes along the side of the peak, with the deep, glacially carved basin of La Borra dropping down below.

Once across the side of the peak and heading out onto the gentle grassy ridgeline, the trail to the summit turns left, while Trail 617 drops into the basin. The trek to the summit is not overly arduous. However, semi-wild horses roam here and sheep are grazed in this vicinity, so watch out for Maremma sheepdogs protecting their flocks.

Once you have soaked in the views from the summit, walk back down to the ridgeline and look for Trail 617, descending into La Borra basin below. This trail is steep, but gentle. The views are incredible, and marmots can be seen whistling and running among the talus slopes. At the bottom of the basin, where the hanging valley drops into oblivion, look back at the incredible peak of Monte Cusna above. When you look down and see the descent you are about to make and look up at the peak you just climbed, you will really be thankful that you did not have to climb up this way.

This descent from the basin is the most difficult and arduous part of the day. The trail drops some 300 meters in only 1 kilometer. Your knees will be getting wobbly along this stretch, and it is a good idea to use hiking poles to avoid slipping on the loose material. Once you approach treeline, the trail will begin to even out somewhat. From the edge of the meadow, looking back up at the wall you just descended, imagine the feeling of going the other direction. You would see this wall and think, "If only I can make it to the top"; only upon reaching the bottom of the basin, you would recognize that there is still another 300 meters of climbing to the summit.

For the next 1.5 kilometers, the trail slowly descends through beech forest, with a few scattered openings, small stream crossings, and some interesting erosional features. When you reach the intersection with Trail 609, turn right and follow this path back about 1 kilometer to the parking area of Febbio, where you started.

38

Monte Cimone Loop

Loop hike to the summit of Monte Cimone, the highest peak in the Northern Apennines.

Distance: 12.2 kilometers (7.6 miles)

Elevation: 1,305–2,165 meters (4,280–7,101feet)

Hiking time: 6 hours

Park: Parco Regionale dell'Alto Appennino Modenese (Parco del Frignano)

Difficulty: Moderately strenuous

Time to visit: May to October

Monte Cimone, the highest point in a 400 kilometer stretch between the Alps and central Italy, stands high above the Po Valley in the Appennino Modenese. As such, it commands an outstanding 360-degree panoramic view across almost all of northern Italy. From its summit, one can view across the Po Valley to the Alps nearly 200 kilometers to the north, the Alpi Apuane and Tuscan coast to the west, the Adriatic sea to the east, and all of the major summits of the Northern Apennines. The hike itself is surprisingly not as strenuous as you would expect, given a rise of 860 meters. Along the way, you get to hike into a beautiful alpine basin. From the incredible vantage point at the summit, high above the smog of the industrial valleys and salt spray of the coast, a meteorological observatory keeps track of major climatological data. This station tracks carbon dioxide and other greenhouse gases data, and correlates it with global warming. In addition, it examines the rates of deposition and chemical composition of Saharan sand that blows across the Mediterranean, during Sirocco events, and how these events affect the Italian climate and the increasing desertification of southern Europe.

To reach the trailhead from Florence, take the A11 Autostrada to Pistoia. Then, get onto the SS66 in the direction of Abetone. At La Lima, connect to the SS12, still headed to Abetone. From Pisa, take the A11 Autostrada to the Lucca Est exit, and follow signs for Abetone. At the Abetone pass, continue down the other side until you

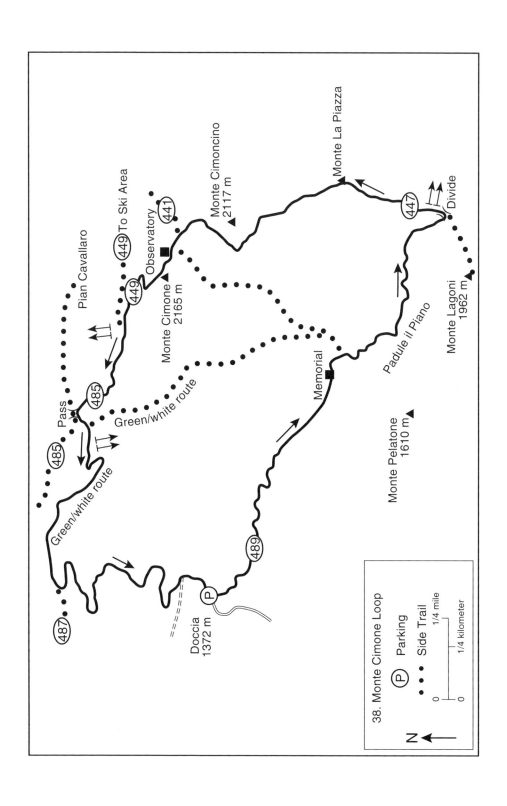

Pian Cavallaro

To Ski Area

Observatory

Monte Cimone
2165 m

Monte Cimoncino
2117 m

Monte La Piazza

449

441

449

485

Pass

Green/white route

485

Green/white route

487

Doccia
1372 m

P

489

Memorial

Padule il Piano

Monte Pelatone
1610 m

447

Divide

Monte Lagoni
1962 m

38. Monte Cimone Loop

P Parking

• • • Side Trail

0   1/4 mile

0   1/4 kilometer

N

Monti Lagoni from Padule il Piano

enter the village of Fiumalbo. Now, this part is tricky, because the turn into Fiumalbo, toward the trailhead at Doccia, is to the right, but turns back almost 180 degrees behind you. In order to make the turn, continue about 100 meters beyond it, pull off to the right at a semicircle, and turn around. If you get disoriented or miss the turn-around spot, you will be forced to drive an additional 6 kilometers before you get another chance. Once in Fiumalbo, cross the bridge and follow the signs out of town. There will be a fork in the road that says ABETONE to the right. Stay left, and follow signs for Monte Cimone and the Parco. This little road will wind its way up for several more kilometers past small farms and summer homes to Doccia, but there are no actual signs for this community. Pull off to the left when you see a large, grassy parking area and campsite, and a green PARCO DEL FRIGNANO sign. To the right is a bar and *ristorante*. There is no direct bus service to the

trailhead, but COPIT S.p.A. offers service to Fiumalbo. Contact COPIT at www.copitspa .it for more information.

The trail begins by crossing the road and heading past the bar. Red/white blazes will show the way, as you take Trail 498 along an old dirt track. The track begins by going through plantations of spruce and an old abandoned field that is now overgrown with shrubs. After about 2 kilometers, you reach the Padule il Piano (translated as "marshy plain"). Just before entering the basin, you cross a stream where there is a memorial for a fallen hiker. The basin is a beautiful glacial cirque covered with wildflowers in early summer. From here, there is a nice view of the summit of Monte Cimone standing high above, and an old track going up the very steep western slope. However, the recommended route is to go across the basin to the ridgeline at the back of the cirque.

As you enter the basin, watch carefully for where the red/white blazes branch off to

Looking north from the summit of Monte Cimone

the left. From this point until the ridgeline, the trail is not always clear, so keep looking out for the red/white blazes painted on the rocks or small trees along the way. Remember, you will be headed up to the back of the basin and then up to the divide, 3.8 kilometers from the trailhead, so keep that goal in mind. At the divide, turn left onto Trail 447. The views here are outstanding and will continue to be so for the next 5 kilometers. At this point you can see the entire basin below, and Corno alle Scale (Hike 40) to the south.

After a break to catch you breath, follow this ridgeline toward the summit. The initial section is quite easy, but upon reaching another pass, the trail steepens dramatically. Continue up the trail and, at 2.6 kilometers from the divide, you will emerge at a trail intersection, just below the weather observatory. At this point you can see that the trail to the right heads down to the ski area below, while the route labeled VETTA goes

toward the observatory to the left. Take this second trail, past the observatory, and immediately thereafter you will find yourself at the spectacular summit panorama.

There is a large concrete slab on the ground showing all of the major features you can see from this location. If it is a clear day, the snowy Alps are visible above the smoggy Po Valley. The Alpi Apuane rise as rugged crags, above the Abetone ski area to the west. The Tuscan coast can be seen to the southwest and the Alpe di Succiso (Hike 35) and Monte Cusna (Hike 37) lay to the northwest.

Once you decide to head back down, look for the red/white blazes of Trail 449 and blue/white markers heading down the other side. The initial descent is quite steep and rocky; it is also very easy to lose the way. Your goal is to eventually reach the pass below, where a gray gravel road crosses from the Doccia watershed, over to the ski areas on the Emilian side. This segment is the most strenuous of the hike. If you lose the trail, you will likely find yourself at a series of small rocky precipices. While not extremely dangerous, it will be much more comfortable to stick with the marked route. The blue/white markers are most conspicuous, and the trail becomes easier to follow the further you head, as it advances across the eastern slope of the mountain.

About halfway down, there is an intersection where the blue/white route and Trail 449 turn right, heading back down toward the ski slopes, while Trail 485 continues along the ridgeline to the left. Turn left to follow Trail 485 until you reach the gravel road. While this trail is not well-marked and is faint in places, at this stage the gravel road is obvious below and the terrain is relatively easy to traverse. Once at the gravel road, turn left and follow it down, all the way back to the trailhead. You will see green/white trail markers on the side of the road. This road has virtually no traffic, and is a pleasant way to return after the rough descent you have just experienced. After about 2.7 kilometers on the road, while in a spruce plantation, Trail 487 will branch off to the right. Ignore this and continue on the road to the left. Just before you get back to your car, the gravel road meets up with a paved road. Turn left onto the pavement, and you will be back at the car in 200 meters.

39

Glacial Cirque of Monte Giovo

*Distance: Approximately 8.5 kilometers
(5.3 miles) for the short loop; 11.4
kilometers (7.1 miles) for the long loop*

*Elevation: 1,365–1,964 meters
(4,477–6,442 feet) or 1,991 meters
(6,531 feet) at Monte Giovo summit*

*Hiking time: 4–5 hours for the short loop;
6–7 hours for the long loop*

*Park: Parco Regionale dell'Alto Apennino
Modenese (Parco del Frignano)*

*Difficulty: Moderately strenuous for
the short loop; very strenuous for
the long loop*

Time to visit: June to October

Monte Giovo is the most prominent Apennine mountain, as viewed from western Tuscany. Its broad, sedimentary-layered summit faces west and feels the full brunt of winter storms coming off the Mediterranean. As such, it is one of the snowiest peaks in the Apennines and its white-capped ridge is obvious all winter from Pisa. Monte Giovo offers some of the most spectacular panoramas there is in all of Tuscany. Monte Giovo and the adjacent Monte Rondinaio contain many significant glacial features left from the Ice Age. Within this mountain complex is an incredible glacial headwall that rises some 600 meters above a large glacial cirque on Monte Giovo, multiple arêtes which connect several mountain peaks, several other smaller cirques, and many beautiful little turquoise tarns.

Monte Giovo also offers some of the most expansive views of the Apennine chain, and on clear days offers incredible vistas across the Garfagnana valley to the Alpi Apuane and out across the Pisa plain, to the Mediterranean sea. While the landscape is extremely rugged in this area, there are a multitude of trail options that range from relatively short loops in the cirque, to an extremely rugged longer loop to the summit of Monte Giovo. This guide will describe both a shorter, easier option and a longer and more strenuous option that should be reserved for those who are experienced hikers, familiar with negotiating terrain on exposed rocky cliff faces. Dogs are more than welcome on the shorter loop, but you should not bring your dog to the summit of Monte Giovo, due to

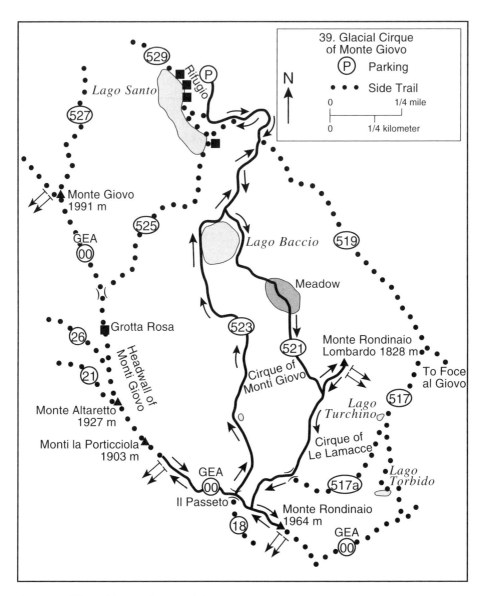

39. Glacial Cirque
of Monte Giovo

P Parking

••• Side Trail

N

0   1/4 mile

0   1/4 kilometer

529

Rifugio P

Lago Santo

527

Monte Giovo
1991 m

GEA
00

525

Grotta Rosa

26

21

Headwall of
Monti Giovo

Monte Altaretto
1927 m

Monti la Porticciola
1903 m

Lago Baccio 519

Meadow

523

521

Cirque of
Monti Giovo

Monte Rondinaio
Lombardo 1828 m

To Foce
al Giovo

Lago
Turchino 517

Cirque of
Le Lamacce

Lago
Torbido

GEA
00

Il Passeto

517a

18

Monte Rondinaio
1964 m

GEA
00

the steep cliffs and the need to use chains as an aid in making the ascent.

To get to the Cirque of Monte Giovo from Pisa or Florence, take the A12 Autostrada to Lucca. Exit here, and follow the SS12 to Abetone. It will take about 1.5 hours to reach Abetone. Once past Abetone, continue onto the village of Pieve- pelago. Just before reaching the center of Pievepelago, look for a turn to the left towards Aulla, Passo delle Radici, and Lago Santo. Shortly after that turn, turn left again, following signs for Lago Santo. Continue on that road for about 10 kilometers until it ends at a parking area. Parking for the day is €2.50. There is no direct bus service to

The glacial cirque of Monte Giovo

Lago Santo, but COPIT offers service to Pievepelago. Contact COPIT at www.copit spa.it for more information.

Lago Santo is a very popular day area for fishing and picnicking, with several *rifugi* offering meals and lodging. To access the cirque, walk down the dirt road which passes the bar at the top of the parking area, and then past a waterfall. When the dirt road curves right to head up to Lago Santo, turn left onto Trail 523 toward Lago Baccio. The trail will slowly ascend through a beech forest, passing Trail 519, and continuing up to the beautiful marshy tarn of Lago Baccio at the base of the Cirque of Monte Giovo. From here, outstanding views of the cirque and the incredible headwall come into view. Monte Giovo can be seen above, with the countless sedimentary layers visible in the cliffs.

The trail branches here at the lake, with Trail 521 headed left and Trail 523 to the right. Take Trail 521 and you will reenter the beech forest for a short way, until emerging into a beautiful meadow with a stream flowing through it. Ahead, you can see the trail climbing steeply up the cirque wall to the ridgeline above. Monte Rondinaio Lombardo is visible, with the cross on its summit. This section of trail is steep, and there will be places where you will have to use your hands to grip onto the rocks. However, if you have a dog along, it will have no problems climbing up the grassy slopes, through the blueberries.

Once you reach the ridgeline, you will see that you are on an arête–a narrow ridgeline that was cut into, by two adjacent glaciers during the Ice Age. The cirque of Le Lamacce is on the other side, with two beautiful little aqua-colored tarn lakes. If you take a left, you can make the short climb to the summit of Monte Rondinaio Lombardo. If you are doing the short loop, this side trip is well worth the time, and is an excellent place to view the extent of both adjacent

A view of the Northern Apennines from Monte Rondinaio

cirques, as well as the summit of Monte Ci-mone (Hike 38) across the Abetone pass. At the far end of the arête is the higher summit of Monte Rondinaio, which is a horn that marked the junction of three separate glaciers. If you are doing the longer, more strenuous loop, it is advised to skip Monte Rondinaio Lombardo, as you still have much more climbing ahead of you.

Once you have taken in the view, return the way that you came and continue along the ridgeline towards Monte Rondinaio. This section is pretty easy, and offers amazing views of Monte Giovo and its headwall. When you reach the *finestra* (or "window"), where Trail 517A descends into the cirque of Le Lamacce, stay right and head towards the arête that connects Monte Rondinaio to Monte Giovo. This section is moderately strenuous, because it is quite rocky. At the top, you will connect up with the 00 GEA trail, which works its way along the crest of the Apennines for nearly 400 kilometers.

Take a left at the 00 GEA, and climb up to the summit of Monte Rondinaio, which at 1,964 meters is one of the highest peaks in the Northern Apennines. Monte Rondinaio stands out as a significant feature for hundreds of kilometers. It is visible as a steep horn along the ridgeline from Pisa, and you can see it from most of the hikes in the Alpi Apuane, the Northern Apennines, and Tuscan hill country that are included this guide. As such, it also offers a panoramic view across to all of these sites. The most amazing view, though, is of Monte Giovo across the cirque. The headwall, with long shadows falling onto the amphitheater below, is reminiscent of being in the Rockies or the Cascade mountains. On an exceptionally clear day, the Alps can be see to the north, across the smoggy Po Valley. This is an excellent place for lunch, and to soak in the grandeur of northern Tuscany.

This is also where you must decide whether to return to the trailhead via the

The Northern Apennines

short loop on Trail 523 or continue on, to the summit of Monte Giovo, along the more strenuous long loop. From here, you have already climbed some 600 meters from the parking area and, although rugged and imposing, Monte Giovo is only 30 meters higher in elevation.

If you choose to do the short loop, descend the slope on the 00 GEA, following the ridgeline toward Monte Giovo until you reach Il Passeto. Here, Trail 523 descends back down the slope to the right into the great cirque toward Lago Baccio. Trail 523 passes through some beautiful meadows, full of wildflowers and blueberries, and past a small tarn. Upon reaching Lago Baccio, there is a nice wet meadow and marsh, containing frogs and rare wetland plants. The trail will follow the left side of the lake and reconnect with Trail 521. Once past the lake, retrace your steps back to the parking area.

To do the long loop, continue straight ahead along the ridgeline on the 00 GEA toward the headwall. Also at Il Passeto, Trail 18 descends down to the left towards the Garfagnana valley. The long loop will reach its most rugged and dangerous section between Il Passeto and Monte Giovo. The trail is very steep, with sheer dropoffs, but does have chains to assist you. Be aware that early in the season, snow and ice may be present along these exposed routes. If you have a dog with you, do not take it along this stretch. The trail will climb up and down two intermediate peaks and then along the top of the headwall until it reaches Grotta Rosa. This marks the end of the scary section. Shortly thereafter, Trail 525 will descend along a ridgeline back towards Lago Santo. This is the recommended return route. However, to reach the summit of Monte Giovo, with its cross upon it, continue straight ahead along the flat summit area. From the summit, Trail 527 descends down slope and eventually meets with Trail 529 near Lago Santo. This is another option down, but would make an already strenuous route even longer.

40

Corno alle Scale Loop

Loop along the crest of the Appennino Bolognese to the summit of Corno alle Scale.

Round Trip: 9.2 kilometers (5.7 miles)

Elevation: 1,415–1,945 meters (4,641–6,380 feet)

Hiking time: 3–4 hours

Park: Parco Regionale del Corno alle Scale

Difficulty: Moderate

Time to visit: May to October

The Corno alle Scale is the southernmost of the high peaks of the Northern Apennines. From this vantage point, one can look out across most of Tuscany, including looking down onto Florence and the Prato plain. This hike is not particularly strenuous or long, and includes walking among the lifts of an active ski area, but it does make for a nice loop along the top of a glacial cirque and on narrow ridges, providing views. The bonus for this hike is the final descent into the beautiful meadows and woods of Cavone, where one feels like they are in a true wilderness.

To access Corno alle Scale from Florence or Pisa, take the A11 Autostrada to the Pistoia exit. Follow the SS64 towards Bologna. As this road climbs across the Apennines, exit at the town of Silla, about 40 kilometers from Pistoia. From Silla, follow the signs for Lizzano in Belvedere and Corno alle Scale along the SS324. Just past Lizzano, near the town of Vidiciatico, look for a left turn for Corno alle Scale on the SP71. Just above the town, the road comes to a T-junction, turn right and continue up the road for 10 more kilometers until you reach the parking area near the small pond and *rifugio* at Cavone. ATC Bologna offers bus service to Corno alle Scale from Porretta Terme. Contact ATC Trasporti Pubblici Bologna at www.atc.bo.it or 051/290290 for more information.

From the parking area, walk up the paved road, past the ski maintenance area. Where the road splits, stay left on the upper road and continue until you see another split on

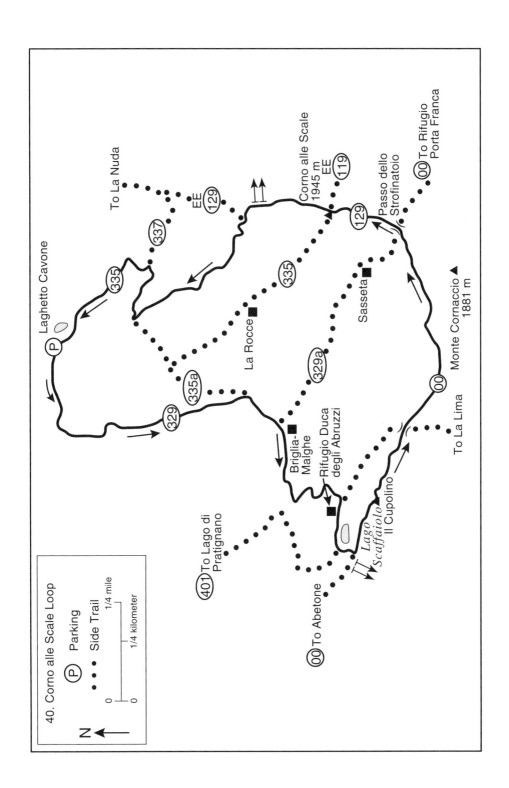

40. Corno alle Scale Loop

P Parking
••••• Side Trail

0 ¼ mile
0 ¼ kilometer

N

To La Nuda

Laghetto Cavone

P

335

337

EE 129

Corno alle Scale
1945 m
EE
119

335

La Rocce

Passo dello
Strofinatoio

129

00 To Rifugio
Porta Franca

335a

329

329a

Sasseta

Monte Cornaccio
1881 m

00

To La Lima

Briglia-
Malghe

Rifugio Duca
degli Abruzzi

Il Cupolino

Lago
Scaffaiolo

401 To Lago di
Pratignano

00 To Abetone

Lago Scaffaiolo

the road. At this point, the lower route will be gated, and the upper one has red/white blazes labeled #329. Trail 329 will take you up past some beech woods, until you emerge in the meadows at the bottom of a glacial cirque. Upon reaching the first trail intersection, near a stream crossing, there will be a sign. To the left is the shortcut route up to the summit of Corne alle Scale, on Trail 329A. However, follow the sign for the Rifugio Duca degli Abruzzi and Lago Scaffaiolo on Trail 329. This route follows a dirt path through meadows and up past a ski lift, then switchbacks up the ridge towards the top. After 2.8 kilometers, you will reach the *rifugio* and the glacial tarn near the ridgeline.

From the *rifugio,* Trail 00 (the Grande Escursione Appenninica, or GEA), follows the ridgeline north toward Abetone and south, on its way to Monte Falco (Hike 41). Initially, the 00 GEA route heads left along the base of the small hill called Il Cupolino. However, you can continue past the lake up to the ridge crest, for the better scenic views. Once at the ridge crest, turn left and climb to the top of Il Cupolino, where there is a terrific view and a nice place to have a snack or rest, away from the crowds at the *rifugio.* From this point, you can easily see the summit of Monte Cimone (Hike 38), the highest peak in the Northern Apennines, and its atmospheric weather observatory. In addition, there are expansive views of the Alpi Apuane, Monte Pisano (Hike 21), the Tuscan hill country, and the Po Valley.

Upon descending, you will meet up with the 00 GEA again at a pass. Continue along the ridgeline as the trail climbs along the sides of the Monte Cornaccio. At Passo dello Strofinatoio, the 00 GEA continues on its way south. In addition, you also meet up with Trail 329A, the shortcut route encountered at the bottom of the cirque. Continue straight, and the climb up to the summit of Corno alle Scale is very short. Upon reaching the summit, you will see the end of a ski

Layered cliffs on the Corno alle Scale Loop

lift on the left, a placard showing what features can be seen from this vantage, and a ridiculous route down the sheer cliffs to the north, labeled EE, or *("Escursionisti Esperti")*–recomended for experts only.

From the summit, walk out to the large metal cross at the end of the ridge. From here, you can look down the steep, layered cliffs of the mountain and out toward La Nuda peak. Another "EE" route descends this cliff to reach La Nuda, but turn left instead and follow along the edges of the cliff. The trail here is not well-marked, but it is a pretty obvious cut into the blueberries and juniper.

Near the bottom of the ski lift, the trail turns right and heads down the cliff into the glacial cirque of Cavone on Trail 335. First descending into beech and larch woods, the trail emerges in a beautiful meadow area complete with a bubbling brook. This small area is the one place on this route that feels like a true wilderness, tucked away from the ski lifts and roads, that cross throughout much of the rest of the park. The route meets up with Trail 337 in the meadow, which climbs up to the summit of La Nuda. Instead, turn left and continue down Trail 335, along the small brook, past wildflowers, bumblebees, and ferns, until slowly a forest closes in above you. The final stretch follows the drainage down, through beech woods, emerging at the Laghetto Cavone and your car.

VI

The Central Apennines and the Adriatic Coast

Introduction to the Central Apennines and the Adriatic Coast

Some of the highest and the most dramatic scenery in Italy, outside of the Alps, is found in the Central Apennines. Near the boundaries of the regions of Umbria, Abruzzo, and Le Marché, is the highest peak on the Italian peninsula: the Corno Grande at 2,912 meters (9,552 feet). On the northern slopes of this peak sits the southernmost glacier in Europe, Il Calderone. In fact, the mountains of the Central Apennines are the highest peaks on the Italian peninsula, the result of intense tectonic pressures from the African plate colliding with Eurasia. The range is primarily made up of limestone and various other sedimentary rocks which accumulated at a time when the area was part of the ancient Tethys Sea. These limestone layers give the mountains a white or light-gray appearance. Many layers have been tilted due the tectonic forces which have shaped this area, and these layers can be seen well on Monte Vettore and the Corno Grande.

Among the most beautiful spots in the area are the Monti Sibillini, which ring the spectacular alpine basin of the Piano Grande, also known less formally as the Pian Grande. Sitting high above this basin is Monte Vettore, which is the fifth highest peak on the Italian peninsula, at 2,476 meters (8,121 feet). This basin and the ridges that encircle it have much to offer. From here, you can watch shepherds tending their flocks of sheep, visit a rare alpine tarn with its own endemic species of brine shrimp, and watch paragliders soaring high above the mountain tops.

Just south of Perugia is another Central Apennine peak, the bald-topped Monte Subasio, which is 1,290 meters (4,231 feet) high. At the base of this peak is the world famous village of Assisi. Here, St. Francis wandered the slopes of Monte Subasio in search of solace and meditation, and developed his love of nature and a desire to shed all worldly possessions.

The Central Apennines have a distinct cuisine based on the foods of the forests, fields, and mountains of the area. The village of Norcia, located at the base of the Monti Sibillini, is famous for its wild boar sausage and truffles. Inside the Pian Grande sits the village of Castelluccio, which is famous for its lentil soup and deep-fried stuffed olives. And let's not forget the outstanding wines of Umbria.

In between the central and northern sections of the Apennines, the mountains are significantly lower and are primarily covered in forests of chestnut and beech. But, just east of Florence, one twin-peaked mountain rises suddenly above all the others. Monte Falco and Monte Falterona, at 1,654 meters (5,425 feet) high, provides the only alpine summits between Corno alle Scale and Monte Subasio, and the source of the Arno River flows down from its slopes. Here, due to the geographic isolation, endemic wildflowers grow. On the slopes below, small villages still earn their income collecting chestnuts and mushrooms in the forests.

To the east lies the Adriatic Sea. Compared to the landscape of the Tuscan coast, the Adriatic coast is gentle, and the soft, sandy beaches make this a very popular summer resort area. However, near Ancona, a mountain rises suddenly up out of the sea, in stark contrast to the surrounding landscape. The spectacular limestone cliffs of Monte Conero (Hike 43) drop 500 meters to the sea, and sea stacks with highly tilted layers can be seen just offshore.

Northwest of Ancona, the tiny Republic of San Marino represents another location where dramatic high cliffs rise above the gentle, rolling hills of Emilia-Romagna, not far from the beaches of Rimini. San Marino is a touristic curiosity. It is one of the oldest and smallest republics in the world, having been founded in 301 AD. People visit here to see the old castles along the cliff tops, buy special San Marinese stamps and currency, and just to say they have visited one of the tiniest counties in the world. But San Marino also offers an interesting hike for someone who wants to get out of the car and see the entire nation on foot!

41

Monte Falco and the Foreste Casentinesi National Park

A hike through the ancient forests of the Apennines to the summit of Monte Falterona.

Distance: approximately 15 kilometers (9.3 miles)

Elevation: 1,296–1,654 meters (4,251–5,425 feet)

Hiking time: 5 hours

Difficulty: Moderate

Park: Parco Nazionale Foreste Casentinesi-Falterona-Campigna

Time to visit: April to November

The Parco Nazionale Foreste Casentinesi-Falterona-Campigna protects extensive stands of beech and chestnut forests in the lightly populated Appennino Cesenese. These mountains contain villages that still maintain traditional lifestyles, where communities still earn their living primarily by harvesting chestnuts and mushrooms, hunting wild boar, and otherwise living off the land. The summits of Monte Falco and Monte Falterona are also important ecological reserves, as they contain the only alpine ecosystems located between the Northern Apennines and the Central Apennines, a stretch of some 180 kilometers between Corno alle Scale (Hike 40) and Monte Subasio (Hike 44). This park also protects the headwaters of the famous Arno River, which flows through Florence and Pisa, on its way to the Tyrrhenian Sea. Much of the ancient forests were preserved for centuries by monks, especially the middle-elevation chestnut forests. However, most of the old-growth white fir and beech stands were harvested during the industrial revolution to build ships and supply industry, and are now returning in expansive second-growth stands.

The trail begins at the Passo della Calla. To get there from Florence, take the Firenze Sud exit onto the SP127. Follow it until the SP34 (the Viale Europa) and head toward Pontassieve. At Pontassieve, turn right onto the SS70 (the Strada Statale Consuma) headed toward Stia and Pratovecchio. This stretch is approximately 25 kilometers and goes through beautiful fields and vineyards,

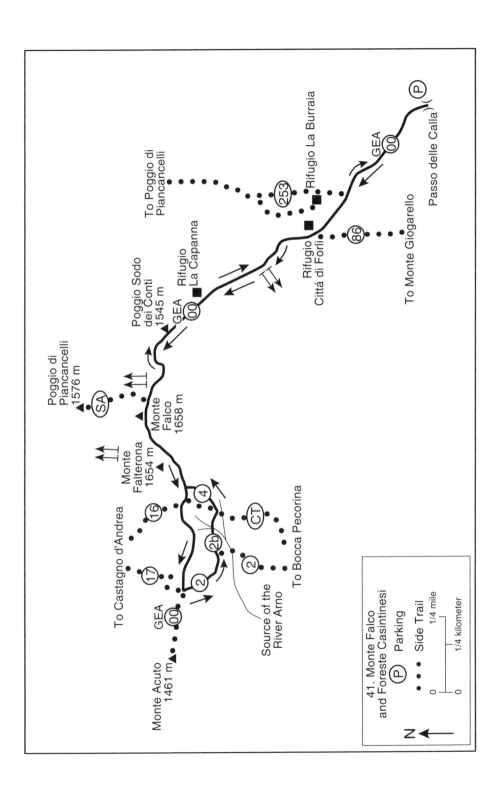

41. Monte Falco
and Foreste Casintinesi

P Parking

••• Side Trail

0 ——— 1/4 mile
0 ——— 1/4 kilometer

N ←

Monte Acuto
1461 m

To Castagno d'Andrea

GEA 00

17

16

Monte
Falterona
1654 m

Poggio di
Piancancelli
1576 m

SA

Monte
Falco
1658 m

Poggio Sodo
dei Conti
1545 m

GEA 00

Rifugio
La Capanna

To Poggio di
Piancancelli

253

Rifugio La Burraia

GEA 00

Rifugio
Città di Forlì

86

To Monte Giogarello

Passo delle Calla

P

2

2b

4

CT

2

Source of the
River Arno

To Bocca Pecorina

Beeches in the Foreste Casentinesi

as it approaches the high ridge of Monte Falco to the east.

Just before the village of Stia, turn right onto the SP74, and follow the signs for Stia. Follow the SP74 into the town center, and then get on the SS310, which climbs up and over Passo della Calla, toward Forlí. It is approximately 15 kilometers from Stia to Passo della Calla. Park in the designated parking area near the buildings at the pass, to begin the hike. SITA bus also offers bus service to Passo della Calla. Contact SITA at www.sitabus.it or 055/47821 for more information.

Passo della Calla (1,296 meters) is very near the southern end of the Grande Escursione Appenninica, as it heads northwest for the next 400 kilometers. At the pass, follow the 00 GEA route north. The first 1.4 kilometers goes through a dense second-growth beech forest. The foliage of these woods provides amazing color through the year, transitioning from lime-green in spring,

to orange in fall, to coating the forest floor with copper in late fall, when the leaves have dropped. The trunks of these trees provide a silvery sheen any time of year. The trail emerges from the woods in a grassy section just before reaching the Rifugio Cittá di Forlí. From here you will see a stand of white fir on the opposite slope, as well as a drainage heading down toward the Adriatic Sea. The slopes to the east are covered in more scattered grass and scrub vegetation. High above the *rifugio,* you can see the summit of Monte Falco and several radio towers on the slopes.

After the Rifugio Cittá di Forlí, the trail ascends approximately 1 kilometer on the western slopes of the ridge, up the to Poggio Sodo dei Conti (1,559 meters). Here, on this hilltop, the terrain opens up into grassy meadows before you reach the Rifugio La Capanna. Follow the dirt track up the slope and back into the beech forest. After approximately 1 kilometer more of climbing,

The ridgeline of Monte Falco

you will reach the alpine summit of Monte Falco (1,658 meters).

Behind the fences, near the summit, are several rare and endangered alpine species. As the only alpine refuge between the Northern and Central Apennines, and a small one at that, it is under grave threat from foot traffic, erosion, and global warming. The national park takes great care to protect these meadows, and you should comply by taking equally great care in being cautious not to damage the delicate wildflowers, while still appreciating them.

From the summit, you can look down onto the flat-topped bluff of Poggio Piancancelli. Its top is covered by a thick carpet of young beech, but grey sandstone layers are obvious on the steep cliffs on its sides. In addition, you can look down onto the village of Castagno d'Andrea, some 800 meters below. This is one of those remote villages that still remains dependent on chestnuts and mushroom harvests for their

livelihood, although tourism is becoming more important as well.

Past the summit of Monte Falco, the trail continues along the ridgeline, descending gently downward and then back into the beech woods. After approximately 1 kilometer, the trail branches. To the right, and up the steep slope, the 00 GEA climbs up to the summit of Monte Falterona (1,654 meters) and another small alpine area. To the left, the signs indicate the Capo d'Arno, or source of the Arno River, which is the trail you will return on.

At the summit of Monte Falterona there is a large cross. The views are spectacular, and on a clear day you can see both the Northern Apennines, 90 kilometers north, and the Central Apennines, some 120 kilometers or so south. From the summit, continue on the 00 GEA along the ridgeline for about 1.2 kilometers, toward Monte Acuto. You will come to an intersection with Trail 17, headed right toward Castagno d'Andrea, and Trail 2 headed left toward the Capo d'Arno. Head left onto Trail 2, and after a little more than 1 kilometer, you will come across a rocky brook tumbling down the steep slope with a plaque just up the slope. This is the spring where the Arno River begins its journey. Continue on Trail 2 until it reconnects with the 00 GEA. From here, retrace your steps back to Monte Falco, and on to Passo della Calla.

42

Republic of San Marino

A hike to the top of Mount Titano in the ancient Republic of San Marino.

Round trip: 7.1 kilometers (4.4 miles)

Elevation: 456–740 meters (1,496–2,427 feet)

Hiking time: 3 hours

Park: Parco Naturale del San Marino

Difficulty: Easy

Time to visit: Year round

The Republic of San Marino, located in east-central Italy, not far from the Adriatic sea, is considered by many to be the oldest independent republic on earth. The country claims to have been founded in 301 AD, by Marinus, an early Christian stonecutter who sought refuge from Roman persecution on Mount Titano. San Marino was occupied from time to time throughout the Middle Ages, but certainly by 1261, when it was recognized by the Holy See as an independent state. The country has enjoyed freedom and independence ever since.

San Marino is the fifth smallest country on Earth, and the third smallest in Europe after Vatican City and Monaco. Although it is tiny in size and only has a population of about 29,000 people, it is visited by some 3 million tourists per year. What makes this country so popular? Besides the novelty of visiting a tiny landlocked country surrounded by beautiful Italian landscapes, San Marino also provides for a wonderful medieval atmosphere. The old city sits high up on the summit of Monte Titano, over 700 meters above sea level, offering spectacular panoramas of the Adriatic Sea and the Apennines. San Marino also offers tourists the opportunity to purchase unique stamps and specially minted Euro coins. In addition, there are precipitous cliffs that will shock and awe the unprepared visitor.

This hike offers you the chance to climb to the summit of Mount Titano through oak and maple forests, walk through the heart of the old city, along the sheer ridgeline past three medieval towers, and through the

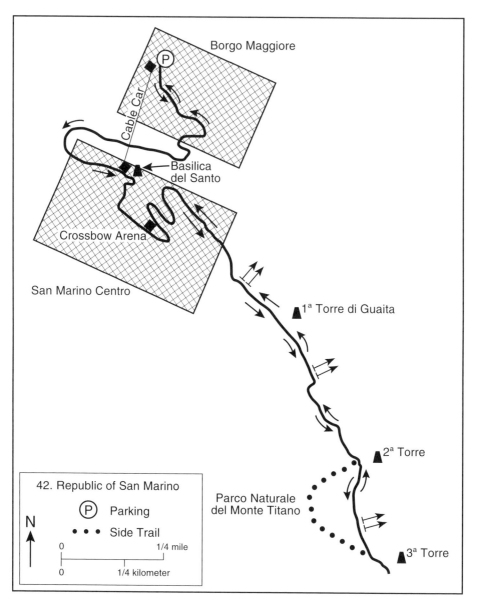

Borgo Maggiore

Cable Car

Basilica del Santo

Crossbow Arena

San Marino Centro

1ᵃ Torre di Guaita

2ᵃ Torre

Parco Naturale del Monte Titano

3ᵃ Torre

42. Republic of San Marino

(P) Parking

• • • Side Trail

N

0   1/4 mile

0   1/4 kilometer

summit forests of the Parco Naturale del San Marino. It is a terrific mix of touristy sightseeing, hiking, nature, and history all crammed into a tiny little package.

To get to San Marino from Florence, take the A1 Autostrada to Bologna. Get on the A14 Autostrada toward Rimini/Ancona. After approximately 1 hour, take the Rimini Sud exit, and get onto the SS72 towards San Marino. Once in the Republic of San Marino, continue on the main road as it climbs up toward the mountain. Keep following signs for San Marino (the city). At Borgo Maggiore, the first of the older buildings you will see on

The crossbow grounds in San Marino

the way up at the base of the steep cliffs, park at the pay parking lot on the right, near the cable car station. It is also possible to reach San Marino by taking the train to Rimini and then catching the #72 bus into San Marino. Go to www.visitsanmarino.com for more information.

From here, walk into the village of Borgo Maggiore, and look for hiking/castle signs pointing toward the cliffs. After a couple of blocks, you will end up at the Costa dell'Arnella, a stone pathway which begins climbing the mountain through the forest. This stone pathway will climb for about 1 kilometer though oak and maple woods, until it reaches the outskirts of the capital of San Marino. A road will branch to the right, but stay left on the path until it enters the city through a stone gate.

Once in the city, you will walk down narrow roads, past government buildings, and past quaint medieval houses. All along the way, you will keep heading up staircases that will take you higher and higher. It may be a little disorienting at first, but you will not get lost in this small city. Just keep following signs for the Palazzo Pubblico and the Basilica di San Marino. At one point you will pass a grassy pit called the Cave dei Balestrieri, where San Marino holds its yearly crossbow competition. This competition dates back to 1600, as a feast to celebrate the founding of the country. The tradition of the skilled crossbow marksmen dates back even further, to 1339, when San Marino needed to have a highly trained militia to defend itself from would-be invaders.

Once near the top of the ridge, you will see the Torre di Guaita, the first of the three towers of Monte Titano. The view from this spot is incredible, but it is not the best you will see. For that, one must continue on, along the ridgeline, toward the 2^a Torre ("Second Tower"). A walkway along a very narrow section of cliff offers spectacular views to the east, but even more impressive

Torre II

views down the sheer rock wall that drops 300 meters.

At the 2^a Torre, pass through the wall and you will enter the Parco Naturale del San Marino. The forested park at the summit of Monte Titano offers several trails through the deciduous oak forests and a chance to escape the potentially huge numbers of tourists. Staying on the main path will take you on to the 3^a Torre ("Third Tower"), which is the last of the three summits of Monte Titano and offers incredible views to the south. Retrace your steps on the way back, but feel free to wander through the city of San Marino along the way. There are numerous shops, some nice restaurants for lunch, and of course, the special San Marino coin and stamp dealers.

The Central Apennines and the Adriatic Coast

43

Sea Stacks of Monte Conero

A steep, rugged descent to an isolated beach with a view of the sea stacks below, known as Le Due Sorelle.

Round trip: 6.4 kilometers (4 miles)

Elevation: 240 meters (787 feet) to sea level

Hiking time: 3 hours

Difficulty: Moderate

Park: Parco del Conero

Time to visit: Year round; extreme caution advisable when wet or, rarely, icy

Le Due Sorelle ("The Two Sisters") are two limestone sea stacks that sit at the bottom of the steep cliffs of Monte Conero, on the Adriatic Sea. Stretching to the south of the sea stacks is a beautiful and isolated beach, which requires a short but very rugged descent down sheer cliffs and involving metal cables. However, the sense of adventure, spectacular scenery, and relaxing isolation of the beach in one of the more touristy areas of Italy, make this descent well worth it. The Adriatic coast of Italy is generally flat, from its border with Slovenia all the way to the spur near Bari. However, Monte Conero provides for a dramatic break in the relief, which is visible from long distances. There are several trails that weave in and around the oak forests of Monte Conero, but the trail leading to the Passo del Lupo and Le Due Sorelle offers the most spectacular views. On this trail, extensive views of the beaches and resorts of the Adriatic coast extend as far as the eye can see. As this is an extremely steep descent on loose, unconsolidated material, avoid doing this hike if it is raining or very windy. The good news is that limestone drains water well, and the day I did the hike was a day after a rainstorm, and the rocks were not slippery.

The Parco del Conero is just south of the city of Ancona. To access this hike from Florence, take the A1 Autostrada to Bologna. At Bologna, get onto the A14 Autostrada south towards Pescara and Bari. Drive on the A14 for 245 kilometers until you pass Ancona, and take the Loreto–Porto Recanati exit. Follow signs to Port Recanati and

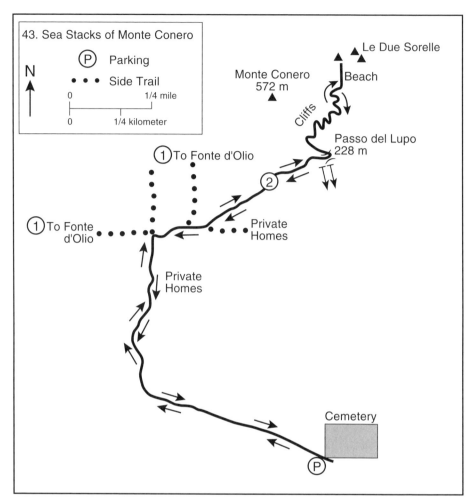

43. Sea Stacks of Monte Conero

Ⓟ Parking

• • • Side Trail

N

0 _____ 1/4 mile

0 _____ 1/4 kilometer

Le Due Sorelle

Monte Conero
572 m

Beach

Cliffs

Passo del Lupo
228 m

①To Fonte d'Olio

②

①To Fonte
d'Olio

Private
Homes

Private
Homes

Cemetery

Ⓟ

then north, toward Sirolo and Numana, on the SP100 along the sea. Continue to follow signs until you reach Sirolo, located on the hilltop above the sea at the base of Monte Conero. The SP1 passes just east of the center of Sirolo and then heads up the slope of Monte Conero. Follow the brown signs for Monte Conero, but just as you are leaving town, look for a blue P (parking) sign and one for San Michele beach, to the right. It is easy to miss, so if you keep driving up the mountain, turn around. The parking area is only a hundred meters or so down this ac-

cess road, across from the cemetery. It is possible to take the train to Ancona and then catch a bus to Sirolo. Contact Autolinee Reni at www.anconarenibus.it or 071/8046504 for more information.

The trail begins on the dirt road that continues north from the cemetery. This road passes several houses and continues up for 1.2 kilometers, before reaching a trail intersection. Trail 1 heads up the slopes of Monte Conero toward Fonte D'Olio, while Trail 2 heads to Passo del Lupo. There is another branch of Trail 1 shortly thereafter, and sev-

Le Due Sorelle Beach at Monte Conero

eral more private homes along this stretch. Continue to follow the trail markers for Passo del Lupo. After leaving the last of these homes, the trail briefly enters an oak woodland, before emerging at the Passo del Lupo, 2.4 kilometers from the start. The view from Passo del Lupo is absolutely incredible. The view south, toward Sirolo and the Adriatic coast is extensive. The aquamarine blue of the Adriatic entices, but seeing Le Due Sorelle, 230 meters below at the base the sheer cliffs of the Monte Conero, is both exciting and intimidating.

From the Passo del Lupo, the trail begins its relentless descent down the cliffs, using metal cables as your guide. The trail is narrow, the footing is unsure in places, and the cables are not always in the places you would like them. There are places where the cliff is so steep that it appears you are overhanging the coast below. For those who like adventure, this is a good trail, despite its short length. The total descent to the beach

is only 700 linear meters. But this short distance takes nearly 45 minutes, due to the slow rate of descent. The trail does not really seem so bad, after the first steep segment and a more gradual second segment, but then you will reach another pass and another set of steep cliffs, and you will have to muster up the courage to get through that section as well. The good thing about this trail is that there are at least a few places to rest along the way.

Once you have reached the beach and can finally start using your eyes for something other than looking at the next step you take, you can look up the cliffs above and enjoy the white sand and limestone layered rocks of the sea stacks. These tilted layers are evidence that as the Italian peninsula rotates counterclockwise, tectonic stresses are tilting the rocks, and the Adriatic Sea is slowly closing in. If you go in the off season (any time other than July and August), there is a good chance that the beach will be completely

Passo del Lupo at Monte Conero

empty. However, I have read that in the peak summer season, boats will dock in the small cove and dozens of people will bathe on the beach, so the isolation may not be as complete as you expected. Along the beach, you can enjoy beachcombing for the various seashells and sponges that have washed up.

Once you have enjoyed the beach and the relaxation, the climb back up begins. While the climb is steep and takes some effort, it is always easier, safer, and less stressful to climb a cliff than descend one. You should get back up to the top much faster than it took to get down.

The Central Apennines and the Adriatic Coast

44

Monte Subasio of St. Francis of Assisi

A hike to the summit of Monte Subasio—the mountain St. Francis would wander to find solace and to appreciate nature.

Round trip: 7.5 kilometers (4.7 miles)

Elevation: 750–1,290 meters (2,460–4,231 feet)

Hiking time: 3 hours

Park: Parco del Monte Subasio

Difficulty: Moderate

Time to visit: March to November

From 1182–1226 AD, Monte Subasio was the stomping grounds of St. Francis of Assisi. It was on this mountain that St. Francis sought out solace, and gained his appreciation of nature. It was in these woods and subalpine meadows, that he reflected upon the disillusionment he had towards the pursuit of worldly goods, and where he sought enlightenment from God. Monte Subasio is a broad, rounded mountain, with a gentle grassy summit area. It sits high above the Spoleto valley (also called Valle Umbra) and is one of the most obvious features while driving along the SS75. Monte Subasio commands outstanding views above the Umbrian hills and offers a beautiful hike near some of the most historical religious sites in Italy.

To get to Monte Subasio from Florence, take the A1 Autostrada south until the exit for Perugia. Get on the Raccordo Highway toward Perugia, and follow the Raccordo through Perugia looking for signs for Assisi and Spoleto. Getting through the stretch around Perugia can be quite confusing, as you change highways two times, but the signs for Assisi are pretty obvious. Near Assisi there are two options to get to the village of Armenzano, which is where the trail begins. From Assisi, drive all the way up through the village, and out the other side, towards Gualdo Tadino. Shortly after leaving Assisi, look for a right turn, following signs for Costa di Trex. At Costa di Trex, follow signs for Spello, going along the eastern base of Monte Subasio. Upon reaching the village of Armenzano, go just past the village on the

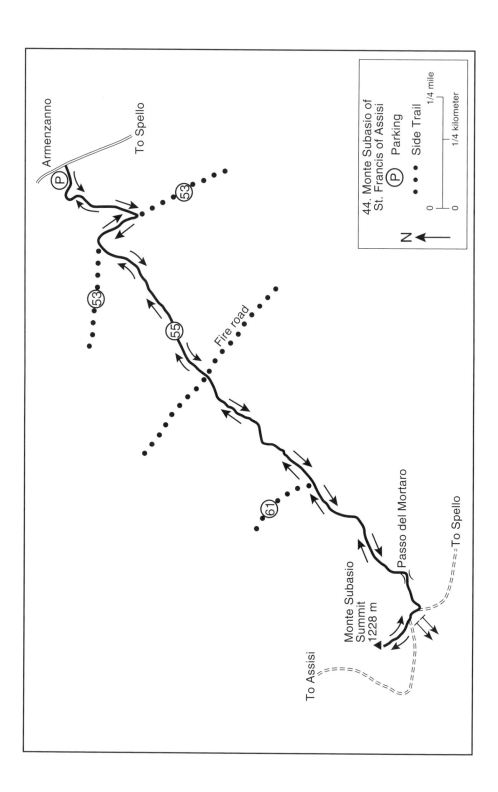

N

44. Monte Subasio of
St. Francis of Assisi

Ⓟ   Parking
••• Side Trail

0   1/4 kilometer
0   1/4 mile

Armenzanno

To Spello

Ⓟ

53

53

55

Fire road

61

Passo del Mortaro

To Spello

Monte Subasio
Summit
1228 m

To Assisi

The valley behind Monte Subasio, Assisi

main road, and turn right into the parking area. The other option is to drive up past Spello, and then continue toward Assisi on the eastside road. Just before reaching Armenzano, turn left into the parking area. There is no public bus service to the trailhead, but it is possible to reach Assisi or Spello by bus. Contact APM Perugia at www.apmperugia.it or 800/512140 for more information.

Trail 55 begins by climbing the dirt road up the slope. After 400 meters, the trail arrives at the first intersection, with Trail 53. Turn right and shortly thereafter, the trail splits again. Turn left and continue to follow Trail 55. The trail begins by heading through deciduous oak woodlands. Eventually, the trail will meet up with a dirt fire road. Go past this road and through the fence, and continue going straight up the trail. The route heading up will take you up a fire break cut into the forest, but thick shrubs along the way make it brushy in places.

Approximately 2.5 kilometers from the parking area, the trail begins to emerge at treeline, at nearly 1,200 meters elevation.

The subalpine area on Monte Subasio is heavily grazed by livestock, and thus is maintained significantly shorter than it would naturally be, if allowed to grow. Throughout the rest of the hike, the grasses are grazed low in places, spiky and unpalatable thistles will become common, and livestock droppings cover most of the slopes. Just after emerging above the treeline, Trail 61 crosses the streambed, and heads left. Continue straight up the drainage toward the summit ridge. The trail disappears in places, as it is overgrown by grasses and small shrubs, but continue up the drainage, ignoring several way-trails and animal tracks that branch off in all directions. There will be occasional red/white blazes on any available exposed rocks and on a few wooden poles.

Halfway from Trail 61 to the summit road, the route crosses a marshy basin. Stay to

The lower trail at Monte Subasio

the right of this area and continue upslope. There will be a pass and way-trail called Passo del Mortaro, just before the summit road. You may be tempted to head right following this way-trail, but continue straight until the dirt road.

Upon reaching the dirt summit road, the first views of the Spoleto valley and the Umbrian hills open up. Turn right on the summit road and follow it toward the summit. There are some radio towers on top of the ridge-line, but the views from this broad, open summit, include virtually all of Umbria, including the Spoleto valley, the Monti Sibillini and Lago Trasimeno to the south, Perugia and the Apennines to the north, and even the Adriatic Sea on a really clear day. From the summit area, you can explore however you like. Watch out for flocks of sheep and their protective sheepdogs, especially if you also have a dog with you. Return to your car the way you came up.

45

Badlands of Civita di Bagnoregio

A hike into the volcanic badlands and the ancient and crumbing village of Civita.

Distance: 6.0 kilometers (3.7 miles)

Elevation: 481–240 meters (1,580–792 feet)

Hiking time: 2–3 hours

Park: Sistema della Forre della Provincia di Viterbo

Difficulty: Moderate to strenuous (brushy and hard to follow)

Time to visit: September to June (avoid midsummer and when wet)

Very close to the junction of Tuscany, Umbria, and Lazio, just a short distance from Orvieto, is the village of Civita di Bagnoregio, a unique and interesting historical site located in a fascinating geologic area. Approximately 370,000 years ago, a massive eruption of the Vulsini volcano created a large caldera that filled with water to create Lago Bolsena. The plume of volcanic material that was lifted into the atmosphere rained down upon the surrounding landscape, creating layers of welded tuff and scoria many meters thick. Another eruption, some 160,000 years ago, only added to this, and the entire landscape around the Orvieto area is dominated by these volcanic clay layers. Over the thousands of years that followed, erosion worked its way through these soft deposits to created a myriad of canyons and a large badland area near Civita di Bagnoregio (or just Civita, to the locals), known as the Valle dei Calanchi.

In historic times, people built villages on these formations, such as Civita, only to see the landscape erode out from under them. The village was originally placed there by the Etruscans some 2,500 years ago. It was an important village for many centuries, as it stood along an important trade route between Viterbo and Orvieto. In 1695, an earthquake leveled the village and caused extensive erosion, forcing most of its residents to flee. Today, it is only occupied by a dozen or so year-round residents, and is completely isolated, except for an elevated footbridge. The future for the village is uncertain, as erosion continues to undermine

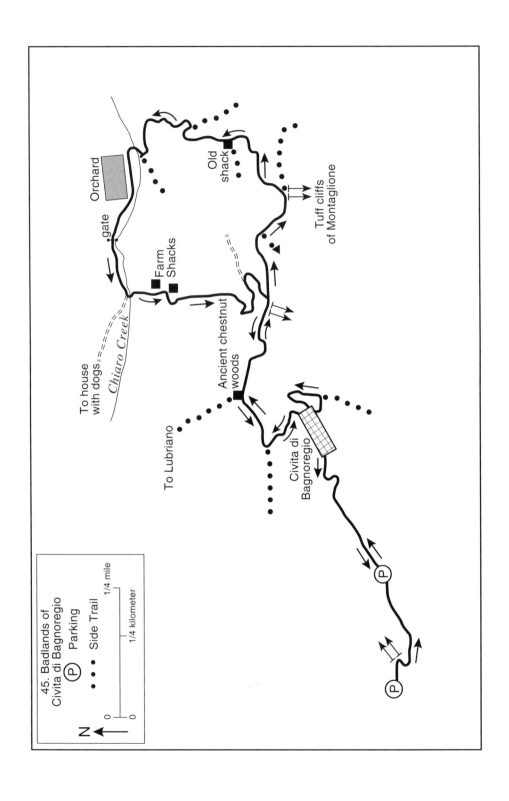

45. Badlands of
Civita di Bagnoregio

Ⓟ Parking

• • • Side Trail

0   1/4 kilometer
0   1/4 mile

N ←

Orchard

gate

To house
with dogs

Chiaro Creek

Farm
Shacks

Old
shack

Tuff cliffs
of Montaglione

Ancient chestnut
woods

To Lubriano

Civita di
Bagnoregio

Ⓟ

Ⓟ

Civita

the stability of the bluff and the village itself. While actions have been taken to stabilize the soil, geologic processes will continue to shape this landscape.

This hike offers visitors an opportunity to visit this unique site, as well as the incredible volcanic landscape of the badlands, below. However, it should be noted that while the loop route is relatively short, it is very brushy and difficult to follow in sections. It is not really maintained, so conditions will change over time. Due to the thick brush, watch for ticks in spring, and wear pants as well, to protect your legs from scratches. If it has rained, expect the tuff on the bluffs to turn into a thick slippery layer of clay that will stick to your boots. In addition, this area gets extremely hot and muggy in midsummer, and I do not recommend it during July and August. So, if you chose to try this route, be prepared for some adventure, and have a sense of humor!

To get to Civita di Bagnoregio from Florence or Rome, take the A1 Autostrada until the Orvieto exit. Get on the SP12 headed toward the village. When you cross the bor-

der from Umbria to Lazio, the road changes its name to SP6. The signs for the village are clear as you approach. Continue all the way through the town, following brown signs for CIVITA. There is an upper parking lot which provides a wonderful overlook point before beginning the hike. If you follow the road down steeply right, it will dead end shortly at the lower parking lot, that will likely fill in the peak tourist season. This hike begins at the upper lot. A small parking fee can be paid at the bar right near each parking lot. But, if the bar is closed, you can assume that parking is free. It is also possible to reach Civita by bus from Orvieto. Contact CoTral at www.cotralspa.it for more information.

From the upper parking lot, walk past the interpretive signs and the small bar to an overlook point. Take the stairs down to the lower road and walk 300 meters to the lower parking lot. From here, you will cross the footbridge across the chasm, the only access to the village. Below you can see flowing patterns of dried mud from recent rainstorms and chunks of tuff that continu-

Volcanic badlands of Civita di Bagnoregio

ously drop from the bluff above. It is quite obvious from the bridge that the village's days are numbered.

Wandering around the village takes little time. There are a couple of bars and restaurants and only one B&B containing three rooms. Walk all the way through the village to the other side, where the sidewalk will begin to drop down steeply, and a panorama of the surrounding badlands opens up.

The path descends, and a faint overgrown trail branches left and downhill, while the main path continues, turning sharply right, and enters a tunnel under the village. Along this stretch, the alternating layers of tuff and scoria, with its embedded pumice stones, become obvious. Continue through the tunnel and emerge out the other side, into a locust and maple stand lined with nettles and other tall herbaceous plants. Ignore the way-trail to the left and continue right, and soon the understory will open up under the shade of large, ancient chestnut trees,

some as old as 300 years. The locals have been collecting chestnuts from this stand for generations, and in fact have specific trees they alone are entitled to. The stand is small and is protected from the intense summer heat by the shade of the bluff directly above. The trail will come to an intersection where a placard discusses this ancient chestnut stand. Turn right, and follow the trail out to the badlands area. Heading left, you will descend into the drainage and then climb up the opposite bluff towards Lubriano and Bagnoregio.

The trail will emerge onto a narrow ridgeline which drops steeply on the right above loose gray tuff. Follow this narrow ridge, and soon a small bluff will appear ahead. This is the heart of the badlands. The fragile volcanic clay does not absorb water, thus it is susceptible to flash flooding and massive erosion during any major rainfall. The route then follows the ridge up toward and then along left of this bluff. Once on the backside

The Central Apennines and the Adriatic Coast

of the bluff, a small way-trail up to the right will take you to the edge the bluff. Continuing along the main route, the trail will emerge again along a very narrow hogback, with steep cliffs descending into the badlands to the right, while the left side remains wooded. There will be a placard at Montiglione—one of the most panoramic locations in this hike, and where the full extent of the volcanic deposits can be examined.

At Montiglione, a faint trail continues further on the ridgeline, providing for closer examination of the geological formations. However, the route to complete the loop heads slightly downhill to the left, and descends through the woodland to Chiaro creek below. The route emerges from the brush at an old abandoned house. Continue straight here, and the route continues to descend toward the creek, through locusts and shrubs. At one of the switchbacks, stay left while a way-trail heads right. Remember, if there is any doubt, keep heading down, toward the stream bottom. Once at the creek, head upstream and cross to the other side at a convenient location. Once on the other side, you should come across what appears to be an old road ending at the creek, and an orchard. Walk along the lower part of the orchard upstream to an old road that parallels the creek. Continue past a gate, and follow the road that begins at this gate, until you reach an intersection where another road crosses the stream on the left and where there is a small horse enclosure. To the right, the road approaches the fence of someone's home.

At the time of our visit, there was a horse, and a herding dog tied up at this site. The dog barked, but it seemed generally friendly. However, up the road we could hear dozens of hunting dogs barking furiously, however they were enclosed within the fence of the home just upstream. Cross the stream, and follow this old road up the slope, back toward the ridgeline above. The road is initially blocked by some old farm shacks, but a small trail bypasses these structures, and quickly rejoins the road on the other side. The road climbs up, switching back and forth, until almost reaching the top, and then parallels the ridge. Look for a trail that heads up to the right, which takes you back to where you began at the summit of the badlands. Retrace your steps back through the chestnut stand and back into Civita, where you can stop for some drinks and recover from the climb back up.

Introduction to Hikes 46 & 47

Pian Grande Ridge Routes

Two hikes along the Crest of the Pian Grande Ridge for views of the Monti Sibillini.

Park: Parco Nazionale dei Monti Sibillini

Time to visit: April to October

The Parco Nazionale dei Monti Sibillini is the northernmost of the six national park areas of the Central Apennines. This region contains the highest and most dramatic of the Apennine peaks in Italy. Monti Sibillini is a spectacular mountain range that sits high above an incredible grassy plain, known as the Pian Grande (or, more formally, as Piano Grande). This broad, flat basin was formed when melting glaciers left a large glacial lake, and sediments covered the bottom. Years of erosion from the mountainsides have filled the basin in even more, leaving the broad, grassy plain that exists today. The lack of trees and the large mountains rising directly above the valley floor reminds me more of the Brooks range in Alaska, than of central Italy. Cut deep into Monte Vettore, the highest peak in the park at 2,478 meters, is a spectacular U-shaped valley and glacial tarn.

Besides being a spectacular geological site, this park is a place of ancient traditions and agricultural activities. You will likely see shepherds tending their flocks on the mountain slopes, with their herding dogs keeping the sheep together. In addition, you may even observe traditional methods of wool-shearing, still done with hand-clippers. In the valley bottom, there are a few agricultural fields near the village of Castelluccio where wheat, hay, mustard, and lentils are still grown.

This park is essentially open to any non-motorized sporting activities you can imagine. The Grande Anello dei Sibillini is a 120 kilometer route ringing the park, that is open for hikers, mountain bikers, and horseback riders to enjoy. There are several *rifugio* available along the way for overnight lodging and meals. In addition, there are several dirt paths inside the Pian Grande available for exploration. In winter, these routes become places for cross-country skiing, both in the Pian Grande and on the ridge crest. There is also a downhill ski area available near Rifugio Perugia. In the summer you will also see paragliders riding the thermals high above the valley. This is truly a park you will want to visit multiple times, and in multiple seasons. The two hikes listed here follow a southern stretch of the Grande Anello.

From Florence, take the A1 Autostrada south until you reach the Raccordo A1 Perugia, in about 85 kilometers. Follow the signs for Perugia, and this route will take you past the Lago Trasimeno (the largest lake in Italy). At Perugia, look for signs for Foligna and take the SS75 south for 27 kilometers. At Foligna, follow signs for Spoleto on the SS3. After 28 kilometers, just before you reach Spoleto on the SS3, look for signs for Norcia and Cascia, and take the SS209. This will lead through a long and smoggy tunnel. Continue to follow signs for Norcia and after 20 kilometers, turn onto the SS320. Once at Norcia, follow signs for

Castelluccio. The SP447 will climb the mountainside for 20 kilometers, until it reaches the pass near the Rifugio Perugia. Park at the pass to begin both the South Ridge and West Ridge routes. It is also possible to reach Monti Sibillini by bus from Spoleto. Contact SSIT at www.spoletina .com or 074/3212202 for more information.

46

Pian Grande Ridge Route—West

Distance: Up to 19 kilometers roundtrip (11.7 miles)

Hiking time: 6–7 hours

Elevation: 1,296–1,883 meters (4,250–6,176 feet)

Difficulty: Moderately strenuous

Both routes are spectacular, but if you must choose only one, take the West Ridge route. The West Ridge route leaves to the left of the pass, along a gravel road, with red/white blazes painted on the rocks. The route starts out with a spectacular view out over the Pian Grande, and Monte Vettore (Hike 48). This route follows an old road along the crest of the ridge in a northwestern direction, as it heads through spectacular alpine meadows, containing wildflowers of all colors when they are in bloom in May and June. The route will pass a small stand of beech and then, shortly after passing a low ridge that juts out into the valley, looking down into a side valley of the great basin called the Piano Perduto. In this side valley, notice a couple of old stone buildings and small campers, used by shepherds when they are tending their flocks. It is likely that you will also see sheep on the ridges while you walk. After about 20 minutes, the road splits, but stay on the lower route, following the red/white blazes the whole way. This route continues above Piano Perduto, with constant views of the Monti Sibillini. Eventually, the trail will go past some water troughs, and up a some steps to a small pass.

At the pass, you can look down the other side of the ridge into the deep valley of the village of Norcia. After a short time, the trail crosses back over, for more views of the Pian Grande. Soon, you will lose sight of the Pian Grande, as the trail goes behind a hill. Here is where you would come up from the dirt road below, if you were completing

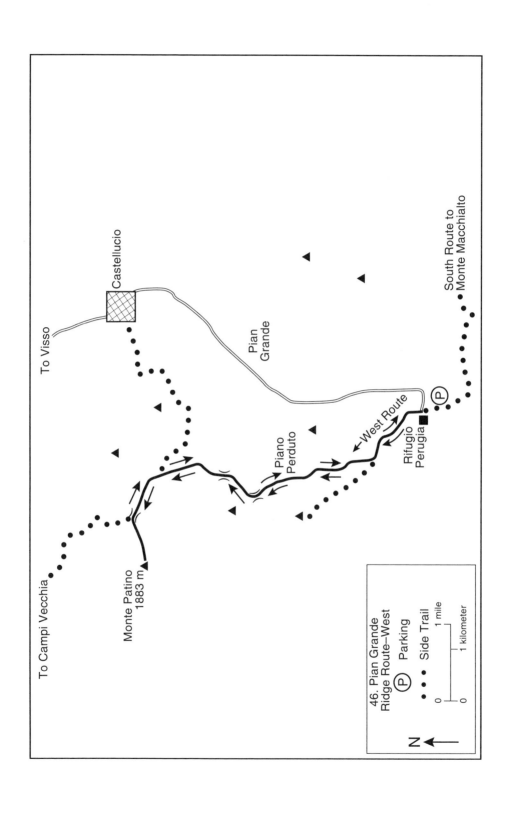

To Visso

Castellucio

To Campi Vecchia

Monte Patino
1883 m

Pian Grande

Piano Perduto

West Route

Rifugio Perugia

South Route to
Monte Macchialto

46. Pian Grande
Ridge Route—West
Ⓟ Parking
•••• Side Trail

0   1 mile
0   1 kilometer

N

Pian Grande

the Grand Loop of Monti Sibillini (Hike 49). To reach Monte Patino, continue on the trail toward the pass, near the base of the mountain, which juts out to the west. Follow the ridgeline out to the summit of Monte Patino (1,883 meters), where you can stop for lunch and enjoy the view down to Campi Vecchio and the valley below. From the summit of Monte Patino, you have hiked over 9 kilometers, so this is a good place to turn around. The Grande Anello dei Sibillini trail continues, by descending steeply down the mountain into the valley, continuing on its 120 kilometer loop.

Along the west route at Pian Grande

47

Pian Grande Ridge Route–South

Distance: 11.8 km roundtrip (7.3 miles) to the summit of Monte Macchialto

Elevation: 1,296–1,751 meters (4,250–5,743 feet)

Hiking time: 4–5 hours

Difficulty: Moderately easy

This hike offers spectacular views out over the Pian Grande and Monte Vettore, albeit in a shorter hike and from different angles. This hike provides closer views of Monte Vettore and the park of Gran Sasso, as well as opportunities to look down to the village of Arquata del Tronto, far below. The trail begins to the right of the pass, following red/white blazes across open meadows, and along a hillside. Continue heading along the slopes for the next 1.5 kilometers until you reach the pass above the ski lifts at Monti del Sole. The trail continues along the ridgeline into some scattered beech woods. There is a spot where the trail descends gradually through some tall grasses and finding the route can prove a little difficult. Continue looking for red/white blazes on the beech trees. However, as long as you continue on the ridgeline, you will rediscover the trail when the meadows open up again.

The trail will emerge at a *rifugio,* at Colle le Cese. The trail then follows a dirt road heading upslope, and branches off to the left into open alpine meadows. The trail gently climbs the rolling hills, offering views over the Piano Piccolo, a side valley of the Pian Grande, the incredible two-horned Monte Vettore, while to the southwest you can see the Parco Nazionale del Gran Sasso, which contains the highest peak and the only glacier in the Apennines (Hike 50).

There is a point where the trail bypasses the summit of a hill on the inside of the ridge before reconnecting with the ridge crest again. The trail continues due east, until you

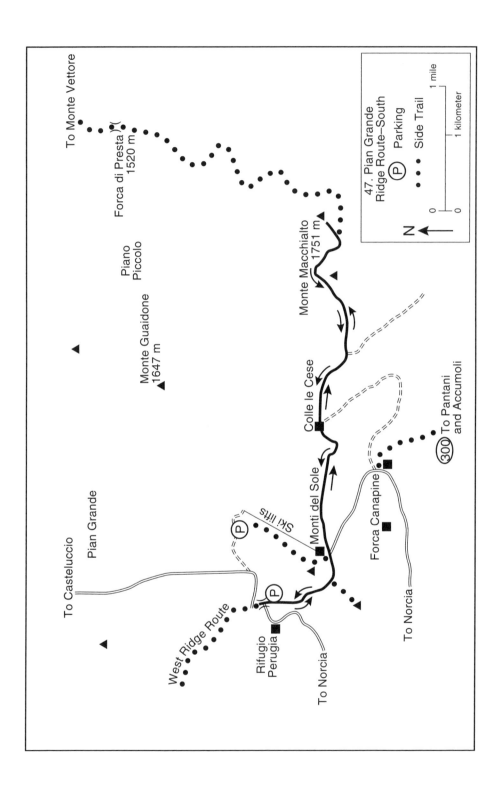

To Monte Vettore

Forca di Presta
1520 m

Piano
Piccolo

Monte Guaidone
▲ 1647 m

Monte Macchialto
1751 m

Colle le Cese

Pian Grande

To Casteluccio

Ski lifts

Monti del Sole

Forca Canapine

300 To Pantani
and Accumoli

To Norcia

West Ridge Route

Rifugio
Perugia

To Norcia

47. Pian Grande
Ridge Route–South
Ⓟ Parking
•••• Side Trail

N

0   1 mile
0   1 kilometer

View of Monte Vettore from the summit of Monte Macchialto

reach a small pass, after a little more than 5 kilometers from the parking area. At this point, you have reached the area where the ridgeline noticeably turns east toward Monte Vettore. The trail heads right along the outside of Monte Macchialto (1,751 meters). This small peak is too attractive not to climb to the summit of it, and the route up through the grass requires no actual trail. At the summit, you have stunning views in all directions. To the east, you can see the ridges of Le Marché and on a clear day, the Adriatic, only 60 kilometers away. To the north, Monte Vettore (Hike 48) is quite close, and it almost seems you could climb it by just going a little further. To the south and west, the region of Umbria opens up and the Corno Grande (Hike 50) is visible. The summit is a great place to turn around and head back the way you came. However, you can also simply descend down the slope and meet up with the trail below, if you wish to continue on the Grand Loop of Monti Sibillini (Hike 49), or intend to climb Monte Vettore.

Wildflower meadow along the south ridge route at Pian Grande

48

Monte Vettore Summit Route

Hike to the summit of Monte Vettore–the fifth highest peak in the Apennines.

Distance: 10–12 kilometers (6.2–7.4 miles) with side trip to Lago di Pilato

Elevation: 1,530–2,476 meters (5,018–8,121 feet)

Hiking Time: 4–5 hours

Park: Parco Nazionale dei Monti Sibillini

Difficulty: Strenuous

Time to visit: May to October

From the floor of the Pian Grande stands a beautiful cone, rising high above the valley. This mountain then extends off to the north as a long ridge with multiple summits that make up the backbone of the Monti Sibillini. The highest peak on this ridge is Monte Vettore, which at 2,476 meters is the fifth highest peak in the Apennines. From the summit of this spectacular peak are expansive views down to the Pian Grande below, Parco Nazionale del Gran Sasso and the Abruzzo range to the south, and out to the Adriatic Sea to the east. Below this high summit, at the bottom of a long U-shaped valley, are two glacial tarn lakes containing an endemic species of brine shrimp. This mountain also offers interesting geological features, such as sandstone slabs and Ice Age glacial cirques and tarns. Inside the Pian Grande, the lentil fields of Castelluccio offer a glimpse into the lives of the farmers who have lived on this high mountain landscape for centuries.

To get to the trailhead of Monte Vettore, drive into the Pian Grande by following the directions for the Pian Grande Ridge Trails (Hikes 46 and 47). Once in the valley, drive almost all the way to Castelluccio, the village located on a small hill at the center of the valley. Just before reaching the village, there is a paved road to the right. Follow this road until you reach the pass at the top of the ridge, called Forca di Presta. To the south, a dirt road heads off to the Rifugio A.N.A., while the trail to Monte Vettore rises to the north. There is no direct bus service to the trailhead, but SSIT (Società Spoletina di

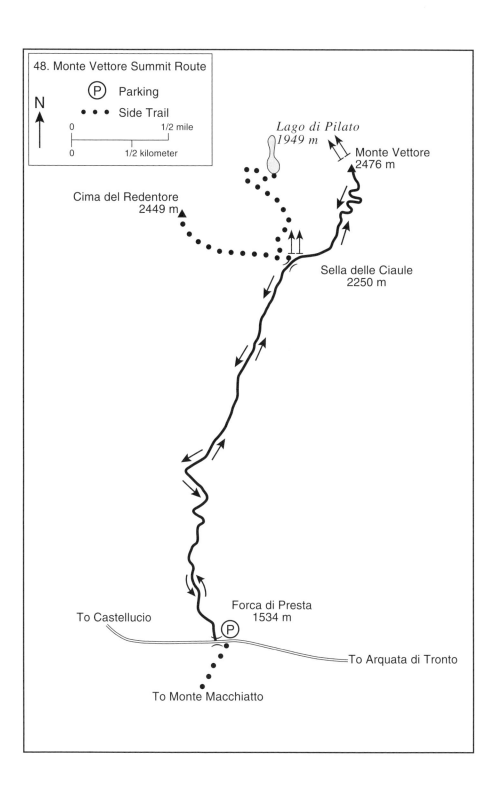

48. Monte Vettore Summit Route

P Parking

••• Side Trail

N

0   1/2 mile

0   1/2 kilometer

Lago di Pilato
1949 m

Monte Vettore
2476 m

Cima del Redentore
2449 m

Sella delle Ciaule
2250 m

To Castellucio

Forca di Presta
1534 m

To Arquata di Tronto

To Monte Macchiatto

On the trail to the summit of Monte Vettore

Imprese Trasporti SpA) does offer bus service to the area. Contact SSIT at www.spoletina.com or 074/3212202 for more information.

The trail climbing to the summit is steep and rugged in places. It is very exposed, as there are no trees at this elevation, thus be prepared for baking in the hot Italian sunshine in summer, or for shivering in the cold winds in late fall. In the summer, it is recommended that you start your hike early in the morning before the peak of the midday sun. This is one of those trails where you feel like you should almost be there, but you just keep trudging along even though the summit seems so close. For the first couple of kilometers, there are spectacular views out across the Pian Grande, as you view Castelluccio, the fields and ridges across the way, and a funny, not-quite geographically correct Italian map made from trees on the hillside. Once you cross over the ridgeback, you get a good view of the summit. However, your

initial goal is to reach the saddle, 700 meters above the starting point of the hike, where a small abandoned *rifugio* sits. The trail gets steeper and steeper and at one section, about 150 meters below the saddle, the trail is very slick with small, loose rocks. You may have to use your hands to keep your balance along this stretch, and it will be even more difficult on the way down.

The saddle of Sella delle Ciaule is the main accomplishment. Once at this saddle, you have only 200 meters left of climbing to do. This is the perfect place for a rest, while you gaze out across toward Corno Grande (Hike 50) across the deep valley, and down into glacial cirque and U-shape valley that separates Monte Vettore from the almost equally high Cima del Redentore (2,449 meters). From the saddle, you cannot see the glacial tarn lakes, but if you descend to the edge of the cirque directly below, you will have an incredible view of them. If you want, you may choose to do the 1 kilometer

View of glacial valley from the summit of Monte Vettore

side trip down to the Lago di Pilato, 300 meters below the saddle, and see the endemic brine shrimp that inhabit these lakes. However, this is a very sensitive ecosystem, so please do not swim or otherwise disturb the water of these tarns.

Once you are ready to ascend to the summit, head up the trail that is east of the *rifugio*. The trail will climb 220 meters in elevation, and take about 30 minutes. It is actually not as steep as the climb up to the saddle, but weak calves may make it feel like it is. There is one false summit with a cross, but once you reach it you will find yourself on a flatter, rocky area where the real summit and another cross are visible, a little higher up. From the summit, the view is truly panoramic and takes in virtually all of central Italy. Although I could not tell whether the Tyrrhenian Sea was visible, due to the haze, the Adriatic was, as well as the Abruzzo range to the south and the snow-capped Corno Grande. If you did not do the side trail down to see the glacial lakes, they are also visible from the summit, although you have to peek over the steep cliff to see them 550 meters below. This is definitely one of the most beautiful and spectacular hikes I have done in Italy! To return, retrace your steps back to the car.

49

Monti Sibillini Grand Loop

Multi-day loop along the crest and across the Pian Grande—with optional climb of Monte Vettore.

Distance: Approximately 30 kilometers (18.6 miles); add 10 kilometers with optional climb of Monte Vettore

Hiking time: 2–3 days

Elevation: 1,296–1,883 meters (4,251–6,176 feet); (2,478 meters on Monte Vettore)

Park: Parco Nazionale dei Monti Sibillini

Difficulty: Moderately strenuous

Time to visit: April to October

The Grand Loop of the Monti Sibillini is a multi-day loop that begins at Rifugio Perugia (see directions for Hikes 46 and 47). This hike follows the ridge crests that circle the broad flat valley of Pian Grande on the south and east sides, before crossing the grassy plain itself and heading into the wonderful medieval village of Castelluccio. From Castelluccio, the route climbs back up to the ridgeline and then follows the ridge crest along the west slopes, before returning to Rifugio Perugia. All in all, this grand loop offers panoramas across virtually all of central Italy, open gentle landscapes bursting with wildflowers in early spring, traditional rural practices such as herding and shearing of sheep, cultivating wheat and lentils, and rugged mountain summits of the Monti Sibillini. This is such an open landscape, that finding your way around and going off-trail are quite easy.

The route begins by following the directions for the Pian Grande South Ridge Route (Hike 47). At Monte Macchialto (5.2 kilometers from Rifugio Perugia), continue down to the trail below, as it heads along the eastern side of the Pian Grande, toward Monte Vettore. The trail will meet up with a dirt road near Rifugio A.N.A. and then the dirt road continues, until arriving at Forca di Presta, 4.2 kilometers from Monte Macchialto. From Forca di Presta, you have the option of climbing to the summit of Monte Vettore or visiting the glacial tarn of Lago di Pilato (both in Hike 48). If you choose to do this option, be prepared to add an extra day to this hike, as it will add 10 kilometers to

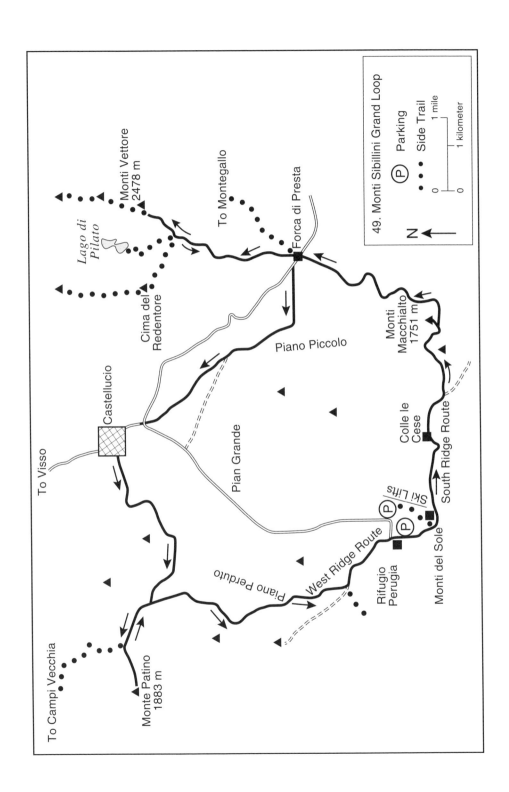

Monti Vettore
2478 m

Lago di
Pilato

Cima del
Redentore

To Montegallo

Forca di Presta

Castellucio

To Visso

Piano Piccolo

Pian Grande

Monti
Macchialto
1751 m

Colle le Cese

South Ridge Route

Ski Lifts

West Ridge Route

Piano Perduto

Rifugio
Perugia

Monti del Sole

To Campi Vecchia

Monte Patino
1883 m

N

49. Monti Sibillini Grand Loop

(P) Parking

•••• Side Trail

0 ———— 1 mile
0 ———— 1 kilometer

Castellucio

your route and Monte Vettore is a rugged climb. One option is to consider camping near Forca di Presta the first night, prior to the summit ascent, or look into Rifugio degli Alpini A.N.A. (or "Rifugio A.N.A.") for lodging options.

From Forca di Presta, head down the steep, grassy slopes until reaching the valley floor in Piano Piccolo. There is no trail, but in this open and grassy landscape, finding your way to the bottom is a piece of cake. You could also follow the paved road toward Castelluccio, but heading off-trail to Piano Piccolo will be much more relaxing and you are unlikely to encounter any other people. At the bottom, there is an unmaintained dirt track that curves around one of the small hills in the valley and heads toward Castelluccio. As the dirt road emerges into the larger Pian Grande, it will begin to turn away from Castelluccio and towards an RV park and horse rental place to the south of town. You may choose to continue on the dirt road

until it reaches the RV park at the paved road, and then turn right, following the paved road into Castelluccio. Or, you may just cut straight across the grassy fields straight toward the village. There is usually a way-trail cut through the grass that is used by horses and livestock.

Upon reaching the paved road at the base of the small hill that Castelluccio is perched on, follow the pavement up into the village. Castelluccio is an excellent place to seek lodging for the first or second night, where you can get a traditional meal of this area, including lentil soup or wild boar, with deep-fried stuffed olives and excellent Umbrian wine.

From Castelluccio, look for a dirt road heading upslope, on the southwest end of town. This road will gently climb for the next 4.4 kilometers up the slopes of the western ridgeline, until it reaches the ridge crest at a small saddle. Upon reaching the saddle, you have now joined the Pian Grande West

Summer wildflowers abound at Monti Sibillini.

Ridge Route (Hike 46). From here you may choose to turn right and head to the summit of Monte Patino. To return to Rifugio Perugia, turn left follow the route as described in Hike 46 for the next 8 kilometers, back to the pass where you began.

Bonus Hike

Lakes of Pantani-Accumoli

A pleasant hike from Rifugio Perugia to the Lakes of Pantani-Accumoli with spectacular views of the Umbrian hills, Monti Sibillini, and Gran Sasso.

Distance: Between 7.0 and 13.0 kilometers roundtrip (4.5–8.0 miles)

Hiking time: 4–5 hours

Elevation: 1,547–1,790 meters (5,075–5,871 feet)

Park: Parco Nazionale dei Monti Sibillini

Difficulty: Moderately easy

Time to visit: May to October

The Parco Nazionale dei Monti Sibillini has so much to offer visitors. It could take years to see all of it. You can probably see from the number of hikes I have included in the guide for this park, that I am impressed with it. We have visited it five times now, with more visits planned for the future. If you are as enamored with the park as we are, then the Lakes of Pantani-Accumoli are definitely worth a visit. Located in a grassy basin, surrounded by several rounded ridges, these ephemeral lakes provide water to cattle, sheep, and semi-wild horses, which graze in the meadows. This hike also offers views of the Monti Sibillini from a different perspective, as well as excellent views of the Norcia valley, the Umbrian hills, and the Corno Grande (Hike 50).

The hike can be accessed from two locations. For a longer hike, begin at Refugio Perugia and follow directions for the Pian Grande South Ridge Route (Hike 47). Upon reaching the Monte del Sole, turn onto the paved access road and follow it downslope until you reach the pass of Forca Canapine. At the pass, look for a dirt road, just above a small *rifugio,* heading southwest. There are signs for Pantani and Accumoli pointing in that direction.

It is also possible to cut this hike in half by driving directly to Forca Canapine. Just before reaching Rifugio Perugia, a road will branch to the right, heading to Forca Canapine and the ski area. Drive the road to the pass, and park there.

The dirt track that leaves from the pass will go past an apparently abandoned

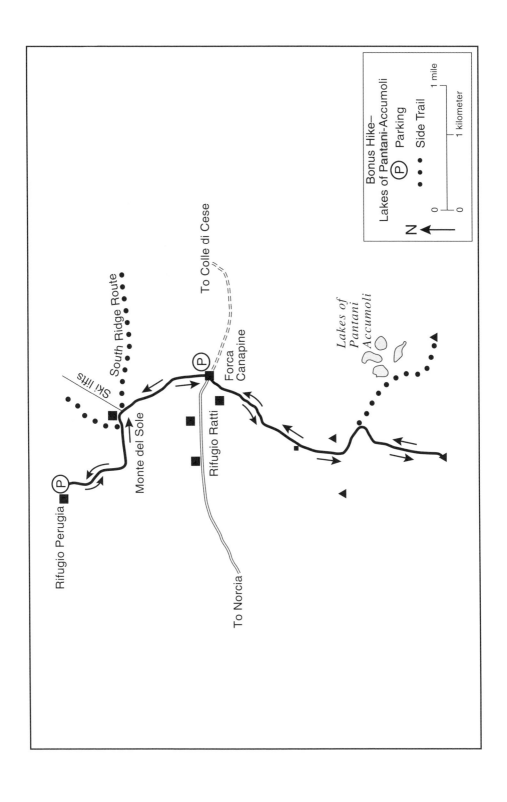

Bonus Hike—
Lakes of Pantani-Accumoli

Ⓟ Parking
• • • Side Trail

N

0   1 kilometer
0   1 mile

Rifugio Perugia

South Ridge Route

Ski lifts

Monte del Sole

To Colle di Cese

Forca Canapine

Ⓟ

Rifugio Ratti

To Norcia

Lakes of
Pantani
Accumoli

Beech forest at Lakes of Pantani-Accumoli

rifugio, briefly passing through a stand of beech, and then into a notch between two rounded hills. The track turns southeast into another notch, and then the lakes of Pantani become visible, approximately 1 hour after Forca Canapine. The lakes will likely have horses, cattle, and sheep milling about them in summer. From here, you can choose what route to take. To the right, a steep slope climbs to a rock cairn on a false summit above. This ascent, alongside of a stand of beech climbing the slope, is by far the most strenuous part of the hike. Upon reaching the rounded summit, spectacular views

On the trail at Lakes of Pantani-Accumoli

open up of the Umbrian hills and Norcia valley, Corno Grande to the south, and Monte Vettore to the northeast. This is an excellent place to eat lunch and enjoy the scenery. Alternatively, you could continue on past the lakes, and up the rounded hill straight ahead to the southeast, for similar expansive views. This route is a little longer. But, in this area, it is fun to just wander across the meadows to find your own little spot of solitude, before retracing your steps to return to your car.

50

Great Cirque of Corno Grande

Loop hike from Campo Imperatore into the great cirque of Corno Grande—the highest peak on the Italian Peninsula.

Round trip: 14.3 kilometers (9 miles)

Elevation: 1,640–2,450 meters (5,380–8,036 feet)

Hiking time: 6–7 hours

Park: Parco Nazionale del Gran Sasso e Monti della Laga

Difficulty: Strenuous

Time to visit: May to October

I have saved the best for last—the Corno Grande stands as the highest and most rugged area of the entire Italian peninsula. The Central Apennines reach a remarkable crescendo here, where the Corno Grande stands like a sentinel, 2,300 meters above the Abruzzo region, inside the National Park of Gran Sasso. It is here that the southern-most glacier in Europe sits (Il Calderone). It is also the only glacier in Italy outside of the Alps. The Corno Grande is the punctuation mark for this book and will challenge not only the body, but also the senses. With towering cliffs, meadows of alpine wildflowers, and extensive ice fields, you will wonder whether you have somehow been transported to Alaska, instead of central Italy. While climbing to the summit of this towering peak is the goal of most, the freedom of exploration that comes from descending into the great cirque and seeing its features up close, makes for a far more interesting adventure, in my opinion.

To get to the Gran Sasso from either Florence or Rome, drive the A1 Autostrada to the A24 Autostrade just east of Rome, following the signs for L'Aquila. Continue past L'Aquila, and take the Assergi exit. Follow signs for Campo Imperatore, and you will arrive at Fonte Cerreto and the cable car lift up the mountain. You may park at this resort area and ride the lift up to Campo Imperatore, if open. If the lift is not operational, or you choose to drive to Campo Imperatore, continue on the same road up for an additional 26 kilometers. There is no direct bus service to the trailhead at Campo Imperatore,

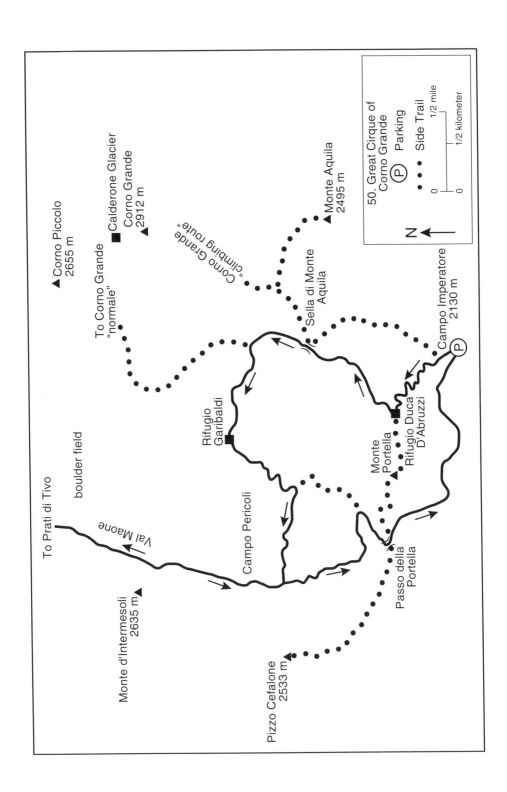

Corno Piccolo
2655 m

Calderone Glacier
Corno Grande
2912 m

To Corno Grande
"normale"

Corno Grande
"climbing route"

Monte Aquila
2495 m

Sella di Monte
Aquila

Campo Imperatore
2130 m

Rifugio Garibaldi

boulder field

To Prati di Tivo

Val Maone

Monte d'Intermesoli
2635 m

Campo Pericoli

Monte
Portella

Rifugio Duca
D'Abruzzi

Passo della
Portella

Pizzo Cefalone
2533 m

50. Great Cirque of
Corno Grande

Ⓟ Parking

••• Side Trail

0   1/2 mile
0   1/2 kilometer

N ←

Along the Campo Pericolo Trail

however, it is possible to reach Fonte Cerreto by bus from L'Aquila. Contact ARPA SpA at www.arpaonline.it or 199/166952 for more information.

Campo Imperatore refers to the broad, flat, plain still grazed by sheep and cattle, and contained by mountains on both sides. Among the mountains, the Corno Grande stands out as a monolith, rising 1,000 meters above the plain. Campo Imperatore hosts a ski area, hotel, gift shop, and general tourist trap filled with many day visitors from Rome. Campo Imperatore also happens to be the place where Mussolini was held prisoner in 1943 before he was freed by German special operations forces led by Otto Skorzeny, in a daring rescue, that included landing gliders and capturing the hotel without firing their weapons. Underneath the mountain, the Autostrada heads toward Teramo, through a 10 kilometer tunnel and there is a particle physics laboratory here, which looks for neutrinos and dark matter, using the mass of the mountain to block most other cosmic rays.

Although the numbers of people in summer can be intimidating for someone who would like a solitary wilderness hike, rest assured that 75 percent of them have no intention of hiking anywhere. For another 20 percent, they have come for one purpose—to climb the Corno Grande. If you avoid this urge to peakbag the highest summit on the Italian peninsula, you can find an amazing level of solitude by descending into the great cirque.

From Campo Imperatore, walk past the astronomical observatory and uphill. You will see a hut at the top of the hill; this is Rifugio Duca degli Abruzzi, and is approximately 40 minutes away. Shortly after passing the observatory, the trail will split. Stay left, and follow the trail as it zigzags its way up the steep slope towards the *rifugio*. The trail to the right heads toward the Corno Grande climbing route. If it is a summer weekend,

The Central Apennines and the Adriatic Coast

you will likely see most people heading in that direction. Upon reaching the *rifugio,* the true grandeur of Gran Sasso National Park is revealed. From the *rifugio,* a 360 degree panorama stops you dead in your tracks. The first thing to catch your eye to the left is the Corno Grande. The deep basin below you is called Campo Pericoli. The steep cliffs of the Monte d'Intermesoli climb high to the left. After catching your breath and taking in the view, head right toward the Corno Grande along the ridgeline.

After a few minutes you will arrive at the trail intersection for the Corno Grande climbing route, and the path to Monte Aquila. To the right, the climbing route will be obvious because of how many people are headed in that direction. Stay left and continue on the trail following signs for Corno Grande *"normale,"* Val Maone, and Prati di Tivo. Not long after this intersection there is another intersection, with Corno Grande *"normale"* staying straight ahead and up the slope, eventually leading to the top of the mountain. Turn left here, following the small path headed into the valley below toward Prati di Tivo. Once you head into this deep basin, there will hardly be anyone on the trail anymore.

In early summer the wildflowers are in bloom, there are patches of snow, and you will be surrounded by 360 degrees of rugged, rocky cliffs in this incredible glacial cirque. It is easy to imagine how this basin was filled with a large glacier during the Ice Age. As you continue down into the basin you will pass the Rifugio Garibaldi where, if you are hungry, you can get some pasta and relax with a beer.

The basin is filled with many hummocks and hills, and the trail is faint in places, but blazes can be found on the rocks, and the general direction of the trail is downward. When you reach the next trail intersection,

follow the sign for Prati di Tivo and Val Maone to the right. When you reach the second trail intersection, take note of this place. To the left is a trail headed up the basin, which will be the return route to Campo Imperatore via the Passo della Portella. To the right, the trail continues down into the Val Maone, which is the U-shaped valley where the Ice Age glacier emptied from the basin.

Val Maone is a spectacular canyon cut between the Corno Grande on your right and the Monte d'Intermesoli on the left. As the trail descends, the cliffs rise higher and higher. There are several sections where the cliff walls are vertical or even overhanging and you are likely to hear the voices of rock climbers hundreds of feet above you. Looking straight down Val Maone, you can see the Monti Sibillini and the summit of Monte Vettore (Hike 48) in the distance. Continuing down the valley, Corno Piccolo will start to appear, although it is hard to accept it as *piccolo* ("small," in Italian), when its rocky cliffs rise some 1,000 meters above you. Somewhere, tucked in between the Corno Grande and Corno Piccolo, and hidden from view by a rocky ridge, sits the Ghiacciaio del Calderone, the southernmost glacier in Europe. Along Val Maone, you may choose turn back at any time. The further down the Val Maone you go, the lower you will descend and the more climbing you have to do on the way back. If the clouds are building up and thunderstorms threaten, you may not want to go very far, as you still have to climb back up over those high, exposed ridges to get back. However, if time and weather are not limiting, a nice place to turn around is at the end of the hanging valley, where a field of very large boulders sits and the beech forests begin, about three kilometers from the last trail intersection.

The climb back up the valley is not difficult, but can be sweltering in the midday

Hiking at Gran Sasso

summer sun, as the heat reflects and radiates from the cliffs. However, once you return to Campo Pericoli, the temperature may be lower due to the ice fields and the growing shadows from the high cliffs above. At the trail marker for Passo della Portella, begin climbing the talus slope toward the steep ridgeline above. There will likely be lingering snow along this north-facing route in early summer, so be prepared to walk on the snow or along the sides of it. About halfway up, the trail makes an abrupt turn left and then slowly rises up to meet another trail headed to Passo della Portella. It is very easy to miss this turn, as footprints in the snow and a steep way-trail ahead beckon you to continue right up, straight to the other trail. While it is not a big deal if you miss this turn, the way-trail is very steep and there is loose talus just before the top. Either way, you turn right at the main trail above, and in no time you reach the Passo della Portella.

From here you cross over to the outside of the ridge where you can look down to the city of L'Aquila, across to the mountains of

Silente-Velino, and even all the way toward smoggy Rome itself. At Passo della Portella, the trails branch in multiple directions. One heads up the ridge to the left, to the summit of Monte Portella and eventually back to the Rifugio Duca d'Abruzzi. Another heads right toward the Monti d'Intermesoli, which is a scary, knife-edged route! Stay straight ahead, and then follow the trail as it curves left, along the sides of the Monte Portella back toward Campo Imperatore. There are no switchbacks or steep sections; it just gradually descends gently back to the parking area, which you are thankful for at this point, after a long day's hike. If you arrived early in the day, upon reaching the parking area, you will likely be astonished by how many cars have driven up from Rome. You can go into one of the hotels for food or a drink, but be prepared for huge lines. It seems unfair that after a long, hot, strenuous hike, wanting nothing more than food and cold drink, all of these people who drove up are taking all the spots. But, as the Italians graciously say: *"Va bene."*

The Central Apennines and the Adriatic Coast

Index

126; Museo Leonardiano di Vinci, 121, 124; parish church of, 125
deer, 37, 49, 111, 203, 214
diga (dam), 98, 100
dining. *See also* restaurants (*ristorante*)
dinner (*cene*), 20–21, 130
Doccia, 226
dogs (*cane*): hiking with, 18–19, 81; hunting, 17; at Maremma South, 41; at Monte Giovo, 229, 231; at Penna di Sumbra, 156; and sheepdogs, 18, 258; snakes and, 21; ticks and, 21
dragonflies, 76
driving: to ampitheatre of Monte Moneglia, 193; on Autostrade, 15–16; in Cinque Terre (Five-Lands), 172; RV's (recreation vehicles) rental, 19
ducks, 39
dunes, 67, 84–85. *See also* coastal dune ecosystems
Dunes of Torre del Lago, 83–86

E

eating and eating terms, 19–21
ecological reserves, 242
ecosystems: alpine meadows, 24–25; beaches, 22; beech forests, 24; chestnut forests, 24; coastal sand dunes, 22; cork oak savanna, 25; garigue, 25; and habitats, 21–25; macchia, 23; Mediterranean fan palms, 25; oak woodlands, 23; pineta (coastal pine forests), 23; rare, 25; riparian woodlands, 23–24; sensitive, 275; white fir forests, 25
EE (*Excursionisti Esperti*) warning, 133, 161–162, 237
egrets, 98
Elba (island), 30, 52, 56–57
Elba–Monte Capanne Summit Loop, 56–60
Elba–Pomonte Valley Loop, 52–53
Elba–Ruins of Volterraio, 61–63
elderberries (*Sabucus nigra*), 24
elm (*Ulmus sp.*), 23
elm and oak forests, 35
Emilia-Romagna, 203
Empoli, 124
erosion, 262
Etruscan mining, 102

Etruscan ruins site, 61
euphorb (*Euphobia arborea*), 186
euphorbs (*Euphobia sp.)*, 25, 76
European beech (*Fagus silvatica*), 24
European black pine (*Pinus nigra*), 23
European chestnuts (*Castanea sativa*), 24
European hornbeam (*Carpinus betulus*), 24
evening primrose, 83

F

falcons, 30
fallow deer, 41, 45, 51
Faltognano, 126
farms/homesteads, abandoned, 77
fault blocks, 204
Febbio, 219, 223
femmina (female dog), 18
ferries: to Capraia (island), 75; to Elba, 52, 56; for La Spezia, 180; at Piombino, 68; for Portofino, 200; for Portonvenere, 180; for San Fruttuoso, 198; for Tuscan Archipelago, 30
figs, 54, 81
finestra (window), 232
fishing, 231
fishing platforms, 80
Fiumalbo, 226
flamingoes, 39
flash floods, 17
flooding, 262
Florence, 124
flowering locust trees, 82
Foce della Faggiola (Pass of the Beeches), 168
Foce delle Porchette, 137, 141, 147, 152
Foce di Faneletto, 169
Foce di Petrosciana, 145, 147, 152
food terms, 20
Forca Canapine, 280, 282–283
Forca di Presta, 272, 278
Forests and Canyon of Tatti-Berignone Loop, 107–111
Forno, 168
Fornovolasco, 137, 143, 147, 151–152
Fort Stelle, 35
Fosso alle Canne, 71–72

foxes, 37, 41, 45, 51, 203, 214
fragile ecosystems, 64, 85
freshwater marsh, 73
frogs, 82

G

Galleria Cipollaio, 160
Gamberame, 119, 121
Garfagnana, 132
Garfagnana Valley, 161
garigue ecosystems, 25
garigue grasslands, 55
garigue saddle, 76
garigue vegetation, 76
gelato, 36, 55, 82, 187
Genoa, 172
geothermal energy site, 88
German Gothic Line, 160–161
Ghiacciaio del Calderone, 287
ghost towns, 73, 77
Giannutri (island), 35
Giglio (island), 30, 35
Glacial Cirque of Monte Giovo, 229–233
glacial cirques, 203–204, 212, 229, 236–237, 272, 287
glacial folding, 142
glacial headwall, 229
glacial lakes, 264
glacial tarn lakes, 203, 236, 264, 272, 274, 276, 278
glaciation, 202–203
glaciers, 269, 284, 287
gneisses, 133, 157
goat-herder sheds (*caprile*), 55, 58
goldenrods, 22, 83
Gorgona (island), 30
Grande Anello dei Sibilini, 264
Grande Anello dei Sibilini trail, 268
Grande Escursione Apennicia (GEA) trail, 203–204, 207, 214, 216, 232–233, 236, 244–245
Grand Loop of Monti Sibilini, 271, 276
The Grand Loop of the Southern Alpi Apuane, 148–149
granite landscapes, 30
granite pluton, 56
Gran Sasso, 284
grapes, 54, 178
grasslands, 64
Great Cirque of Corno Grande, 284
greater flamingo, 37

Index